Peace on Earth

Peace on Earth

The Renaissance of Christian Humanism
(Towards a More Coherent and Humane Society
in the "Global Village" of the Third Millennium)

Edwin Jones

RESOURCE *Publications* • Eugene, Oregon

PEACE ON EARTH
The Renaissance of Christian Humanism

Copyright © 2016 Edwin Jones. All rights reserved. Except for brief quotations in critical publications or reviews, no part of this book may be reproduced in any manner without prior written permission from the publisher. Write: Permissions, Wipf and Stock Publishers, 199 W. 8th Ave., Suite 3, Eugene, OR 97401.

Resource Publications
An Imprint of Wipf and Stock Publishers
199 W. 8th Ave., Suite 3
Eugene, OR 97401

www.wipfandstock.com

PAPERBACK ISBN: 978-1-4982-9061-6
HARDCOVER ISBN: 978-1-4982-9063-0
EBOOK ISBN: 978-1-4982-9062-3

Manufactured in the U.S.A.

For Andrea

Pope John XXIII   Robert Schuman   Arnold Toynbee

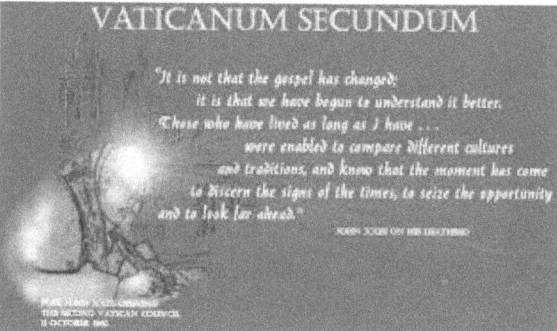

Pope Francis

Contents

Preface | IX

- I   A Tale of Two Cultures | 1
- II   The Place of Religion in Culture and Civilization (Arnold Toynbee and his "A Study of History") | 22
- III   The Meaning of Christian Humanism | 37
- IV   The History of Christian Humanism | 48
- V   Robert Schuman and the movement for Peace and Unity in Europe (1950–2015) | 64
- VI   Pope John XXIII's Encyclical, "Pacem in Terris," (Peace on Earth), 1963 | 81
- VII   Pope John XXIII and the Second Vatican Council (1962–1965) | 90
- VIII   Pope Francis, "The Great Reformer" | 106
- IX   Epilogue | 162

Appendix I. Britain and Europe | 165
Appendix II. The Encyclical Laudato si' (Praise be to You) | 171
Bibliography | 173

Preface

AT THE CENTRE OF this Essay is a consideration of one of the most profound problems which has always faced humanity, as individuals and in all levels of human groupings, from the birth of "Homo Sapiens" to the global world of our present time. It is the struggle between good and bad in humanity itself. There are, broadly speaking, three views about human nature, concerning this question. It may be convenient to take three very clear examples to indicate what I mean.

The first view is that human nature is totally corrupt and cannot do any good. My example here is Martin Luther who initiated the "Reformation" in the sixteenth century. As a result of this view he was horrified by the "Renaissance" which celebrated the wonderful aspect of the achievements of human beings; and he believed that education should have only the Bible as its text book. It also meant that he supported the German princes in their violent treatment of the "Peasants Revolt" (1525) in attempting to achieve what we would now call their "human rights." In politics this idea tended to support right-wing views. I hasten to add that this would not be true of modern Lutheranism.

The second example is Rousseau, the French philosopher in the eighteenth century's "age of enlightenment," who believed that human nature is perfect in itself, except that it can be led astray by outside influences. So education should not interfere with the child's "natural" development; indeed the child should not be ordered to do anything: 'not the least jot or tittle' as he wrote in his "Emile." This idea influenced and exalted "child-centred" education in the USA in the nineteenth century and Britain in the twentieth. It was also a view that tended to support the left-wing in political disputes.

The third view is much older, going back to Aristotle and confirmed by later Christian teaching. This said that human nature is innately good, but it has been warped by an element of self-centredness, selfishness, greed and pride, which theologians have called "Original Sin." This meant that education should be concerned with keeping the balance between teaching "self expression" for what is good in human nature, and "self-denial" to contain and restrain that warped element in us all, to a more or less extent, and which should be recognised and rejected.

Another element in us, as taught in this tradition, is that human beings have, to a more or less extent, the free will to decide what we choose to do in matters of right or wrong. The strength of this "free will," however, can range widely in different people and in different circumstances; but we can all be more or less responsible for our decisions. This is the underlying assumption of the law which is needed in all human societies to decide on these matters and to keep order within human communities.

Self-consciousness and religion have been part of human life from its very beginning in whatever ways they have been expressed. As opposed to all other animals, humans have always recognised their own vulnerability and have always sought to belong to some greater power than themselves. They have always recognised, innately, that they are spiritual as well as bodily creatures; and therefore different from other animal life. Consequently, their needs have always been spiritual as well as bodily, and this, too, has always distinguished them from other animal life. They, too, have always shown evidence of having a conscience, to distinguish right from wrong. Alone among animal life, they have been concerned with life after death; and have demonstrated a belief in it. Some of us would say that this could not have been the case, if there was not a corresponding truth to respond to it; that is to say that food and water did exist; and if food and water did not exist there would be no human beings. This is why astronauts look for water on any particular planet to discover whether or not there had been human life on it.

Most of us would agree that human beings have a spiritual life as well as a material existence. The fact that we all have spiritual needs must mean that spirituality exists to answer these needs. The existence of needs show that the answers to them exist. It is a logical consequence that all human spiritual needs, such as love, meaning in life, desire for after-life, which

Preface

do not exist in animals, but are equally important and inherent in human beings, have corresponding truths which answer to these needs. Why else would these innately- felt needs exist? It follows that if the answers to these needs are denied them, then the spiritual nature of human beings will decline, leaving man at the mercy of the warped aspects of human life. This, I think, explains why Toynbee discovered quite separately from our approach, but from his extraordinary and brilliant investigations into the history of world cultures and civilizations, that religion, to his surprise, created culture, rather than the opposite which he had expected.

The wonderful Book of Genesis in the Bible explains in its own metaphorical way, so that humans could understand it, that God "breathed" into the animate but not yet spiritual body of the first humans and so created the "soul" needed to achieve the fully human being. It is no surprise then that archaeological finds tell us that such evidence as human worship of God and belief in an after- life, shown in burial grounds, arrives with the first appearance of "homo sapiens," the first fully human being.

It is not surprising either that modern science has made extraordinary steps towards understanding the human body and brain (neuro-science); they have not come near to knowing the human "soul," which was created in the "image of God." The greatest and wisest scientists seem to have accepted this "mystery" as being beyond the range of the human brain. We have got no further in this than Aristotle, in my view the greatest "mind" in the history of mankind, who was the founder of modern science and virtually every other branch of human learning. Aristotle actually believed in the immortal soul and in what he called a "Form" which had some of the characteristics which we might describes as those of "God," but accepted that he could not understand it, only its characteristics. I always think that he would have been delighted to have lived a few centuries later to receive by revelation what he could not have discovered for himself; and to have received this Christian Revelation of God –in- Christ which has created the faith of Christianity and the "Good News" of the Gospel.

The soul is not material and therefore scientists cannot handle it. There is no conflict between science and religion. Such conflicts, where they have existed, have taken place because lesser scientists and theologians have stepped in to areas of learning that they do not understand and "where angels fear to tread." Many fine scientists are Christians and are content in regarding their discoveries as wonders of God's creation: "The heavens are telling the glory of God."

Preface

In this Essay we are proposing the third and oldest view of human nature, described above, and the philosophy on which it is based. It corresponds to what we call, "reality," from the viewpoint of the holistic approach to truth. We all know by experience that this third description is an accurate description of ourselves and of all other people we know. It is taken for granted, for example, by Dylan Thomas through the mouth of the Rev. Eli Jenkins in "Under Milk Wood."

"We are neither wholly bad or good, who live our lives under Milk Wood; And He I know will be the first, to see our best side, not the worst"

There are consequences which follow from this view of human nature and the premises following from it. One such premise is that we are all involved in a continual struggle between these two elements in our nature. For the good to develop, arrangements have to be made for management of this problem in the life of individual human beings and in all levels of group human management which we call "politics." In both cases, the answer to human development is contained in the ways used by human beings and human governments, to understand the nature of human beings and then adopt means, ways and strategies by which the "good" in us can be encouraged and the "bad" discouraged.

This is the role of conscience and self-discipline in individuals, and of "politics" and "law" at governmental level. The three main ways by which we can plan the proper development of both individuals and very large groupings of human beings, are to be found in three main areas of thought which are primarily concerned with this problem –Theology, Philosophy and Law (dealing with the human mind); and Medicine (dealing with the body). This has been recognised from the beginning of the story of mankind, which we call "History."

These were the main elements of education for the most part in Western civilization. It is one of the great weaknesses of our society today , in my view, that children are not taught now in British schools that these are among the chief and most important aims and components of public education. Professor Angela Hobbs, Professor of Public Understanding of Philosophy at Sheffield University, has demonstrated recently that this can be done very well from the earliest stages of education.

In my view the first and most important part of education is to produce fully human and well balanced human beings. In my long practical and professional experience, all other aims of education follow and take their own place appropriately from this premise of thought. Then all other areas of human endeavour and expression –the Arts and the Sciences– take their very important place in contributing to human development in their various ways. But if this first aim is not achieved, or even diminished in importance, then an educational system cannot produce what should be its chief purpose ; and this can produce disastrous personal and social effects for any individual and for any culture or civilization.

Bringing all this together, we come to the very important element of "Education" in society which is meant to guide us to become fully human people and good citizens. Indeed a properly conceived education is to the advantage of all humanity if this necessary provision is extended throughout humanity and contains the whole of the new "global" village which the world has become in this new Millennium. It has been said with some, but incomplete, truth, that "History is a race between education and catastrophe"; though we have also to take into account other influences such as the primary influence of parents in "educating" their own children in their own homes, not necessarily in academic subjects but in the most important aspects of human life. Then, again, why do parents, who are usually the most concerned and want the best for their children, also often want to send their children to "Faith" schools?

The essay will be touching on all these areas of human life. Its intention is simply to contribute in some way to the many important decisions we have to make, concerning the best way forward in our planning for a better future for mankind in this new Millennium on which we are all embarking. It will certainly be trying to introduce more clarity and understanding into the situation, concerning many aspects of human life, when important decisions have to be made at this time in world history.

In this sense it has a particular relevance for many areas of human life which need to be addressed quite quickly, from the height of us all "becoming more fully human" in a the new world of the "global village," to the more particular questions such as how British people should vote in the coming referendum on staying in or leaving the European Union?" In fact both of these questions are much inter-related and inter-dependent. I think that they should both be put to the people of Britain for their consideration, with the proviso that they read this Essay first {!} .These are bound to become very relevant and very important decision-making processes in the next two years, during which time I hope that this Essay will have a contribution to make to the preparatory debates.

Preface

There is much confusion, perplexity, and fear in the Western world as it enters the third Millennium. People are suffering from the experience of living in a "fragmented" society, without a common set of values which are essential to a productive and settled culture. This is what Eric Hobsbawm, a life-long Marxist, was saying in his last work published after his death in 2013, "Fractured Times: Culture and Society in the Twentieth Century." We must remember, too, that Winston Churchill proclaimed on 6th February, 1945, looking back after the end of the Second World War:

"As the sun goes down today, we are experiencing the worst period of suffering in human history."

Something had gone seriously wrong with human development, progressively in the last four centuries of continual warfare between the new nation-states, ending in two highly destructive World Wars, when contrasted with the comparatively "mild skirmishes" of the less imperfect medieval period which preceded it. What are we to do about the present situation? Are we going to proceed blindly on in desperation? Or can we make a real effort to learn lessons from the errors of the past and make a rational, intelligent and courageous attempt to find a new and much more positive way forward?

For example, can we now accept the premise that, because of the interdependence of all aspects of humanity and the Universe, a primary lesson is "What is morally wrong cannot in the end be politically, economically or socially right"? Aristotle seems to have been the first thinker to understand this, but modern man in the twentieth century had long forgotten it. This helps to explain much of what this Essay is about.

Eric Hobsbawm (1917-2012) had lived through many changes. He had seen the rise and fall of Fascism in 1945. He was a Marxist and remained faithful to it until the collapse of Communism at the end of the twentieth century, when he allowed his life-long membership of the Communist Party to lapse, and the Party itself was dissolved a short time later.

Hobsbawm's reactions are interesting because they represent those of many others in society who felt that Christianity had come to an end and other philosophical systems –Communism, Fascism, unregulated Capitalism, and others, had failed to meet the needs of human beings. Hobsbawm believed that Christianity had also come to an end; but, at the very end of his life, he seemed to retain a wistful memory of the old Christian dispensation. His last work is an expression of a disillusioned state of mind. He

Preface

prefaces his last book, with a significant quote from a poem of Matthew Arnold, "Dover Beach" (1867):

> "And here we are on a plain darkling
> Swept with confused alarms of struggle and flight
> Where ignorant armies clash by night."

Matthew Arnold was the most prominent commentator on culture and society in the Victorian era. He had written the famous "Culture and Anarchy" (1869) which warned of the dangers involved in the waning of religious belief, which he saw starting to emerge in England. He also worked as an inspector of schools and visited schools on the Continent which had a better quality of education than in Britain, in his view.

He argued that the Christian faith was at the roots and development of our Culture; and if this waning developed, it could mean isolating ourselves from the great European and Christian heritage which was based on the Christian Revelation of the "Good News" of the Gospel, bringing light out of the darkness of the previously intellectual but pagan Greek world.

The quote, taken from Arnold's poem, was highly significant in this context. It suggests that Hobsbawm, at the age of 95 and a year before his death, would seem to be making a comparison between the Greek pagan culture and the new culture emerging in England in the second half of the twentieth century which he was describing in his last book. The quote is taken from the following context in this Poem when Arnold was meditating, while watching and listening to the tide ebbing and flowing, in and out on the beach in Dover:

> "Sophocles long ago
> Heard it on the Aegean, and it brought
> Into his mind the troubled ebb and flow
> Of human misery, as we
> Find also in the sounds, a thought.
> Hearing it by this distant northern sea;
> The Sea of Faith once at the full
> But now I hear
> Its melancholy, long, withdrawing roar.
> The World
> Hath really neither joy, nor love, nor light
> Nor certitude, nor peace, nor help for pain

Preface

And we are here on a darkling plain,
Swept with confused alarms of struggle and flight
Where ignorant armies clash by night"

When Arnold, in this Poem, mentions Sophocles (495-306 BC.) reflecting on the miserable state of mankind, he had been referring to one of the three great Greek tragedians of Greece who were living in pagan times, before the coming of Christ, when there seemed to be no real meaning or purpose in life, and the great emphasis in their culture was on the tragedies of the human condition.

Arnold was expressing a similar misery at the prospect of another age arriving without hope or meaning or joy in human life, if the tide of Christian faith was withdrawn. Suicide was well known in Greek culture and one has to say that the number of suicides in Britain in the period since the 1960's has risen greatly, and is now being reported as rising among young children and adults in their teens for the first time, as is the problem of mental illness of various kinds. In a very recent international study of the well-being and happiness of children across the world, Britain is bottom but one (South Korea) in the world listing.

Perhaps the most unfortunate aspect of Hobsbawm's bleak view of the future is that he seems to have no hope or suggestion of what might be done to create a better situation for mankind. He actually says in fact that: "I have no manifesto to propose."

He has nothing helpful to say, so that in this Preface he has to confess his own inability to suggest any way out of our bewilderment about the future, except that he has little hope:

"However, we no longer understand or know how to deal with the present creative flood drowning the globe in image, sound and words, which is almost certain to become uncontrollable in both space and time" .

And, again:

"Who can tell on what terms reason and anti-reason will co-exist in the on-going earthquakes and tsunamis of the twenty first century"

While agreeing with much of Hosbawm's description of a "fractured" and "fragmented" culture and society at the present time, something which even our Prime Minister, David Cameron, has had to accept, my own view is that there could be a much more important and positive response to our problems.

Arnold Toynbee described the present situation as a "Challenge and Response" situation in which we have to face perhaps the greatest challenge

Preface

in human history, which is to decide how we can shape for ourselves and our posterity a better future in the third Millennium. Perhaps the greatest threat facing the modern world is that of annihilation produced by mankind itself, resulting from its failure to overcome its own selfishness, pride and seeking of power over others. This has led to continuous wars on the one hand; and on the other the abuse of mankind's "home," the natural environment, which as a result is now threatening another form of annihilation through climate change.

The challenge lies in devising new ways of seeking human development in the coming millennium. This will demand great courage, intelligence and determination to the utmost, but is by no means beyond the human capacity. We have the free-will to make the necessary decisions if we can first understand what needs to be done and are then prepared to make the necessary response this challenge before us.

In this Essay I am suggesting that the best and most positive response to the challenge is contained within a certain system and ideology, "an aesthetic which is both in the European inheritance and of world relevance now", which I have named "Christian Humanism."

Ours is a typical situation described by Arnold Toynbee in his unprecedented study of the rise and fall of the World's cultures and civilizations, entitled "A Study of History," written by him during a lifetime's unprecedented research into his detailed study of 52 world cultures and civilizations. In each of these he found that there had been a rise, then decline, then fall, in each and every one of them, with one exception. This is the Christian culture and civilization which has lasted already for over two millennia as the basis of European society and has continually spread throughout the world over these two thousand years and more.

Toynbee's work is an astonishing achievement of modern scholarship by a brilliant mind. There is nothing pre-determined in Toynbee's analysis, because his work has convinced him that human free will exists, to a more or less extent, in all human beings. There are changes in emphasis as his research advanced and even a complete change of mind on a centrally important matter. For he assumed at the beginning that religion was an aspect of culture, whereas he became convinced by the end that the opposite is true—that culture is an aspect of religion. Therefore, it is possible for a declining culture to die and this has been the usual pattern; but, very importantly for us human beings, it can be revived under certain circumstances.

Preface

The most important circumstance was one in which a spiritual or religious revival, led by a spiritual and creative leader, can achieve it.

One of the most important of Toynbee's conclusions was contained in his critical review of Oswald Spengler's earlier book, "The Decline of the West" which appeared between the two World Wars and had encouraged the Nazi Party in Germany by proclaiming that a strong military leader was needed. Spengler predicted that Western civilization as we knew it would wither and die as had all other civilizations before it.

In his critique of this book, Toynbee denied this, proclaiming that the West had a unique element in its make-up which was lacking in the other civilizations, and would prevent this from happening. He had come to the conclusion that the Christian religion had, at its centre, a unique capacity for renewing itself against all the challenges which it had faced in its history of already two millennia of existence.

In his detailed study of 52 civilizations, Christianity, as represented by the Universal Church which Christ founded, seemed to contain a kind of "dynamo" in its make-up which gave it a unique capacity to renew itself continually when faced with various challenges throughout its history of more than two Millennia in the World.

This was an important discovery which had arisen from his disinterested but exceptionally scholarly research into the rise and fall of human cultures and civilizations. It so happened that about the same time, but quite separately, the world's most famous psycho-analyst, was stating that his work on the individual human psyche (soul, spirit, mind) had made it so obvious to him that God exists that he no longer spoke of "believing" it, but of "knowing" that this was true.

Carl Gustav Jung, the Swiss founder of modern psycho- analysis had come to the same conclusion as that of Toynbee, but from a different standpoint. Jung came to believe that the human "psyche" which he had studied longer and more intensely than anyone else, required more than the secular society on its own, in which to exist. Again, the spiritual or religious aspect of the "psyche" required a transcendental answer to satisfy its spiritual needs.

He said: "That is the great problem before us today. Reason alone no long suffices." (Anthony Storr, "The Essential Jung: Selected Writings," 1983, p.397). Moreover, just like Toynbee, working from his unsurpassed knowledge of world history, Jung, working from his unsurpassed knowledge of the individual human and psycho-analytical angle, both came to the same conclusion, that it was the continuing existence of the original Universal Church which was the essential element in answering these needs, both individual and societal. (See Toynbee, p.210; and Jung, Op.Cit, pp.321-323, 326-327).

Both these were great minds, neither of whom was ever committed to this Church; nor, to my knowledge, did they ever meet or know one another. For both of them this special force or "dynamo" for renewal was part of the original Institution which Jesus had established, for a purpose which could never be destroyed:

"Thou art Peter and on this rock I shall build My Church; and the gates of Hell shall never prevail against it"

Moreover, and intriguingly, Jung, like Toynbee, but quite separately and from another field of research and learning, came to the same conclusion, about the "living" and "dynamic" nature of Christianity, which enables it to last to the end of time. Toynbee discovered in his studies the existence of a "dynamic" force within this Church which would never cease from renewing and reforming it whenever this was needed; while Jung wrote that the present lack of belief in the West was owing to a failure of humanity in recognising it:

"This is not to say that Christianity is finished. I am, on the contrary, convinced that it is not Christianity, but our conception and interpretation of it that has become antiquated in face of the present world situation. The Christian symbol is a living thing that carries the seeds of further development. It can go on developing; it depends only on us, whether we can make up our minds to meditate again, and more thoroughly, on the Christian premises" (Ibid. p.379)'

Also, in Jung there is the stated danger of western civilization relying too much on the analytic approach to truth, leaving aside the holistic approach, which has created a very important deficiency in the humane culture of our civilization. Altogether, there is an intriguing "pattern" which emerges, quite separately, from the different work and disciplines of these two great thinkers on a central and essential aspect of the human situation, approached from two separate and vitally important analyses –of the individual mind (Jung) and culture or civilization (Toynbee)- in the human condition and its essential requirements.

Toynbee has drawn the conclusion that there existed some kind of "dynamo" effect in Christianity from his historical researches over a vast period of time since its birth. Christians themselves had simply assumed

Preface

this as part of their faith heritage because their Founder, Jesus Christ, had promised his very small group of early apostles, when He was founding this Church that "I will be with you to the end of the World . . . and the Gates of Hell shall never prevail against it." They could point to the fact that they had come to believe this because they had personally witnessed His dying the brutal and unmistakeable death of the Cross, which He had foretold but which they could never quite believe or understand. Then, to their utter astonishment and fright originally, but then filling them with great confidence and delight, they witnessed that He had risen from this death to a new life as He had again predicted would happen after three days, to meet and talk to them again.

It was only such a super-human and unprecedented experience, which could have changed them into people who were no longer afraid and were quite ready to die for their faith in Him, and actually did so. He had also said that this Church which He had founded in a remote part of the World would grow, like a mustard seed, to become a great tree, which covered the whole world. This was another promise which countless generations of Christians have seen happening, as another example of His reliability.

This was enough for them to explain in terms of their own faith in Christ, why His Church would last until the end of time. Their faith had shown them that this "Dynamo effect," described in another way, is the work of the same Holy Spirit of God which had also enabled Jesus to rise from the Dead. But still, it was interesting to discover now from Toynbee and Kung that there is a detached and scholarly, confirmation of all these transcendental elements as divine answers to human needs.

However it was a finding that did not make Toynbee popular in the new "After Virtue" culture which entered the British scene after 1960; and which was responsible for a new era of disbelief in all these happenings. Toynbee, who was not a member of any particular faith group, was also describing the same phenomenon now from the viewpoint of a detached scholar who was determined to get to the truth of what was happening.

There was no sign after more than two millennia, of it ever ending; and all this while this Church had experienced and overcome every conceivable attempt from outside and inside the Church itself, to destroy it, during this uniquely long history of more than two Millennia. Moreover, this Church, represented by Pope Francis and the Synod of Bishops is even now (October, 2015) calling upon the Holy Spirit, for inspiration and guidance into what is the best way forward in dealing with some particularly

Preface

difficult ways of bringing together Church teaching on the mercy and compassion of God, with previous teaching on marriage and the family.

Toynbee also found patterns associated with these religious and spiritual revivals, such as "Challenge and Response"; and "Withdrawal and Return." Christians had "responded" positively to the "challenge" of accepting a transcendent power which satisfied their spiritual needs; Christ had "withdrawn" for forty days in the desert, before "returning" to His task of founding His Church. Moreover, this Church had "responded" positively to every "challenge" over two Millennia. These patterns which accompanied such responses are also very relevant also to our particular study. The unique element in the case of this Universal Church is its continuance and growth as a spiritual institution for more than two Millennia.

It is also at the present moment, the beginning of the new and third Millennium, that another reform and revival of this Institution have become essential to meet the needs and challenge of the modern world which it exists to serve and guide. The world had been rapidly changing in the twentieth century and it is essential that the Universal Church should undergo a change and reform in order to be able to assimilate the consequences of these "signs of the times," while at the same time retaining its old but undying system of beliefs and values enjoined by the Christian Revelation.

Suddenly there appears to have arrived unexpectedly, from outside the normal context, a new earthly leader of this Universal Church in our own time, well able and equipped in all respects, to respond to this recent challenge in the interests of the Catholic Church and of the whole world which it seeks to serve. This, of course, is Pope Francis, the dynamic leader who has suddenly but very clearly become "well known, in every corner of the world as a figure of radiance and charisma" (National Geographic, August, 2015, p.36), unknown before perhaps since the time of St. Francis of Assisi whom Toynbee had stated to be the greatest human being who had been seen in the Western world.

Such considerations make it possible for me to now to attempt to offer a new "manifesto," which is much more positive and hopeful, for mankind, concerning, the way forward towards creating a better future for all people of good will in Western Europe, and indeed in the new much "smaller" world established by amazing developments in the technology of human communication, a world which we can now call the "global village." It seems that history is gradually making its way to the full conception of humanity seen as a "global family," learning ever so slowly that it must learn to live as such if it will ever achieve its goal of World peace. Patriotism and love of one's own country is good, but love for the whole human family must take precedence when necessary. The old type of aggressive nationalism cannot be part of the concept of World peace which is built upon justice and equal care for all. Each country, however, should retain its own language, culture, and special "genius," for the common good of all.

The first step in reform and renewal will be to look at the nature of human beings which does not, it seems, change very much, to examine what constitutes human "needs" which may not coincide, however, with our "wants." To do this we have to examine the work of some of the greatest "thinkers" in human history. We must also look at the necessary constituents of human "culture" and civilization. This will require a brief look at the history of mankind from its very beginning on this earth; for knowledge of the past can help greatly in guiding us forward into the future, if we are prepared to learn from it.

One premise in this Essay is that human nature remains the same in its needs but not in its wants. Wants are simply what people imagine are needs. Though most of human wants may be "neutral," many wants are at the expense of our needs and therefore not good for us. Again, contrary to a popular belief, human beings do not become more intelligent as time goes on. They simply accumulate more knowledge as times change. So we really need to know what our real needs are and to recognise them; and we should never think that we are cleverer than our ancestors, for example Aristotle, but rather recognise what they can teach us, especially about our real needs which do not change.

One of Toynbee's greatest discoveries in his monumental "Study of History" was that human beings actually need religion, even when they do not realize or accept it. This means that the human who does not accept it, usually finds some other outlet to fill this vacuum. R. C. Zaehner, the Oxford Professor of Eastern Religions, working separately from Toynbee, had come to the same conclusion and expressed it in "The Religious Instinct" (New Outline of Modern Knowledge', 1956). He explained that this instinct, inherent in human nature, can express itself in distorted or warped ways, if it is not grounded in an authentic religion, based on a strong foundation of faith and human reason. People, as individuals or communities, can worship "false gods" to fill a spiritual vacuum in their own lives and in their own nations.

Preface

For instance he recognized Hitler and the Nazi movement as a warped expression of a false god in Germany, arising from the collapse of public and individual morale after the defeat in the First World War, together with their treatment by the victorious victors and the collapse of their own economy in the 1920's. A spiritual vacuum resulted which was filled by Hitler and the Nazi movement, which seemed to satisfy their need to belong to something bigger than themselves, to which they could respond. This became a good example of the way in which the religious instinct, if thwarted or misdirected, can become one of the great obstacles to world peace, whereas an authentic religion will be the greatest help to world peace. Zaehner's findings had fitted in well with those of his contemporary, Toynbee, from another angle of research. Incidentally, Zaehner himself became a member of the Universal Church.

All this is what we mean by learning from the wisdom of the past; just as young people can learn from the experience of their parents. We cannot afford to look down on the past, as the Whig historians used to do, as if they were on a higher step on the supposed "ladder of progress." Consider the fact that more people were killed in the two World Wars in the twentieth century, than at any previous stage of human history; or the fact that the divide between rich and poor people suffering from extreme poverty in the world has increased and is increasing to unprecedented levels. Is this what we can describe as progress? Real progress for mankind is to establish better relationships across the globe, for peace and justice on earth in terms of the fair distribution of the earth's great and God-given resources for the common good of His global family; and it is surely on this that we shall be judged for real progress.

The possible alternative, another World War, or the effects of climate warming, with the possibility of destroying humanity this time, should have sufficient effect on humanity to frighten sane people from continuing to accept warfare or climate warming, as a something which can possibly be considered on any human agenda for progress; and to concentrate its sanity and God-given reasoning power on ways of avoiding such catastrophes.

Some may wonder how chapter 3 (on the European Union) and then various incursions into the division of the history of Germany in the twentieth century into two completely different cultural experiences are relevant to our theme. It is worth examining this at the beginning of the Essay in order to clarify their relevance.

Preface

Professor Sir Ian Kershaw has rightly made his name as an expert on the history of Germany during this long period in his series of specialised books on the subject. He has shown quite clearly that the result of the First World War (1914-18) and the consequent defeat and treatment of Germany were among the main reasons for the coming of the Second World War. He recognizes the cultural change in Germany after this War and has examined the "secular" reasons contributing to the political change so much so that he has confidently predicted that there would be no repeat of these happenings leading to yet another such War.

In particular he has stated that a main reason for the change is the fact that there were now strong and new institutions protecting Europe in this latter period. In particular he praises quite rightly the Institutions of the European Union and Germany itself, as being responsible for this new period of peace and unity. All this is true, but in this Essay we are exploring another way of approach to why all this happened. It is the approach which was adopted by Arnold Toynbee whose interpretation involved a different and wider form of truth which we, too, are following in this Essay. It involves a much greater emphasis on the underlying roles of religion, culture and civilizations, as giving greater depth to our understanding than simply looking at the facts involved on the secular scene, though in no way omitting these facts, and taking them into account.

Our conclusion is that the greatest reason for the appearance of these two great Institutions was the "Renaissance of Christian Humanism" in Western Europe which took place in the second half of the twentieth century. That is why these chapters are very relevant to our theme.

What we are suggesting in this Essay is that we need to make a fresh start from a different set of premises, if we are going to create something better than we have achieved in the past. We can only do so by recognising where we went wrong in the past and be sufficiently determined and hopeful to put it right for our posterity in the New Millennium which we are all facing. To achieve this we need to proceed into the new Millennium hopefully, determinedly, creatively, imaginatively and courageously in putting into practise what I have called our new "Manifesto."

When we refer to "mankind" or "man" in this Essay we have to accept that it is a generic use of this term, meaning always "men and women," since this was the terminology used in various documents to which we shall l be referring. We have to use an accepted premise of thought, expressing the equality of sexes in the future.

Preface

Again, when referring to the "Universal" or "Catholic" Church, we are referring, unless otherwise stated, to the "Christian faith" in the broadest terms. True, the longest (over 2 millennia) and largest (1.2 billion) representative body of Christianity is this Universal Church which, however, regards all baptised Christians as part of the "Body of Christ" and the Kingdom of God; and desires, as did Christ Himself, the unity of all Christians .The term "Christian humanist" is likewise used to include all Christians who share this particular outlook on expressing the Christian faith.

Again, the term "all people of good will" is always taken to mean those humans of all faiths and none, who have the innate desire to do what is good, as their conscience tells them. This is one of the first premises of thought operating in the mind of Pope Francis as he begins his work of reforming the Catholic Universal Church to bring it up to date with the needs of the modern world which it exists to serve.

All the quotes from Arnold Toynbee's great work are from his last, single volume edition of "A Study of History" (1972) (Oxford University Press and Thames and Hudson, Ltd.) in which he develops, summarises and up-dates all his important findings from the previous huge 12 -volume editions which are hugely impressive in their scholarship, but have been read by a comparatively few scholars who have had the time or energy to read them in their original 12 long and extremely detailed and erudite volumes. We should all be grateful, I think, for Toynbee's usual consideration for others a in this one volume edition, before he died.

We shall see, too, that Toynbee himself had the talent and capacity enabling him to find a distinctive, but not always discerned, place for himself in the ranks of British and World historians. He raised the level and capacity of historiography to another level, dealing with the story of worldwide civilizations and cultures, rather than smaller units such as national histories. In so doing, he made a great step forward in historical writing by introducing the idea of looking at and comparing different "patterns" of detailed events, which, when discerned across different times and in different parts of the world, themselves produced different types of truth which are very important in understanding the past and indeed ourselves as well.

This, too, is why the great psycho-analyst, Carl Gustav Jung, considered his own area of study, the human "psyche," had much to offer the study of history as well as psychology. All this, however, was yet to happen, because modern historians are still not fully aware or yet sufficiently

Preface

appreciative of the importance of Toynbee's work in pioneering this step forward in understanding the past as well as ourselves.

The reader will note that Toynbee's work which up to and including the last World War, was popularly regarded as "one of the greatest achievements of modern scholarship"; but precisely from the beginning of the 1960's when a new culture was operative in Britain, his work was downgraded, for no rational or obvious reason. In 1985, the "Oxford Companion to English Literature," remarked that: "His view that the fragmentation and waning of Western Civilization could already be detected, and that hope lay in a new universal religion which would re-capture "spiritual initiative" aroused much controversy." In 1986, the "Oxford Reference Dictionary" commented that:

"His (Toynbee's) greatest work is his "Study of History" in which he surveys the history of civilizations, tracing a pattern of growth, maturity and decay in them all, and concluding that the present Western civilization is in the last of these stages. His suggestion that its fragmentation and waning could be saved by a new universal religion, with one spiritually oriented world society, was not well received." In 1995, "The Companion to British History," commented very briefly that "His work is generally regarded as being too schematic." Significantly, I have not seen any criticism of his actual scholarship and factual accuracy. By "schematic" I think critics are showing an ignorance of Toynbee's jumping ahead to new ways of approaching the truths of history, apart from just seeking "facts"as has been the practice up until now in British historiography. I have some doubts whether such critics actually knew anything about his work or his actual way of working, except that his emphasis on the central importance of religion in the secular society was thus counter-cultural for the present time and should not now be encouraged.

The criticism, ironically, was referring in fact to one of the merits of his work which some of us have now come to appreciate at a later stage of discerning the truth and significance of what lies behind the "patterns" to be discerned in history, which have to be compared and analysed, in such a deep and scholarly work, Toynbee undertook a phenomenally difficult task as a lifetime's work, the enormity and scale of which can never be over-estimated.

It was, however, the first and only historical work of its type which was written with both an "analytical" and "holistic" approach to the investigation of mankind; and as such it could not be comprehended by British historians at large, particularly in the cultural climate of British culture after 1960, as we shall see below.

It seems evident to me that the new culture in Britain disliked any mention of "religion" which seemed to be out of fashion and anti-cultural at this period after 1960. Toynbee would seem to represent rather a threat to this new purely secular world scene. There is, however, an interesting reflection here, because another reason for this downgrading of his work in the late twentieth century, is that he was in touch with new ways of understanding historical truths, fifty years ago, of which historians of today have not yet began to be aware.

In fact on new edges of research in Science, Mathematics and the Arts, and in the new age of computer science and technology, researchers are now beginning to find new ways of finding new truths by discerning "patterns" of symmetry emerging from a wide range of subject areas, regarded in the past as totally separate areas of learning. This approach is being applied recently to the inter-connection of areas such as the symmetry between robotics and dance, humans and animals, choreography and walking, dynamics and shapes of the human body, the beauty of patterns in subjects such as science and mathematics when compared with similar structure of beauty in a range of patterns associated with the world of arts, such as Music in particular; and between religion and mathematics. This might now be on the cutting edge of modern research; yet Aristotle was aware of it more than two thousand years ago. Sometimes in human history we simply have to re-learn wisdom from the past which has been forgotten.

Historical writing, on the whole, has not yet arrived there, except in the case of Arnold Toynbee who was capable of understanding the value of the "holistic" approach in seeing inter-dependent and inter-relationship between all aspects of human life when the vast range of inter-locking facts can reveal underlying patterns and symmetry, hitherto hidden in a variety of separate and analytical studies.

Part of this was owing to Toynbee 's knowledge and understanding of all other parts of the World, including Eastern and Asian cultures and their distinctive approaches to truth and expressing it, in which he was helped by his enviable knowledge of other languages. He was one of the least "insular" of historians in the history of English historical writing; and possibly the first one who lived and thought as a "citizen of the world" as it began to approach the new era of the "global village," in which I believe his distinction and importance will again come to be truly appreciated and his contribution to the story of humanity, made more meaningful and important. His own genius, as in many other cases, was that he was ahead of his own times and therefore did not get the recognition which he deserves.

This Essay has been written in my retirement and is the result of long thought about various issues in which I have been personally involved and gained a long experience professionally, in the areas of education, law, history, historiography, philosophy and theology. My thanks are due to all who have shared with me these experiences, including colleagues, students and pupils, from whom I have learned much and reflected on at length.

I owe a special thanks to my wife, Andrea, and family of four children and nine grandchildren, who have all played an important part in our many discussions on these matters, which have been of interest to us all. I pay tribute, also, to the very helpful global news made available by the splendid team of global reporters engaged by "The Tablet" journal.

My wife, Andrea, has a specialised knowledge in both Science, particularly in Zoology, Biology, and Psychology, which has been invaluable in filling gaps in my own education. Finally, particular thanks to Maria, my daughter, who has helped me greatly in my insufficient knowledge of computer technology, so as to make this enterprise possible. Thanks, also, to my grandchildren, particularly Florrie and Tomas, who are particularly accomplished in this field. I am very fortunate indeed and very grateful to them all for their patience and help.

There are many important decisions to be made in the near future by us Britons, including the referendum on staying in the European Union and the development of our particular culture in the new Millennium. I hope that this Essay will be some contribution to the preparatory debates which are very necessary pre-cursors to our decisions.

I

A Tale of Two Cultures

WE KNOW FROM ARCHAEOLOGY and anthropology that, from the time that "homo sapiens" emerged in the world as a self-conscious being, he (she) has believed instinctively in a transcendental and supernatural life. The first great step forward in human thinking beyond this, was taken by a trio of three great Greek philosophers who won a monumental battle against other Greek thinkers who had a very pessimistic and nihilist view of the capacity of human intelligence. The "sophists", for example, believed that human reason was not capable of discovering truth, but they contented themselves with simply winning arguments without worrying about anything else. Pyrrho (360-270 BC.) founded the group of "sceptics" who accepted the idea of "nescience", meaning that human reason could not achieve certain knowledge of anything. Therefore human reason, for them, had no proper basis for discovering truth, and therefore could not be trusted. Peace of mind could be gained only by accepting this and not trying to do the impossible.

Both sophists and sceptics held a doctrine of intellectual despair, but others wanted to exploit their innate curiosity and reasoning powers as human beings. If the former had won the battle, so to speak, the future of civilization and culture in Western Europe would have been stifled at birth.

The great psycho-therapist, Dr. Carl Gustav Jung, warned us in the twentieth century that "man cannot tolerate life without meaning." Jung has been called "one of the great doctors of all time and one of the great thinkers of his century"[1] and one of his interesting comments, of relevance

---

1. Freeman, In Preface to Jung's *Man and Symbols*, 1964.

to our theme was: "To find the solution to most of modern man's problems, we have to turn to the medieval (world)."

Jung (1875-1961) was a Swiss thinker of world fame. A psychologist who proceeded to fame as a psycho-analytic specialist, he, too, like Toynbee in another area of study and discovery, deduced from his detailed study of the human "psycho" that the human being requires religion and belief in the transcendence of God, to meet the demands of his or her spiritual nature; and so did societies and civilizations. Jung concluded that modern problems of many kinds came from the waning of religious belief in the western world. In 1933 he published his "Modern Man in Search of a Soul" (1933), but perhaps his most important book was "The Psychology of the Unconscious" (1912). He concluded that the human subconscious was an important entrance into the realm of spiritual transcendence. Here there are undiscovered patterns of knowledge from different areas of human studies which can provide future truths yet to be discovered. When modern research begins to cross different subject areas, important new discoveries such as the revelation of patterns can be made through such "holistic" thinking. It can bring science and the arts together in appreciation of a previously unknown beauty.

Jung himself believed that his own work had important conclusions which would be very important for the history of psychology and religion. His "Undiscovered Self: Present and Future: The plight of the individual in modern society"[2] for example, is redolent with connections to Toynbee's work, without either party knowing it. They were both too busy with their own work. I have no record of Jung ever meeting or knowing of Toynbee; but it seems clear that there are interesting patterns of knowledge, to be discerned in the work of both, leading to new truths concerning human beings and the nature of mankind.

Again, from Toynbee's study of cultures and civilizations, when seen in the light of other studies from different angles, such as those of Carl Gustav Jung, R.C. Zaehner, and T.S. Eliot, produced patterns of thought, leading to new truths when brought together, but this was to be a later stage of Inquiry into the pursuit of truth; and indeed my research seems to have been the first time for it to be used in my own study of its place in historiography.

This seeking of truths from patterns of thought, had not yet started in other studies in the 20th century and have only began to come to light in

---

2. See Storr, *The Essential Jung*, 349-403

the late twentieth first century through developments in science and mathematics. In this sense there has been an interesting coming together of Arts and Sciences, when scientific research has began to show the beauty, as well as new knowledge, that can be found in these patterns. This can then make contact with the "beauty" to be found in the creation of the Cosmos and the Universe. It was part of the greatness of Aristotle, of course, that he knew all about the need for "holistic thinking" more than two millennia ago. He would have found it difficult to understand the narrow and analytic approach that the Western World has taken up in the modern world. Again, his genius was to be so far ahead of his own times. Again and again modern researchers discover that he has been there before them and his place in intellectual thinking is being continuously enhanced.

This may well be a development which can lead us out of the idea of truth being found only in science, which has dogged British culture since the vastly inappropriate name of "the enlightenment" –usually defined in scientific terms- of the seventeenth and eighteenth centuries took charge of our thinking. Similarly, scientists such as the Czech geneticist, Gregor Mendel, Abbot of a Monastery there, who discovered the laws of genetics and inheritance, could have taught the British that there is complete harmony between Science and Religion, with nothing to fear at all from one another when they kept to their own particular approach to the truth. Indeed, when properly understood they can be mutually inspiring, as they were to Aristotle.

Fortunately for us there was another positive and much more enduring system of thinking in the Greek world, provided by three of the greatest philosophers of all time. Socrates (469-399 BC), Plato (428-347 BC) and Aristotle (384-322 BC) were each the pupil, in chronological order, to the other. Each of these pupils stood on the shoulders, so to speak, of the previous one. Together they lifted expectation of human reason to its highest point of understanding. They showed that human reason could reach certainty, as far as it could go in its purely human capacity.

Socrates never wrote a book, but fortunately his pupil Plato published his teacher's methods in his "Dialogues." Socrates showed that human reason could reach the truth by dialogue and continual cross examination to discover any error in the argument, leading to a final certainty. His "Socratic" method of learning has still been in use through the ages and up to the present. His belief in the human need for freedom and human rights put him in bad odour with the Athenian state which organised his death.

Socrates' pupil, Plato, went on to found the "Academy of Learning" in Greece and produced important work on metaphysics and ethics. A central idea of his teaching was the idea of "Forms" which are outside the secular world. These are real, but timeless and motionless. He believed that mind, not matter, was the fundamental basis. Material things were simply imperfect copies of abstract and eternal "ideas." His thinking played an important part in future culture and civilization in Western Europe influencing the work of St. Augustine, for example, during the Christian era.

Then came Plato's pupil, Aristotle, who I believe, reached the peak of human learning and understanding by bringing this combined learning together by his holistic approach and sheer width of mind and vision. Using reason he argued that man could discover the truth concerning the nature of man and the universe, by a close study of human nature and the working of the universe. Knowledge is gathered through the senses. It was this which substantiates the claim by modern scientists that he was the founder of modern science. His range of knowledge was immense. His philosophical work was incorporated into Christian philosophy by St. Thomas Aquinas in the twelfth century and was also influential in the work of Islamic scholars at this time.

Aristotle widened the whole field of Greek learning, and in the 22 treatises which have survived, his work covers ethics, philosophy, logic, psychology, astronomy, politics, biology, meteorology, physics and literary criticism. His work on politics and ethics demonstrates his belief that human happiness comes from conformity to the needs or laws of human nature and the natural world. He said that it was incumbent on human beings to work in accordance with the natural laws which were to be discerned in nature. He taught that human help for one another is incipient and ingrained in human nature. Humans should react by developing the character qualities, such as fortitude, justice, temperance, wisdom, prudence, moderation, which were needed to obey such "laws."

These character qualities were called "virtues" which were needed to guide good "ethics." These were needed to produce good human beings, who through them could achieve a sense of their own fulfilment; and would also produce good results for the common good of a well-ordered and manageable democratic State. From this was born the culture of "virtue-ethics" which has provided one of the two great pillars of the culture of Western Civilization for over two millennia.

A Tale of Two Cultures

But Aristotle did not stop there. At a higher level he believed that everything derived from a single form of "prime matter"; and this was shaped by some transcendent "Form." The principle of human life was what he termed "the soul" which was the "form" of the living creature, not a substance derived from it; and since soul transcends matter, it must be immortal. Basically, he believed that all human life had a purpose –that of becoming what was intended for them; and people should progress to become what they were meant to be.

This procedure could only make sense, however, if there was a transcendent (or spiritual) "Form." This "Form" represented the Ultimate Good at which human development was intended to aim. It was this "Form" which provided the natural law inherent in human nature and the world. This law provided the criteria against which "ethics" , the discernment of "right" and "wrong" could be identified, assessed, and promulgated in the good and ordered society.

For Aristotle, all human knowledge was contained in a great unity of form and design; its parts were inter-connected and inter-dependent. There were no false and artificial divisions between these parts as far as he was concerned. His genius was in his ability to combine two parts of the human brain which have been identified in the twentieth century, in the new and intriguing science which we call "neuroscience", the study of the human brain and how it works for the mysterious and varied elements of the human mind.

Neuroscience has revealed much of interest to our theme. It confirms, for example, Aristotle's belief that man has an inherent inclination to help his neighbour; and that man "feels good" when having done this; it even improves his standard of health and living, by doing good; and this result increases as this action becomes "habitual." We also know from this science that the mental processes involved in approaching such elements as religion and transcendent matters, coincide with the ways in which theologians works, which indicates that this is an inherent part of human nature, created for our benefit and to fit our human needs.

But an even more profound discovery has emerged from neuroscience. We know now that the human brain works in two distinct ways which we describe as "analytical" and "holistic." The first is concerned primarily with detailed study and analytic literalism of observed facts in science and mathematics. It meant that the only real approach to truth was the "scientific" in the minds of the "Enlightened" Western world; and this has remained in them up to the present moment - an analytical process, judged by what we can see through the human senses - touching, tasting, feeling, seeing and listening.

The second, the holistic approach to truth, is concerned with a far wider outlook on life and human knowledge, and has continued to dominate in the Eastern world. It uses many kinds of approaches to truth in different aspects of human intelligence, such as intuitive, emotional, empathetic, imaginative, symbolic, metaphorical, and most importantly the religious or transcendental area of human intelligence and awareness.[3] The is valuable, but not necessarily the of a matter, which can be better discovered by placing that fact in a wider framework of many other facts and values which have then to be placed in perspective to discover the truth in all areas of life.

Both of these approaches to truth are important and ideally come together in a balanced outlook which best serves human beings in coming to terms with "reality"; but of the two, the holistic is the more important in keeping in touch with reality. If this aspect is omitted, man is more inclined to be narrow minded and inward looking, with a loss of perspective which can lead to mental problems. For truth and the important element of humour are often to be found in looking at the world through the media of perspective, that is in terms of the small or great importance of its different elements. It was a French thinker who once stated that "Le rire est avant tout une correction" (laughter is above all a form of correction). We laugh when we can recognize that something is totally out of perspective; and we are in danger if we cannot discern this. This is why despotic rulers cannot tolerate being laughed at.

The human being is constituted of body and soul. We are not simply pieces of material, put together. Aristotle had come to acknowledge this as a central part of his philosophy; but western man has been led astray in modern times partly, I believe, because of an element of inappropriate pride, by the thought that man can know everything of importance through science and has no need of God, his Creator. This single-minded approach has greatly affected his discernment of the reality in human life and all its aspects. This pride, together with selfishness, are two examples of that warping of human nature, which the Greeks described as "hubris", the pride which comes before a fall. This in fact was a main theme which featured widely in the great Greek Tragedies.

3. Jung. *Man on his Symbols*.

A Tale of Two Cultures

Of the two approaches then, the "holistic "approach to truth is more important than the analytic, because it takes account of other and equally valid considerations such as contextual background, feasibility, emotional effects, general perspective, and religious values, which may or may not make an idea "practical" or appropriate in relation to the "real" life of human beings. This has connection with what we call "common sense." There is a connection between a holistic outlook and mental health because truth lies in perspective; but the ideal state of mind is where health for the human mind is achieved with a proper balance between both approaches to truth, as practised by Aristotle. A person whose mind is narrowed by a purely analytic approach to knowledge is in some danger of losing his or her sense of perspective, or common sense, and sense of humour, which can endanger mental health.

This phenomenon is reported to have increased rapidly in the period after 1960 so that it is now a major problem in modern society, in the culture which has become known as "After-Virtue", or the "Permissive Society." Here mental illnesses are frequently reported to have increased greatly, in all age groups, but particularly and most sadly in the case of suicides and other mental problems among young people. Toynbee actually says that this is a characteristic phenomenon which he has seen repeated in the process of fragmentation in the civilizations and cultures which he has studied and where religious faith has waned. He writes:

"I also find a corresponding psychological schism in the souls of people who happen to have born into this unhappy age. Discordant psychic tendencies which are perhaps always latent in human nature now find free play. People lose their bearings, and rush down blind alleys, seeking escape."[4]

So the rapid advance of science in the Western world since the seventeenth and eighteenth, and particularly in the huge advances of scientific and technological knowledge in the twentieth and twentieth first centuries, has unfortunately led to the false idea that science and the analytic approach is the only form of credible knowledge, leaving aside other and even more important values and truths which stem from the "holistic" part of the human brain.

The psychiatrist and neuroscientist, Iain McGilchrist's book, "The Master and his Emissary: the divided brain and the making of the Western world", was acclaimed by "Network Review", the Journal of the Scientific

---

4. Toynbee, *A Study of History*, 211.

and Medical Network which stated that: "this quite remarkable book will radically challenge the way you understand the world and yourself." It confirmed the insights of Aristotle and the Christian tradition, and is opening new paths for future development in this field.

The Christian Revelation tells us that "God is love" and His presence is revealed in all aspects of life where love is involved. True love is the only answer to all God's actions, whether we understand them or not. Life on earth is the preparation for our real birth, through what we call "death", by entering a process of complete human fulfilment and happiness which we call "Heaven." This has been possible because Christ chose to die that we may live. Our part is simply to know, love and serve God and our neighbour in this life, which is the essential part of this preparation for the next.

The Revelation showed too that God had created human beings in "His own image." This included the gift of human reason but transcended it with the supreme power of "love." So the first two commandments of God, which really contains within themselves all the others, are: "Love God and love your neighbour as yourselves", later explained even more fully by Christ as "Love God and love others as I Have loved you." This concept was beautifully and elegantly exemplified by Shakespeare centuries afterwards when he wrote "To err is human; to forgive divine"; meaning that making mistakes is part of being human in spite of reason; but forgiveness is a share in the divinity of God and part of man's spiritual and transcendent nature.

This capacity of "transcendence" is termed in Christianity as being born "in the image of God", making the human being unique in the animal world and capable of rising to greater transcendent and spiritual heights; but the warped character of human nature is also capable, if unrestrained, to fall to depths which are below the purely animal level. This was what Toynbee had in mind in his assertion that:

"the religious experience . . . transforms "Chaos" into "Cosmos" and, therefore, renders human existence possible –prevents it, that is, from regression into the levels of zoological existence."[5]

Again, to demonstrate this in another way, many modern minds might not understand what the theologian of the eleventh century, Anselm, meant when he wrote with complete assurance that: "Credo ut intellegem" (I believe, that I may understand). What he meant is that he knew that his reason could take him far, but he would need "Faith" and "Love" to carry him higher into the transcendent realms of higher knowledge; and this

---

5. Toynbee, *A Study of History*, 343.

could be gained only by prayer and also by the Sacraments of the Church which are meeting points with, and sources of spiritual power from the God of love, to help us fulfil our spiritual needs and awareness.

This transcendental power is the grace of God, which reaches its height in the sacrament of the Eucharist in which we receive God himself into our very being in the form of bread and wine. John Betjeman expressed this in the last line of his poem on where he describes the greatest joy for Christmas celebration as being the knowledge given to the whole world, that:

"God was man in Palestine, and lives today in Bread and Wine."[6]

This was indeed an event which was so great that it divides the whole of mankind's history into two parts which we still describe, after two Millennia, as BC and AD, before and after the coming of God in Christ which we call the Christian Revelation, and is celebrated throughout the World today. All this explanation is needed to understand why the Christian Revelation was to provide the second, and even more important, pillar of the culture and civilization of Western Europe. It also produced an immediate change in Greek culture, in various ways. For example, until the Christian Revelation, the greatest disaster for the Greek man or woman under the "virtue-ethics" culture of Aristotle, was the public shame to be endured if he or she was found out in some crime against its ethics. It was being found out, rather than the crime which hurt most, because it was not redeemable and often ended in suicide.

This was caused by a sense of shame that could not be removed, not of a feeling of "guilt" against the law of love, because this under the Christian dispensation was redeemable when the sinner confessed. In the latter case it was recognized that the God of love is eager to forgive the erring sinner who is genuinely sorry, but now forgiven and can start again with a "clean sheet." There is no need for any thought of suicide. This is only one detail of the more joyful life which the Christian ethos of love can contribute to a culture and its human beings. That is why Christ is often described as "the Light of the World", who brought us out of darkness into light.

The Christian Revelation showed that "God, in Christ, was reconciling the World unto Himself" and contributed a personal relationship of love between God and the individual person. It provided the warmth and joy which human beings need. It gave a greater meaning, purpose, identity, and inalienable dignity and self-worth to all human beings. They could be

---

6. Betjeman, *Christmas*.

joyful in knowing that God had a personal love and interest in each one of them, which is the real basis for his or her necessary sense of self-worth. This self- worth is an answer to one of the most important of human needs, which derives from man's spiritual nature.

Each one of us is different from anyone else and his or her importance comes from his or her special creation as a unique human being, created by God for an eternal and joyful destiny with Him. So, we have to treat one another, with that special respect and importance which we call love. This is the basis of human worth, which is exactly the same for all human beings, and makes us equal in the sight of God. This is the ultimate basis for modern democracy and human rights which are inalienable, for each and every human being.

So, the "Reason" of Aristotle and the "Faith" of the Christian Revelation became the two great spiritual pillars on which the future culture and civilization of Western Europe was created. These two elements are also the necessary ingredients of an authentic religion. This did not mean, however, that everything was perfect in this situation. There was still the problem of the warped aspect of human nature, in spite of the inherent goodness existing in us all. Human pride and selfishness and jealousy still exist but at least people know under this dispensation that there a purpose life and that they know the difference between good and evil, and what they both entailed. And perhaps most importantly, God's compassion and forgiveness is available to all of us when we sincerely ask for forgiveness.

Because of human free will which had to be the case to complete the fully human nature of man, there will always be trouble of various sorts deriving from human weakness in the face of temptation and we shall be looking at this phenomenon in human culture and civilization later. This weakness at the individual level is quite different, however, from what we mean by cultural change which can involve a radical difference to the whole of a community, in terms of values, beliefs and assumptions of thought, together with a marked change in behaviour. This can undermine and overthrow the basic premises of value, meaningfulness, coherence and mutual trust which are necessary parts of a real culture or civilization.

The culture of "virtue-ethics" has lasted for two millennia, in spite of dangers and attacks from within and without; but in the twentieth century a great change took place when a new culture quite suddenly appeared in Britain which we shall now examine in some detail.

A Tale of Two Cultures

Britain had shown great strength and durability in leading the defence of the World against the attempt of the Nazi Party in Germany, led by Hitler, to dominate the World with its anti-religious Fascist ideology. It is generally agreed that much of this strength was drawn from its determination to defend the culture, civilization and Christian values which had underlain its way of life from time immemorial. Winston Churchill had emphasized this in his never-to- forgotten speech in 1940 when Hitler was overcoming surrounding states in Europe, leaving Britain and its Commonwealth isolated in defence of "Christian Civilization." In this situation, Churchill predicted that it was destined to be "Britain's finest hour", a speech which certainly enhanced the innate "bull-dog" sense of courage and determination in the British people.

With the notable help of the United States of America, this threat was overcome and Hitler defeated; and a period of peace followed. Then another hidden danger, of equal menace, appeared as Russia, dominated by Stalin and his Communist Party, showed its intention of threatening to dominate Europe with its materialistic Marxist ideology.

The last World War had begun when Hitler invaded Poland, but when it ended. Russia, a supposed ally of the West, had occupied not only Poland, but also East Germany and claimed these territories as its own. It became obvious to the West that Stalin intended to extend his "Empire" and its anti- religious ideology over the rest of Europe. The USA wanted Britain to lead again and to help build a new and stronger Europe against this new menace, assisted again by the USA, with its formidable global strength. There was much negotiation about this over the next decade, but by 1950 it had become obvious that Britain did not want this role of leading Europe again. We shall be returning to what happened next below.[7]

There were various reasons for Britain's reluctance to get too involved in the defence of Europe again. It had largely lost its own vast Empire overseas by this time and needed a new role in the World, but it had a long history of four centuries of separating itself from the rest of Europe and was tempted to "mind its own business", so to speak, in the period of peace after 1945. It had been the first of the new "nation states" in the sixteenth century and there was a strong feeling of wanting to re-establish its old status as a nation-state which until recently had its own great Empire, and not becoming simply a part of Europe. This was the result of a powerful

---

7. See Appendix 1.

tradition established in the sixteenth century by Henry VIII and still alive to this day in the psychological make-up of many English people.[8]

Another element in the situation was the curious belief that the "nation state" is a necessary and implicit part of human life, an essential and natural part of being human. But this in fact is not the case. The nation state is simply a passing result of certain circumstances which arose at one period of human development; and now its day has passed as we enter the new world of "the global village." The new world is offering us a much better life as fellow members of the human family which now has a better chance of achieving peace in the world if we can take the new opportunities available through the principles of "solidarity" and human rights, preserving political unity while also preserving the uniqueness of various cultures throughout the world by the concomitant principle of "subsidiarity" (decisions to be made at the lowest appropriate level of responsibility).

Britain was enjoying its period of peace after the long War and celebrating our success in it; enjoying, too, a period of much better material prosperity than it had before the War. This period of material comfort, security and immense technical advancement, particularly in the area of mass media entertainment, caused a sense of inordinate pride in human achievement. There was also this old enjoyment of "splendid isolation"; perhaps with a touch of the old sense of "superiority" over the "foreigner." There were echoes here of the old Greek tragedies concerning "hubris." Indeed the author of the masterpiece on the origin, growth and decline of cultures, Arnold Toynbee, makes mention of one characteristic of the process of the breakdown of civilizations which is pertinent in this case:

"I then have to account for the failure of creativity, and ascribe it to the spiritual demoralization to which we are not bound to succumb, and for which, therefore we have to bear the responsibility. Success seems to make us lazy or self-satisfied or conceited"[9] and, the great Bard himself, Shakespeare, a notable expert in understanding human nature, once mentioned that "security is man's chiefest enemy." Those of us who lived in wartime know exactly what he meant. When the bombs were falling, there was an astonishing sense of neighbourliness in all types of people, and the need to "get together" and actually enjoy mutual inter-dependence, was great. After the War everything wonderful in comparison secular society with the past, except for the behaviour of people who felt that they should be free

8. Jones, *The English Nation*.
9. Toynbee, *A Study of History*, 127.

to do what they liked, without regard for others; and then there came the opportunity and temptation to adopt a drastic change of life and their way of living it. The temptation to free themselves from the old conscientious restrictions of the Christian tradition, allowed the warped elements of human nature to make their public appearance on an unprecedented scale.

All this produced the background for the appearance of a new culture, led initially by a minority of celebrated figures in the new mass media and the world of entertainment, but soon spreading more widely in the 1960s, to include powerful political people, and then the Police. These began to take advantage of the new culture which had became popularly known as the "permissive society" or perhaps better rendered as "the me-first" society, to become involved in various nefarious activities, the sexual abuse of young and vulnerable young people.

This was beginning to mark the start of a completely new culture in which other people were afraid to raise their voices against those who were offending.

All this was in direct contrast to the values the old culture governed by "virtue- ethics which had proclaimed its reliance on the two greatest commandments of the old culture: "to love God and "to love thy neighbour as thyself."

The Christian attitude to sex, for example, is that it is a wonderful gift from God, that combined intrinsically with love, joy and the human family, can be of central importance to a humane and human culture. The new attitude resulting from the "permissive society" was that sex could be used and exploited simply as an instrument of pleasure and personal gratification; and it became used in this way. It then became an instrument of abuse leaving a trail of human misery in its wake on a very great scale. It reaches its worst excesses when exploited by paedophile groups, abusing children, and degrading humanity to something way below the purely animal way of life.

All this demonstrated a remarkably naïve and ignorant awareness of how powerful a danger sex can represent, when let loose from the restraints which our ancestors learned to respect. This was the seed-bed from which the attitude of sexual behaviour declined radically and quickly. The sexual abuse of young children reached a stage throughout Britain of becoming regarded by people in supposedly caring positions of authority as "socially acceptable" and many in this position were afraid to interfere with powerful or celebrated nationally famous people who exploited their status for doing did what they liked with women and children. The spread of "gangs" of perverted people, exploiting the system and abusing children at a "sub-human" level, has reached such dimension that present Prime minister, Mr. Cameron, has described it as a "national threat" of the highest kind.

In more general terms, on the 10th of August, 2015, "The Guardian" Newspaper reported as its main headline that an international study across the countries of the world, had revealed that English children were second from the bottom in terms of their well-being and happiness.

It all in this period 1960 and has ever since. A report in June, 2015, based on the thousands of cases paedophile activity, has described the situation as a "revolution" in which it is estimated that one in thirty five men in Britain are now likely paedophiles, with no inhibitions.

In the same month a report shows that the prosecutions of attacks on females, involving, rape, violence in families, and other elements, has reached a its highest point in Britain in 2015. Now the Government has asked an outsider, an eminent Canadian judge, to make an independent inquiry into the continual rise of sexual abuse of all kinds, but especially against children, which has grown since 1960 to the level of a national threat. In September, 2015 a new post was established, a "Czar" in charge of mental problems existing in the teenager section of society caused by the now "pornographic nature of this society."

The decline in culture was not, however, confined to one area of life in Britain. It affected the behaviour of all aspects of human life as the very word "virtue" became scorned and avoided. From that time onwards, there has been a marked change in the behaviour of professional bodies across the board; and especially that of bodies, supposedly looking after children and vulnerable or elderly people in British society.

All our institutional bodies were created to exist primarily for the common good of a human and humane society as it had been envisaged by the old "virtue-ethics" culture of the past. As such, they were known and respected by all. Under the new culture all of these professions have all been castigated repeatedly by a relentless series of reports into areas of unprofessional standards; and often revealing levels of cruelty, selfishness, greed and corruption which have led at all levels to man's inhumanity to man. At all levels, too, there has been evidence of abuse and disregard of whistle-blowers' who have attempted to reveal any wrong doing.

The Banking system has been affected drastically by wrong doing of a selfish and greedy nature which became so endemic, that it was a major cause of the financial and economic collapses of 2008. Similarly there has

A Tale of Two Cultures

developed during this period a huge increase in the practise of fraud and "scams" against vulnerable people, to such an extent that the BBC has produced a regular programme entitled "Scam Britain."

Neither has any of this behaviour been stopped. As I write (March 16th, 2015), for example, there has been revealed yesterday a sex abuse against children, where hundreds of victims have been suffered in Sheffield and Rotherham and where both the police and social services have failed in their work of protection –only the most recent in a series of such cases in other parts of Britain.

Similarly, today, also, other evidence has been revealed of past hideous and inhuman offences against children of all ages by senior politicians, with the connivance of police of the London metropolitan, who have either taken part themselves or have concealed the offences of their colleagues. Significantly all these offences have been traced back to the beginning of this culture which started about 1960.

Virtually every week there are reports from all areas of life in Britain and its professional institutions, providing further evidence of the continuing effects of this new culture on the behaviour and attitude of its people. On,20th May,2015, for example, the newspaper headlines on BBC news are telling of the "shocking report" which has just been produced, on the inhuman treatment (lack of care, neglect and no compassion) of terminally ill people in Britain's NHS hospitals, to such an extent that they would be much better advised to die at home or anywhere else. I am sure that there are good nurses who have better standards and suffer from this kind of report, but one must also accept that, on the whole, it is telling the truth; for it has no reason for doing otherwise, as is the case with the other reports such as this in different areas.

What is significant, too, is in spite of these many reports, deciding that "a new culture" was needed in each type of profession involved, they do not seem to have stopped the damage being done. Now, for just one of many such examples, in August, 2015, a report has been produced that the number of serious abuses in the supposed care of elderly, vulnerable and mentally inflicted patients, has continued to increase greatly in this area of concern, reaching its highest ever point.

A classical example of this failure to be able to correct a general cultural demise within one isolated section of such a society, is the manifest inability revealed by a certain Bank, one of the main culprits in previous misdemeanours, to put itself right after having had to pay back millions of pounds as punishment for their past fraudulent behaviour. The Bank admitted its fault, recognising that it had placed too much emphasis on money making at the cost of losing its ethical standards.

It replaced its main executive leader (investment –private money making banking) by a leader from the retail (public service banking) who made a valiant to attempt to put things right in the Summer of 2015. The new man did well, applying reformed ethical standards to reform the whole system. By early Autumn 2015, however, he was suddenly sacked because the Governing Board, were receiving too many complaints that certain people were not making as much money as they had been in the "bad old days."

Similarly there continues the same increasing number of frauds and scams, usually at the expense of the old and vulnerable members of society; the cases of lack of care towards the old and vulnerable in hospitals; the rise in violent crime, home and family breakdowns and sexual abuse of women and children.

The new culture which arose about 1960 was analysed by the philosopher Alastair Macintyre in his study entitled "After Virtue" (1981), explaining that the waning of religious belief meant that "moral judgments are linguistic survivals from the practise of classical theism which have lost the context provided by these practices." In short it means that the age old "virtue-ethics" which had been in control for over two millennia, had been replaced by the attitude that God could be left out of the "context" so that people should be free to what they liked; and this unleashed all the dark forces of the warped element in human nature.

One of the most telling and possibly most invidious results of the change of culture after 1960, in my view, is also the most logical. "After Virtue" implies that the "belief" in virtue itself has been abandoned; and it is true that the very word itself has gone out of fashion and is no longer in common usage, as if people are embarrassed to use it. But with it has gone all kinds of human qualities which were associated with it. "Trust" for example is one of the most obviously important qualities in determining the quality and efficiency of a flourishing culture and community. One of the most noticeable features of our society in the period since 1960 is this lack of trust in one another and in the professions. This can affect the whole ethos of a culture, so that people often cannot express and demonstrate the best part of themselves and their human feelings, because they may be misunderstood by a sceptical and suspicious audience.

A Tale of Two Cultures

One of the most extraordinary element in the situation is that after each scandal has been discovered, whether in Banks, the Police, Politicians, Health Service, Care homes, Sports organisations, Local Government, and all other aspects of professional life, the same complaint has been reported: that each of the professions involved needed "a cultural change."

But no-one has suggested that the more obvious "elephant in the room" is the general change in culture and its effect on human society and behaviour in Britain between 1960 and continuing up to the present day. Nor has anyone dared to say that the general cause of it has been the omission of God and any form of religion from a part in the new secular culture. It is quite remarkable that no-one seemed able to deduce the glaringly obvious conclusion that human society cannot remain fully human and humane for long without the help of a religious element which holds together.

It does suggest, however, from the evidence put before us every day, that there must be truth in Toynbee's statement that without a belief in God helping them to respond to man's spiritual nature and needs , it is not possible to create or sustain a human and humane culture and civilization. Law in itself cannot take the place of human conscience and its natural response to good and evil, though British prisons are notably bursting at the seams, to an extent that it is often not possible to provide the improving strategies which have been suggested to help prisoners to reform.

This, of course, does not mean, however, that individual people cannot live the good life; because the innate conscience exists in all of us; and many still live good lives, but they often now provide the victims of the new cultural faults. Human nature is innately good, but it can be led astray, especially when it attempts to live without its Creator. Nor are we saying, of course that there are no people now behaving differently to this new culture; and of course the imperfection of human nature means that there were always some people in the previous culture who behaved contrary to its values.

But the real change in cultures involves a behaviour, not always by the majority initially, though spreading rapidly, but including virtually all professional groups who constitute the "pillars" upholding society; and this is what marks out the nature of the change which began in 1960 and which was demonstrated beyond all doubt after it contributed largely to the world's economic recession of 2008, which was produced by an extraordinary increase in human greed, selfishness, and dishonesty in the world of financial dealing. The interest of the nation's economy and the common good was lost in the face of this new social culture and its "me first" or "after virtue" assumptions of thought

All investigating bodies into the scandals produced much the same answer that "this cannot be improved without a change in the basic culture of this or that profession or public Many new heads of management were appointed to introduce the needed reforms within a variety of professions. The problem was recognized and attempts to tackle it took place in each of these professions, but to little avail. What it lacked was a proper recognition that we were dealing with a "whole" cultural change which was having the same affect across the whole of our society. This is a far more difficult problem to solve. Even Parliament and the Government have been involved in scandals in various ways and are not trusted. The real truth was not faced and the nation seemed to have "slept walked" into the new culture.

Still, now in 2016, there is ample evidence of the continuation and even increase of this basic weakness in British society. We have been told recently of the discovery of a huge failure in the proper care of the most vulnerable people has been discovered in the huge area covered by the National Health Service in the south of England, with the added rider that this may be the case elsewhere as well. Immediately after this, another report has revealed a "gigantic increase" in the number of cases of domestic abuse in the last two years, so much so that there is real doubt as whether the police can cope with its demands. Again the same cry has gone out that: "only a change in culture" in this particular area can halt the slide downhill. The "elephant in the room" is still completely unrevealed, presumably because it has not been discovered.

The result is that in Britain, as opposed to Germany in particular and the European Continent as a whole, "Christianity is now at the Cross Roads", in the words of Linda Woodhead, Professor of the Sociology of Religion and Britain's leading authority in this field, who gave the British Academy lecture in January, 2016, based on her recent research into the subject. She said that "The ties which once bound religion and society have frayed." The "YouGov poll" which she has been conducting shows a continuing fall in religious belief in Britain, reaching 46% in December. She adds that "No religion is the new norm and there is every indication that its majority will continue to grow." Only a minority show a "Richard Dawkins" type rejection of religion. Only 13% held anti-religious views and under half said that they are atheists. This predominant attitude seems to confirm the view that society in Britain has "slept-walked" into a no- thinking acceptance of the "permissive society" by stating that they are non-religious. In the meanwhile standards of secular society have continued to decline rapidly since the culture of "virtue-ethics" was replaced by "the permissive society." Violent crime, abuse within families, sexual abuse, scandals arising from the inhumane treatment of the most vulnerable people in hospitals and care homes, extraordinary levels of victimisation of vulnerable, helpless and elderly people, are all part of the present way of life.

This is where Toynbee's work is so valuable. His detached scholarship enabled him to find and write the truth in splendid isolation. He has shown, demonstrably and incontrovertibly in my view that the major reason for the decline and fall of a culture is its abandonment of the "religious" and ethical element which is capable of holding all parts of society together into a coherent whole in which people can trust one another. One of Toynbee's major findings in fact from his research into the 52 civilizations and cultures is that human beings cannot remain humane as a group in society if they are deprived of religion and belief in a transcendental God. He wrote that it is the religious experience which: "transforms "Chaos" into "Cosmos", that is it prevents human behaviour from falling into levels of zoological existence."

Toynbee alone had been able to point to the otherwise invisible 'elephant in the room' in Britain after 1960. It was precisely this counter-cultural aspect of his work which made his great work, "A Study of History" become quite suddenly down graded in Britain after 1960. It is a signal example of the way in which the study of history can become a victim to cultural change, at the expense of truth.

The change in Britain was certainly remarkable in this respect. It was simply a change from a society based on "virtue-ethics" to one which could actually be named and identified as an "After Virtue" society, the highly appropriate name of Macintyre's book on the subject. Little wonder, then, that a regular programme on the British BBC is now entitled "Fraud Britain" in which it describes and warns of all the mounting effects of dishonesty, especially at the expense of its most vulnerable citizens; and is advising on ways in which they may be protected.

This, of course, is not saying that all human beings will behave in the same way. The innate goodness of human nature is always struggling against the temptations offered by the warped elements of selfishness, greed and pride. Some very strong-willed people will be able to resist cultural changes. A greater number, I would think, will be much more affected by them. We are not talking here of blame or no blame in individuals. We are talking of the prevailing ethos and climate of a whole society; and it is when there is a great change in this respect that we talk about the rise or decline of a civilization. It is difficult to measure accurately; but it becomes very clear usually to those who have lived through these times and experienced the changes of attitude, assumptions of thought, and behaviour which creep in to accompany such cultural change.

This waning of religious belief in fact was the reason for the decline and fall of human cultures and civilizations put forward by Arnold Toynbee, the distinguished historian of the decline and fall of civilizations throughout human history, in his famous "The Study of History", written in 12 volumes over a period of thirty years. It was also the reason that his unique achievement came into disfavour during this period after 1960, because it showed that this change of British culture fitted in exactly with what he had shown in his work about the history of past cultures, which before and during World War II, had been called "one of the outstanding achievements of British scholarship."

While it made his message counter-cultural and therefore unacceptable to contemporary society, the quick decline in cultural standards throughout this new society was proving at the same time that what he was saying was true and the evidence was staring British society in the face; but it was literally blinded to what it did not want to see.

It is of some interest and relevance to our theme, too, that looking back it becomes apparent that the first attacks on foreign immigrants in Britain, after the War, started in the mid-1960's and continued with greater force in the 1970's and from then onwards. Up until 1960 there had been a much better attitude, generally speaking, in Britain towards foreigners, but this changed rapidly as a concomitant of the cultural change from "virtue-ethics" to the self-centred and "me-first" attitude proclaimed by the new "after virtue" vulture.

Arnold Toynbee had discovered much about the cycles of rise, decline and fall of previous cultures and civilizations. His work did, however and very importantly indicate also that the decline could be stopped and the civilization revived under certain circumstances. This was an extremely important finding which forms the basis for hope in the chances of recovery, as long as human beings, using their free will, react positively to the challenge facing them.

A Tale of Two Cultures

This Essay describes the way in which a new culture, could be created in Britain, if the majority of people wanted it. This new culture which we call "Christian Humanism" has already changed the lives of the German people who realized that a drastic change was needed in their society after the awful experience living under Nazi regime which very nearly destroyed them altogether.

Their position was much worse than anything experienced in Britain; but they were given the right leadership by a "Christian Humanist" Government (See Chapter 1V) and their own determination and value system to rise from the disastrous culture established by the Nazi Government which had been imposed on them, to become now the new leaders of Europe, following a noble vision of the future which was given to them by an ideology which we are calling "Christian Humanism." They had the "vision" of leading European people to Peace on Earth instead of the dreadful wars which they themselves had experienced. They actually succeeded and gave this peace to 500 million people for an unprecedented 60 years, which hopefully will continue. This was a "Vision" led by the philosophy of Christian Humanism in the European Union..

The British people, in my view, also need a new and noble vision for their future, without which ancient wisdom tell us "the people perish." I think that a referendum put before the British people asking them to decide which type of culture they want : "Christian Humanism" (as portrayed in this Essay)) or "After-Virtue", they might well provide a result which would be interesting, because I have great faith in the potential of the British people, once they understand where they stand and why. They have the chance to take a leading part in the same "Vision" of keeping peace in Europe and possibly spreading it to other Continents, while uplifting their hearts to achieve a much better culture for themselves, following the inspiration of Christian Humanism. The Anglican, Archbishop Justin Welby and Cardinal Vincent Nichols would constitute a very strong team to represent the Christian Humanist element in a secular society seeking help to improve its own culture by education and other strategies.

II

The Place of Religion in Culture and Civilization
The Work of Arnold Toynbee

UNTIL AND DURING THE Second World War, the place of religion in culture and civilization was recognized as a norm of human life and Winston Churchill could tell the nation that it was fighting to defend the Christian civilization of Western Europe; and all this was true. Indeed our victory in this War was in one sense a last demonstration of the strength of that Christian faith which King Alfred had described as the greatest aspect of British life in the 9th Century. Alfred the Great, scholar and creator of the English Nation, stated that he had founded this English Nation on Christian values taught by the Universal Church and they would provide the only sure basis for its survival against all nihilistic enemies in the present and the future. In an exegetic attached to his translation in 890 of Boethius's "De Consulatione Philosophiae" (a Christian martyr, 525 AD), there is still to be found his bold and challenging belief: "I hold, as do all Christian men (and women) that it is Divine Providence that rules and not fate."

There had been a long decline in this faith since the sixteenth century for two reasons. One was that the disintegration of "Christendom" caused by the "Reformation" had led to the rise of various forms of Christianity. This was bound gradually to reduce its influence. The Founder of the Christian Church had known this from the beginning and had stipulated that it should be united. Christ had prayed that, "They (his followers) may be one,

The Place of Religion in Culture and Civilization

as Thou Father in Me and I in Thee; that they may all be one in us, That the World may believe that Thou has sent Me." (John 17-21)

The "Reformation" in the sixteenth century meant that a divided Christianity became closely involved in the rise of the new nation states in Western Europe which started a series of increasingly severe internecine wars in which religion was closely involved with politics; and in which Christians of different denominations were fighting and killing one another. This led to the rise of the principle of "cujus regio ejus religio" (the religion of each nation was to be chosen by its state leader), which ended the savagery of the "Thirty Years War" in Europe in 1648; but other such wars continued, ending in the two World Wars of the twentieth century. All this was bound to bring religion into disrepute. It was so far apart from the early Christians who impressed the people around them by their love for one another.

Secondly there developed from the age of the "Enlightenment" in the seventeenth and eighteenth centuries a feeling that the rapid rise in scientific or "analytic" knowledge was all that human beings needed; instead of the "holistic knowledge" of another kind which included religious truth. The great error in thinking was the presumption that man could do without religion and that science and religion were incompatible. In fact science had its own roots established by Christian thinkers in the medieval period and there never has been any necessary conflict between them. This problem had never even occurred to Aristotle or Thomas Aquinas. Suffice to say that science has not been designed for, and cannot in any case, prove or disprove the existence of God. We shall be looking further into this matter below. The question is whether or not human beings and the societies they create can do without religion.

Olivier Roy is the French Director of "Religio West", the European-funded research project of a 4-year study on religion in Europe. This project, looking at various phenomena in this area has concluded that they have a deeper link that goes beyond Catholicism, Islam or Atheism. They all reflect the tensions that arise in secularised societies because of the contemporary disconnect between religion and culture. Roy has developed his analysis in his *Holy Ignorance*[1] that: "secularism fostered the emergence of shallow fundamentalisms in reaction to societies seen as pagan."

He has argued recently that the Catholic Church may find it difficult to deal with secular norms and rules which had been introduced into

1. Roy, Holy Ignorance.

European culture recently, and he asked: "Are we an autonomous faith community turned in on ourselves, like a monastery. Or do we have a universal vocation?". One of Pope Francis's chief attributes is that he often reveals the simplicity of a saint, getting immediately into the essence of things. He answered "Our universal vocation is love, its charity. It's not about rules." Roy conceded: "This is a logical response. Francis says very clearly that imposing rules does not work" (but that love and mercy and forgiveness does work).[2]

Roy concludes that, "Religion will not disappear. I think religions will either 'sanctuarise' (look in on themselves) like a sect, or 'spiritualise' (look outward to a spiritual revival accompanied by a secular 'renaissance'). It is this second response that Toynbee predicted can happen under the guidance of a creative leader who can evoke a spiritual and religious change. This was his hope, arising from a reform of the Catholic (Universal Church), up-dating its outlook to meet the needs of people in the modern world. Working in and for a secular society, it could be the means of restoring new life to a humane and up-dated 'virtue- ethics' culture."[3]

During the twentieth century there were other thinkers who contributed largely, but from different angles, to this question of the relationship of religion to culture. T. S. Eliot (1888-1965) was an American, educated at Harvard, Paris and Oxford Universities, who became a British citizen in 1927. He was an outstanding poet, playwright and literay critic who became prominent with the publication of his long poems, "The Waste Land" (1922) and "The Hollow Men" (1825) which were brilliant depictions of what he called "desolate modernity." He was editor of the very influential journal of culture, "The Criterion", from 1922-39.

By the 1930's he had become convinced that culture was connected essentially with religion and became very interested in Christianity. This was evidenced by works such as "Ash Wednesday" (1930), followed by a series of highly praised dramatic works such as "Murder in the Cathedral" (1935) on the life and death of St. Thomas Becket. There followed a remarkable series of brilliant works such as "Four Quartets" which dealt with the pursuit of eternal truth. His pre-eminence in cultural life brought him great public recognition. In 1948 he was awarded the Nobel Prize in Literature as well as Britain's highest civilian award, the "Order of Merit."

2. Ibid.
3. Ibid.

The Place of Religion in Culture and Civilization

Our present interest, however, is his work entitled "Notes Towards the Definition of Culture" (1948) having published in 1940 his "The Idea of a Christian Society." In this work he put forward the view that any meaningful culture must have its origins in religion. This should not have been surprising since the very word "culture" is derived from "Cultus" which means precisely "religious worship." He says that all authentic cultures are based on an accepted form of communal religious beliefs and moral values, finding expression in all human creative activities. These gain their meaning, purpose, and cohesion from these beliefs and values. On the other hand, a "fragmented" society is incapable of achieving the cohesion of meaning, purpose and expression needed to produce an accepted culture in communal terms. This certainly sheds some light on the new "culture" which appeared in Britain in the 1960's and the chaos which followed.

The prime "witness" to our theme, however, is the intriguing work of Arnold Toynbee (1889-1975), who had two great pursuits in his life. One was peace in the World; and as a young man he was a chosen representative of Britain in peace talks which were held in Paris in 1919; and again after the Second World War. The second pursuit was his study of the way in which civilizations and cultures in different parts of the World had risen and then declined; and he was determined to discover what process lay behind this pattern. He was to do this for 52 civilizations which he studied in detail for thirty years. He did not attach himself to any particular political, economic or religious party, but simply wanted to discover the truth, which might be helpful to mankind.

Toynbee came from a distinguished family of scholars. His uncle, also named Arnold Toynbee, was a well known economic historian who had invented the name "Industrial Revolution." After his death, a legacy to his name was left by the establishment of "Toynbee Hall", in the east end of London which specialised in helping ordinary people to study history, to better their understanding of the past and lessons for the future.

The young Toynbee was educated at Winchester and Balliol College, Oxford. As a youth he had been appalled by the loss of life among friends and families he knew. This led to a life-long aspiration to try to understand why wars took place; what caused them? Could anything be done to stop them and to stop man's criminal actions against his fellows? His uncle had been a captain of a ship trading with China and India and had captivated him with stories about the East. He read about the Greek historian,

Thucydides, and his description of the Great Peloponnesian War between Athens and Sparta which happened back in the 5th Century BC; and he felt that there may have been a comparison with what he was experiencing in the War of 1914-18. Could he learn something by comparing what caused them both? Could he learn something by this comparison, which could help to avoid the terrible effect of man's inhumanity to man, of which war was a major cause?

This was the start of his life-long research into seeking patterns of human behaviour in different parts of the world and at different times in world history? As he wrote:

"I now saw that classical Greek history and Western history were two specimens of a species which had a number of other representatives . . . I do not want my children and grand-children to have the same fate. The writing of this book has been one of my responses to the challenge that has been presented to me by the senseless criminality of human affairs."[4]

The rest of his long life was devoted to this cause. He started a distinguished career as a scholar at Winchester, and then as Professor of Byzantine and Modern Greek language, literature and history at King's College, London. His high motivation and success led to his later appointment as Director of Studies at the Royal Institute of International Affairs, and Research Professor of International History. By now he had established his reputation as the most distinguished British scholar of World history; and from 1934 to 1961 he studied and published 12 volumes of his masterly work entitled "The Study of History" which was acclaimed during this period as "one of the most outstanding achievements of modern scholarship." Nor was he a closet-academic, as shown in his role as a British representative in Peace negotiations, after both World Wars.

There were two other aspects of his work which is of special interest to those interested in the history of historiography. One was the obvious feature that he was the first British historian to relieve himself of the idea that had dominated western historiography and western culture since the days of the "Enlightenment" in the seventeenth and eighteenth centuries. This was the exciting new notion that discoveries in science meant that "scientific truth" (or the analytic approach) was not the only form of valid truth. In the eastern world there was a wider, "holistic", approach to truth (as well as the "scientific" form of truth), essential to an understanding of cultures and especially religions and the spiritual nature of man.

4. Toynbee, foreword of *A Study of History*. 10.

The Place of Religion in Culture and Civilization

We are only now beginning to re-learn this in the West, and Toynbee was the first British historian to employ this ability displayed in his researches. He had a very wide knowledge of Eastern cultures, religions and languages. He understood that there were other approaches to historical truth, apart from the narrowly scientific. He would appear to have been the first British historian to have understood it and as yet no other British historian has yet used this important tool in historiography.

So, for example, Toynbee knew and could discover and interpret the significance of myths, symbolisms, metaphors, allegories, parables and other such "holistic" routes to uncovering truths which he could discern, but would mean nothing to other western historians who regarded them as "too schematic" and have been concerned only with "facts." So there came the common saying that "History is concerned with facts, no more and no less"; but the truth is more often than not discovered by a more "holistic" approach to anything.

Even Toynbee's style of writing and use of language is sometimes new to the western reader and here I have tried where necessary to explain difficulties in supportive "brackets." Toynbee was the only British historian capable of writing about the cultures and civilizations of the east and to be able to discern patterns which compared with western cultures, so as to produce global answers to the understanding and behaviour of cultures and civilizations across time and space in mankind's history. His aim was to find out what it was that caused cultures to decline and often lead to warfare; and to discover what could be done to avoid this happening again.

The second very interesting feature of Toynbee's work was his special interest in researching the "patterns" seen within vast amounts of factual information crossing wide areas of knowledge and gained from diverse areas of time and space. We are only now, in the twenty first century beginning to understand the importance of researching in this way, which can reveal exciting new "truths" in both the sciences and mathematics, as well as in the arts. It is what top mathematicians feel when they speak of "the beauty of mathematics", when these patterns emerge. It is like the answer given by the famous scientist, Louis Pasteur, when a student found him kneeling, while staring intensely in front of a microscope. To the concerned question "Are you all right, sir", his answer was "Oh yes thanks. I was kneeling in praise of the beauty of Creation." Toynbee appears to be the first British scholar to apply this approach to the "patterns" which can be discerned from a vast range of historical data derived from cultures and civilizations across the world.

It is significant that the attitude of many other historians to Toynbee's work changed radically after 1960, showing that even historians can be affected, consciously or subconsciously, by cultural change. Toynbee was not only "counter-cultural" in terms of the new culture, but he was far ahead of them in the history of historical writing as a whole. No other British historian could have discerned these "patterns" and then compared them with western historiography in so much detail. Again those who did not understand, simply described his work as "too schematic" and may then have chosen to avoid the onerous task of reading it anyway, since they did not like the conclusions to which he seemed to have come.

These qualities become even more evident in the final edition of "The Study of History" when, in 1972, after sustained meditation in retirement on his great work, Toynbee decided to publish a one volume edition, bringing together his main findings on cultures and civilizations. This edition also includes some 500 illustrations, maps and pictures which are actually very helpful in clarifying and explaining certain features that he is describing; and it is to this edition that we shall be referring in every reference made to his book in this Essay, unless otherwise stated.

Toynbee was attempting an unprecedented aim in historical writing. His aim was to search for patterns of human development in 52 cultures and civilizations covering the whole world and covering a time span of over two thousand years. It was to take occupy him for 30 years of intensely detailed and demanding research, and a long lifetime of continuous reflection. It was a massive undertaking, quite possibly unique in the history of historical writing.

This was no ordinary history dealing with a sequence of events. He wanted to compare the development of cultures, taken at random of time and space, to see if there was a pattern of stages of rise and decline emerging from the mass of data gathered from his thirty years of intense study and research; and to gain an understanding of the factors involved in these patterns. All this was to enable him to contribute to the present and the future, by a much better understanding of what had happened in the past, so that we could have a tool to use by which we might be able to avoid future disasters to mankind. So, we can certainly name Arnold Toynbee as an outstanding Humanist of the traditional type, in the twentieth century.

The Place of Religion in Culture and Civilization

In spite of the downgrading which Toynbee suffered during the coming of the "after virtue" culture in Britain, one historian knew better. Noel Annan, himself an experienced historian and politician who had published his own description of the culture which ensued in Britain in the next generation after World War II, reviewed Toynbee's last edition (1972) with much deeper perception and admiration.

He reviewed it for the "The Guardian", making the following assessment of Toynbee. He started, significantly, by defending him against his critics in 1972, by ascribing their "outcry" to "their rage at his refusal to be a propagandist", obviously meaning a propagandist for the contemporary "after-virtue" culture. He then went on to write to assert that Toynbee was "a genuinely civilized, dispassionate cosmopolitan" and continued:

"How fortunate for us that 'A Study of History,' one of the most striking analyses of life in our time, has been written by a man of such humanity and wisdom and with such a passion for inquiry. Today one feeling for his thirty years labour must predominate. Admiration for an achievement which has made his name a household word and history something new and exciting to countless people who needed a wider horizon than the old European landscape. Admiration for the tenacity in completing a task from which he has not permitted war or private troubles to deflect him. Admiration for his humanism, for his sympathy for ages and people long departed from this earth, and for his magnificent feat of synthesizing such diverse and intractable material. The scholar's calling is, after all, is to create order where none before existed; and to that calling Professor Toynbee has been faithful."[5]

This last sentence in Annan's tribute is interesting. One of the recent developments in science has been the "complex" theory. It came originally from pure research in Chemistry, the science of the elements and the laws of combination and behaviour under certain circumstances and conditions. Over time its progress has led to the award of several Nobel Prizes for those who have been able to extend the borders of knowledge in this area. Their achievements have been in demonstrating how the laws established in the pure science have been extended to various other aspects of knowledge, so as to indicate their common relevance in application.

These laws have been used to bring order out of disorder among other elements of studies, such as human nature and the natural world; and these have been shown to be inter-connected and inter-dependent. The theory

---

5. Toynbee, *A Study of History*, written on back cover flap of 1972 edition.

has now become a tool of research by application, not only in the established sciences, but social science and other fields of knowledge. It applies to the question of human relationships in society and how to bring order out of disorder in the modern world of politics and economics. Annan had obviously perceived it at work in the historical research of Toynbee.

In 1972, Toynbee wrote in his Preface, to this last edition, that:

"The two World Wars and the present worldwide anxiety, tension and violence tell the tale. Mankind is surely going to destroy itself unless it succeeds in growing together into something like a single family. For this we must become familiar with each other; and this means becoming familiar with each other's history. For Man does not live just in the immediate present. We live in a mental time-stream, remembering the past and looking forward –with hope or with fear- to an oncoming future."[6]

When he had started his enterprise back in 1934, he expected to find that such accretions as religion, all stemmed from cultures; but as his long researches advanced he was forced to change his mind and came to the conclusion that cultures themselves originated from religion.

Regarding the birth of civilizations and culture, he writes: "I find this in the insights of mythology and religion."[7] This "mythology" is for him, like symbolism, provides access to another type of truth.

Toynbee's certainty concerning the central importance of religion and the belief in God, to the survival of a human and humane secular culture becomes clearly evident. He writes, again, concerning matters which are significant for our theme. So, concerning "Universal States": "Although the historic . . . states have so far always been local and ephemeral, they seem to be the foretastes of a future regime in which the whole of mankind will live in political unity."[8]

And on "Universal Churches":

"Their purpose is to find a direct personal relation with the transcendent in and behind the Universe . . . but some have been betrayed by their institutionalization into becoming rigid in structure and intolerant in outlook . . . I also try to show that only the postulate of a supra-human reality will make some proven human feelings comprehensible to us."[9]

---

6. Ibid., 10.
7. Ibid., 73.
8. Ibid., 215.
9. Ibid., 319.

The Place of Religion in Culture and Civilization

And on the importance of "Contacts between Cultures": "In our present-day world it is imperative that different cultures should not face each other in hostile competition, but should seek to share their experience as they already share a common humanity."[10]

With regard to the growth of civilizations, Toynbee writes that "I find that in general the growth of a society can be measured in terms of the increasing power of self-determination won by the society's leaders ... the minority of creative persons"[11].

And the breakdown of civilizations : "I then have to account for the failure of creativity, and ascribe it to the spiritual demoralization to which we are not bound to succumb, and which, therefore, we have to take the responsibility. Success seems to make us lazy, or self-satisfied or conceited."[12]

And the fragmentation of a civilization:

"I trace the fragmentation of society into a dominant minority, an internal proletariat, and an external proletariat consisting of the barbarians on its fringes. I also find a corresponding psychological schism in the souls of people who happen to have been born into this unhappy age. Discordant psychic tendencies which are perhaps always latent in human nature now find free play. People lose their bearings and run down blind alleys, seeking escape."[13]

But such disintegration and resulting breakdown are "not inevitable and irretrievable (unless) the process of disintegration is allowed to continue."[14] The process of recovery, if it occurs, is stimulated by a spiritual force connected with a religious revival or renaissance:

"The attempt to analyse the processes by which the power of growth may be recovered from the seemingly fatal catastrophe of social collapse will have shown that the 'recurrence of birth' which we have identified at last is not merely a rebirth of society on any mundane level, but the attainment of a super-mundane state, and the simile of birth can be applied illuminatingly to it because this other state is a positive state of life –a life shot through with the image of God. That is the palingenesia (spiritual rebirth) which Jesus proclaimed as the sovereign aim of his own birth in the flesh:

---

10. Ibid., 379.
11. Ibid., 127.
12. Ibid., 141.
13. Ibid., 211.
14. Ibid.

'I have come that they might have life, and that they may have it more abundantly'".[15]

And with direct relevance to the importance of religion in human life: "One manifestation of religion is that it is a consequence of consciousness"[16]; and in a telling remark of a general nature, we find a resonance with our findings concerning the nature of the new "After Virtue" culture in Britain after 1960:

"It is the religious experience which lays the foundation of the World. It is ritual orientation, with the structure of sacred space which it reveals, that transforms "Chaos" into "Cosmos" and therefore renders human existence possible -prevents it, that is, from regression into the levels of zoological existence."[17]

(In one of the most recent revelations of inhuman treatment of elderly and vulnerable patients in certain hospitals in North Wales, in 2015, it was said in the report that "they were treated like animals in a zoo").

Again, "I also believe that history shows us how men may learn to make choices that are not only free, but effective, by learning to achieve harmony with a supra-human reality that makes itself felt though it is impalpable"[18]; and:

"Why is it then, that Man has had religion ever since he awoke to consciousness? And why is religion the built-in feature of human nature as it seems to be a feature which seems to be Man's principle concern so long as the human race survives?"[19]

As far back as 1918, Oswald Spengler, the German philosopher, had written "The Decline of the West." It was a book which was later to be much admired by the Nazis because it predicted that the only answer to this decline would be the emergence of a strong leader who would create a totalitarian state to rule the West. It seemed in 1939 that his prediction might well have come true; but the events of 1945, the suicide of Hitler and the collapse of the Nazi Government, proved him to be wrong.

Toynbee showed that Spengler, like all other "determinists", was basing his prediction on a false premise. In his case it was that he presumed that societies are living organisms, whereas in fact:

15. Ibid., 254.
16. Ibid., 343.
17. Ibid., 343.
18. Ibid.
19. Ibid., 350.

"In subjective terms they are the intelligible fields of study; and in objective terms they are the common ground between the respective fields of activity of a number of individual human beings whose individual energies are the vital forces which operate to work out the history of a society, including its timespan."[20]

Toynbee believed that determinism, shared by other attempts to foretell the future of mankind, such as; Marxism, Communism, and Nazism, all failed because such totalitarian regimes misunderstood the concept of human freedom and its importance as an essential aspiration and need of humanity. He believed in the existence of human free-will, to some extent or another, in all human beings.

Toynbee is also looking towards the World as a "global village." He writes of the past that states "have so far always been local and ephemeral . . . (but) they seem to be foretastes of a future regime in which the whole of Mankind will live in political unity"[21]; and the importance of cultural contact: "in our present-day world it is imperative that different cultures should not face each other in hostile competition, but should seek to share their experience as they already share a common humanity."[22]

He looks to the future and the need for a universal Church to help in bringing mankind together as a family in the "global village", recognising the spirituality which they all share in their human condition:

"Their (Universal Churches) purpose is to enable men to find a direct personal relation with the transcendent in and behind and beyond the Universe . . . but some have been betrayed by their institutionalization into becoming rigid in structure and intolerant in outlook . . . I also try to show that only the postulate of a supra-human reality will make proven human feelings comprehensible to us."[23]

Toynbee saw real signs of an ominous decline in Western Culture and Civilization, for reasons made clear above. However there was no inevitability about it. The chaotic end would come only if this decline was not stopped. It could be stopped by a "creative" and "spiritual" leadership, combined with the revival of a spiritual initiative or renaissance, inspired by a renewed "Universal Religion."

20. Ibid., 154–55.
21. Ibid., 215.
22. Ibid., 379.
23. Ibid., 319.

Toynbee had kept in touch with World events during his retirement and was particularly interested in what was happening in the Catholic (Universal) Church, where it seemed to him, that a hugely important change was taking place which could affect not only this Church, but the whole of Western Europe. He wrote:

"The twentieth century has seen a movement for self-reform in the Roman Church which recalls the fifteenth century Conciliar Movement and the eleventh century awakening that found its leader in Hildebrand, Pope Gregory VII"; and then adds:

"Far more important has been the Church's spiritual "aggiornamento" (up-dating) by Pope John XXIII. In his brief reign (1958-63), this saintly and genial Pope has "made history." He has given vent to the most dynamic of any of the movements of the Western clergy and laity since the eleventh century spiritual revival."[24]

Toynbee's opinion was that previous such efforts had failed because certain popes had "failed spiritually" in not rising to the spiritual demands of their high office and therefore not finding the "creativity" to achieve necessary reforms needed to bring the Church up to date with present spiritual needs. He thought, as a result, that there had been too much emphasis on power, status, and legalism, rather than the love, humility, simplicity and "self-abnegation" of the saints of this Church, which was necessary to do this task. He saw such great potential in this Church. There is a kind of intuitive prediction in his statement that:

"At all stages of its history the Catholic Church has been a seed-bed of saints. Saint Francis of Assisi is the greatest soul that has appeared in the western World."[25]

He was never to know of course that there was going to be another Francis, with the same spirituality as his medieval predecessor, to become a new reforming leader of this Universal Church in 2013.

Toynbee remarks that, during the "Reformation", this Church had forfeited its former ecumenical leadership: "The price had been the replacement of the medieval Western "Respublica Christiana", by a bevy of idolized nation states. For the Western Civilization, as well as for the Roman Church, this had been a grievous change for the worse..."[26]; but:

---

24. Ibid., 210.
25. Ibid.
26. Ibid.

The Place of Religion in Culture and Civilization

"This tragedy (the 'Reformation') need not repeat itself. The saintly Pope John XX111's large-hearted policy may prevail, and, if it does, this will benefit the whole of Western society by giving a special inspiration to the oldest of the Churches. On the other hand, if the present spiritual revival within the Roman Church were to be frustrated once again, the price would be paid; this time, by the Roman Church's own "Establishment.""[27]

Pope John was loved throughout the World and his encyclical "Peace on Earth" (1963) is a great sign-post for direction into the new millennium. He also called into being the Second Vatican Council, "to open the windows of the Church and allow fresh air to enter." The work of this Council was hugely important in laying the foundations of necessary reform in the Catholic Church; but Pope John died in 1963. Arnold Toynbee died in 1972.

It is quite extraordinary that Toynbee who was not a Catholic but seemed to think that wonderful things could ensue if only the Catholic Church had a leader like St. Francis of Assisi who could reform the image and direction of the Church now, as this Saint had done in the past, was to have his dream accomplished in reality, fifty years later; because this actually was going to happen, though Toynbee and the new Pope Francis knew nothing of one another.

The next three popes elected during the following half century were good men who made important advances in Church theology and philosophy, but were not fitted for the task of implementing the necessary reforms anticipated by Vatican II which, in short, were intended to bring it up-to- date with the needs of the modern world which were changing at an unprecedented rate in the twentieth century.

There was some disappointment and consternation in the Church over this period. Hans Kung, the Swiss theologian who had been one of the "periti" (advisers at Vatican II) wrote a critical book expressing his disappointment and impatience. It was entitled, "Can We Save the Catholic Church?" which put him in some difficulties within the Church. One of his colleagues at Vatican II, had been the French theologian and "adviser", Yves de Congar, another reformer who described his friend Kung as a man who "charges; he goes straight ahead like an arrow."

Then suddenly, something quite extraordinary did happen. In March, 2013, the incumbent Pope Benedict XV1, decided, for the first time in modern history, that he should retire, feeling too old and ill to do the task of leading the Church adequately.

27. Ibid.

Quite unexpectedly, just as with the election of Pope John half a century before, a new Pope was elected, in 2013. This was a new and quite different type of man, the first Pope from South America, who was an identical type of Christian humanist as Pope John had been. He was also completely capable and fitted for the job of implementing all the reforms designed by the documents of Vatican II. He was to become an extraordinarily able exponent of change in the direction and image of the Church in readiness for the needs of the new Millennium in both Church and secular society.

Hans Kung, who recognized the extraordinary quality of this stranger, celebrated his election by changing the title of his book to "Can We Save the Catholic Church? Yes We Can Save the Catholic Church." We shall come back to these events below, but now it is time that we took a closer look at what we mean by "Christian Humanism."

III

Meaning of Christian Humanism

CHRISTIAN HUMANISM STANDS FOR the two Christian commandments which Christ said really contained all the other requirements. These two said:

"Love God and love your neighbour as yourself."

For the Christian this means that the second part of this commandment is the proof of the first part. We cannot see God, but we can find him in our neighbour. Loving our neighbour is the proof that we love God. Our "neighbour" of course means all other human beings, without exception. This does not mean that we must "like" our neighbour, for liking is simply a matter of our feelings. Love is a matter of the "will" which is a gift from God, by which we can serve Him by expressing our good will to all our neighbours and their needs in as many ways as we can.

These two branches meet all our duties to God and are the main inspiration behind Catholic Social Teaching and Community Organising. They provide the best possible argument for the inalienable dignity and sacred nature of each and every human being, created by God in His own image. The human being therefore has innate and inalienable human rights. The equality of all human beings is guaranteed by their relationship with God who has created them to love Him and one another. Indeed He tells us that the proof that we love Him is the love (good will, help, kindness, forgiveness, mercy) which we extend to one another. Moreover this kind of love extends not only to those we like, but to all, even our enemies:

"Love your enemies, do good to those who hate you ... Treat others as you would like them to treat you ... If you love those who love you, what thanks can you expect? . . . and if you do good to those who do good to you, what thanks can you expect? Even sinners do that much . . . Instead love your enemies and do good to them . . . You will have a great reward, and you will be sons of the Most High, for He Himself is kind to the ungrateful and the wicked" (Luke, 6, 31-35).

This kind of love is at the heart of Christian humanism, and is the only solid, inspiring and supernatural base for any kind of humanism. There is no other sense in which we can say that all humans are equal or worthy of such dignity, rights and duties. One problem with putting humans on too high a pedestal is that the warped human nature is never capable of it; and this leads to the destruction of human dignity. As Lord Acton commented with regard to human weakness: "Power corrupts and absolute power corrupts absolutely."

Here is the absolute and inalienable premise on which we can build the whole structure of human rights, democracy, freedom from persecution, religious freedom and all the other logical consequences of the argument. It is the basis of all good human relationships and it is also the only true basis on which we can make real progress along the road to world unity and peace. It was the recovery of the spirit of these early teachings of the Church in the documents of Vatican 11, led by Pope John XXIII and the implementation of all this 50 years later in the reforming policies of "The Great Reformer", Pope Francis, which constitute what I am naming "The Renaissance of Christian Humanism."

Of course this is not easy. We call upon the grace of God to strengthen us sufficiently to achieve it. We are not perfect and our Creator understands this. So He forgives us when we fall and help us to start again every time, if we are truly repentant; but we must then be able to forgive others in the same way. The genius of Shakespeare describes the process very succinctly:

"To err is human; to forgive divine."

What we do know by personal and historical experience is that this ability to forgive, for example, is an essential pre-requisite of progress and development in human relationships whether in marriage, friendship, or international relationships.

The word humanism came into being to describe the way in which the theologians and philosophers of the Church in the "high middle ages" (the twelfth and thirteenth centuries) discovered and made use of the Greek texts containing the thinking of the ancient Greek scholars, such as Socrates, Plato and Aristotle. These were found to have reached extraordinarily high standards of mental development which illuminated the background of pre-Christian times.

Aristotle, for example, recognized that there was a transcendent being or power who or which governed everything; and working with this premise, he had made great and insightful researches into the nature of man and of the universe, which proved to be very useful to the great Christian theologian and philosopher, St. Thomas Aquinas. This was apart from the fact that he is now recognized the founder of modern science.

There was no reason why Aristotle's work should not be assimilated into Christian teaching, since Aristotle was in one sense a herald of the coming of the Christian Revelation This led to a strong branch of medieval learning at this time, which was termed "Studia Humanitatis" (Human studies), and was the origin of the term "Humanism", of which there was only one kind, that is what we now term "Christian humanism."

The was regarded as an essential part of religious studies, because it fitted in completely with what has become known as incarnation theology, stressing that Christ was truly God and Man; and that man is born in the image of Christ. It was not until the middle of the twentieth century that atheists created the idea that there was another kind of humanism which could act as an alternative attitude of mind, omitting the idea of God. They began to talk for the first time of themselves as "humanists" and in 2002 the "British Humanist Association" formulated their main beliefs.

Their beliefs turned out to be almost the same as Christian beliefs, except for its omission of God as their Creator. In fact the only outright argument against Christian humanism is that they said religion was unacceptable because it was committed to a fixed revelation, so that there could be no development of human knowledge. This however is not true, because the Christian concept of "development" means that all human knowledge is important and its own dogmas are "live" and "organic" and very capable of "developing" by extending its truths to a wider and more profound understanding of human needs as opposed to wants.

So, for example, the two greatest and all-containing commandments of God are based on its central component of "love", because "God is love": "Love God and Love your neighbour (all human beings) as yourself." This can develop as contexts and cultures change so that there may be new and different ways of expressing that love, to meet the needs of the times.

With regard to science and its development, there is no problem. Science and religion are concerned with different types of truth. Science can never prove or disprove the existence of God. Religion can only clash with science if it is being abused for immoral objectives, breaking the law of "love" and therefore having a dehumanising effect. The contexts of religion and science are quite different. For God time and space do not exist. We simply cannot imagine it, just as a fish could not make any sense of living out of water.

This is where we come to the nature and purpose of faith. God-given Reason and God-given Faith work together to make the complete human life. Reason works to achieve the needs of man's secular life; Faith transcends this to reach those truths which are required to meet the needs of man's spiritual nature.

So, what is the validity of the new "humanism" which omits God from its place in it? Strangely enough the main problem would seem to be not with the content of what it contains; but because it lacks any rational basis for sustaining it. Therefore it is putting the whole content of its humanism at the risk of being destroyed; as if they are cutting the ground of reason from under their own feet.

We must now elaborate on what may seem to be a controversial statement. Secular humanism bases itself chiefly on three aspects of humanity which makes it unique –its reasoning power, its ethical or moral capacity and therefore its special dignity above animal creation. In all these respects, however, if there is no transcendent power involved, none of these can be rationally sustained. They are all essentially contingent and conditional.

Reason cannot be shared by all humanity under these conditions. Some humans can lose their reason, some are children who have not yet reached the "age of reason", some elderly people can lose their reason. People have very different capacities of reasoning. This is no rational basis in this for establishing the reliability, or dignity or equal value of all human beings.

Ethics and moral values can be very different in humanity. People can differ radically in what they think is right or wrong; or in their capacity for discerning it. Stalin and Hitler had different understandings of "right" and "wrong"; and on what grounds can one state that they have no right, in purely human terms, to behave differently than others. This provides no rational basis for establishing the special human dignity or the equal value of all human beings. Only with the help and admission of a "transcendent", outside power, such as God, can such a belief or principle be established on a rational, logical, constant, absolute and incontrovertible basis. This is why this framework for "Christian humanism" has lasted for more than two Millennia.

So human dignity and inalienable human rights, cannot rationally be defended on such conditional and contingent grounds as supplied by a secular humanism. It is in a completely vulnerable position; and there is no durability and reliability in it for humanity. Its aims are good, but there are no rational grounds for establishing any rational basis for them. This does not mean that agnostics and atheists cannot themselves be equally good and reasonable as others; it simply means that they have no rational grounds for defending their position.

It is only the idea of a transcendent and loving God, who creates all humans in his own image and likeness, and who commands us to "love all neighbours (other human beings) as ourselves" which can establish in an absolute way the dignity, sacredness and equal value of all human beings and their inalienable human rights throughout the world.

All human beings are of equal status in God's eyes, worthy of equal dignity and worth because they are children of God who claims them as his own. He makes each one of them unique and wishes each one "to know Him, love Him and serve Him in this world and to live happily with Him forever in the next." This is the basis of that "humanism" which has lasted for over two Millennia in Christianity. It presents the strongest possible grounds for acceptance by the whole of humanity, of its natural and inalienable human rights. It can also supply the meaning, purpose, aim, and ultimately the happiness in life for all human beings. This is what they are all created for and are asked to share with one another. Christians believe that human nature is "innately good", though it has been warped by what has been called "Original Sin."

It is interesting that, after a long, thorough, and costly inquiry led by Janet Smith, an independent report has recently (January, 2016) resulted in explaining how so many people, including young children, suffered in the 1970's and 1980's from the sexual abuses of Jimmy Savile, a prominent "entertainer" in the BBC. People cannot understand why its ravages were known, but not reported. The Report has come to the conclusion that it was because of a "deferential" culture in the BBC which meant that managers were afraid to say anything against those who were celebrated and successful in the eyes of the public.

This is interesting because it tells us that, still, 56 years after the event, British people seem ignorant of the real reason why Jimmy Savile and many others were able to indulge in behaviour which would not have been conceivable before. This was because the whole moral climate of society had changed. Ultimately it was because of the general change in British culture which meant that "religion" and "virtue" and moral standards had been replaced in the popular mind by the "permissive society" which had established an "after virtue" and "me-first" ethos. Many of us can look back to a time when, generally speaking, children were free to wander without fear of harm in a society which looked after them; whereas now parents dare not let children out of their sight. The breakdown of family life, surely one of the great building blocks of society, increased greatly after 1960. There are many other examples of the way in which life became very different after 1960, in all the ways which we discussed earlier. The lack of trust in one another decreased. The whole climate and ethos of society changed; and this is the view of most people who have lived long enough to have experienced these changes. Now, they are almost taken for granted.

Even now, nobody seems able to suggest that it was only one example of the huge cultural change that was affecting the whole of society, including all the professions ,in all its aspects at this time, simply as a consequence of the "permissive society", inaugurated in the 1960's, which decided to leave God out of the picture. The new secular humanism seemed defenceless against it. Even now, nearly half a century, later, Britain does not seem to be aware of the cultural change-and its consequences- which took place in 1960. The British people have literally "slept-walked" into it. It is important that the British public should become aware of all this, because the root cause of these changes still and are still in the process of developing in this Country. By this I mean the creation and development of an atheistic or agnostic society.

In my view the public should be aware of it and be able to evaluate the consequent negative results which we have already experienced and which would seem to be increasing. There are, at the moment attacks by certain pressure groups on the presence of Christianity which has largely shaped our culture until now. Some are attacking the demonstration of Christian belief in secular life. Others are attacking the concept of "faith schools" which in fact played an important part of the start and development of British education in the past. Others have sought to reduce or omit religion as a main subject, in Schools especially; and this is actually happening now.

Some evidence of this is the revelation recently of a significant decline in the Church of England's active numbers to a record low. The Archbishop of Canterbury, Justin Welby, a good leader whom I regard as a Christian humanist, warned leaders of the Anglican Church, meeting in Canterbury in January, 2016, of an "emergent anti-Christian culture" with its 12% decline in Church attendance to an all-time low of less than a million. He proclaimed:

"The culture is becoming anti-Christian, whether it is on matters of sexual morality, or the care for people at the beginning or the end of life. It is easy to paint a very gloomy picture."

The Catholic (Universal) Church has become the largest religious group in Britain, in the light of attendance at any Church, though this has been helped by the attendance figures of migrants from the Continent of Europe.

The values of the past "virtue-ethics" still provide the origin for most of our laws, but less attention is paid to them in the "permissive" society. The law was meant to deal with a minority of people who did not possess the standard of morality and conscience to behave properly for the common good in the sight of a loving God. This is because they no longer belong to a culture which educates people in the belief of a loving and transcendent God to whom we are answerable. Now it seems that the only preventive to sin and crime among the majority is the danger of being caught, which is the reason that British prisons are bursting at the seams. This in itself prevents the prisons from achieving their main purpose of reforming prisoners.

Nevertheless I believe strongly in the innate goodness of humanity and the sometimes hidden belief of the majority of people, in the Christian faith and values of the past, especially since there have been very important developments in this faith and its values in the present age, taking account of needs of the modern world, in the new "renaissance of Christian humanism."

Such a general change of culture indicates a matter of the first importance in any nation's future. It seems evident that there is an even more importance attached to any country's culture, than to our impending referendum to decide on whether we should continue to stay in the European Union. I would seriously suggest that the coming referendum should contain two separate sections, to test the majority opinion in Britain on both these vitally important matters. Personally, I am confident that the majority, given this opportunity to clarify the situation, and on considering the future for themselves and more importantly for their children, would choose a culture based on "Christian Humanism" as it is revealed in this Essay and has actually been implemented in Germany.

An example of a determined change of culture is that of Germany after the Second World War. The Nazi regime had certainly established a culture of its own which certainly was to bring the German nation to defeat and to its knees in the eyes of the World. It was the outstanding leadership of some Christian-Humanists such as Conrad Adenauer (Catholic) and Angela Merkel (Lutheran), which introduced a new and developed Christian Humanist culture which brought Germany from disaster to the leadership of Europe in an amazingly short time. It contains the right balance between a secular society in which religion is given its proper role of respected advice and importance; and its results have been apparent in all aspects of their life. They had learned a great deal from the drastic change of cultures; and their "response" to the "challenge" before them is evidence of how much their determination to change achieved for them.

An interesting aspect of this is that initially some agnostics and atheists in the twentieth century, felt it necessary to be aggressively offensive towards religion in the second half of the twentieth century, which did not help the common good in any way; but more recently this attitude has changed in people who have retained their own non-beliefs, but retained an admiration for what it has achieved for the people of Britain. I refer now to Alain de Botton and his book entitled "Religion for Atheists." He is Chairman of a newly founded group entitled "The School of Life." He is putting forward a simple idea which does not seem to have been considered before and is quite different from the old aggressive rather frenzied atheistic approach, demonstrated by people such as Richard Dawkins.

De Botton's main theme, as an atheist himself, is that atheists and agnostics have a great deal to benefit from a religious culture which had proved itself to be of great help to humanity. "Christian Humanism" is really the new name for an age-old and simple "Humanism." His idea is that if we are speaking of a society of people of good will and an interest in the common good, there is no possible reason why people should not be working together with all types of opinion as long as there is a spirit of tolerance and respect for all. Christian humanism, adapted to meet the needs of the modern pluralistic world, is also intent on peace on earth.

This attitude could be an answer, as well, to the many inter-religious problems which have created problems for the modern world, showing how authentic religion can be the greatest agent for peace in the world. If, however it is misled by extremist and intolerant groups, it can then be a cause of some of our greatest problems. So it is a "sign for the times" that there should be a new meeting of minds involved which can be a great stimulus to peace and human progress in the new Millennium. This is an advance, full of hope and promise, which could be more important for the future than the rightly acclaimed advances in science and technology which have enabled humans to land on the moon, not to say that this has not been a great advance as well.

Moreover de Botton's approach is that the religious element in society is of great benefit to atheists. He is appreciative of all the good work which Christians are well known to do for the common good. He sees no reason why atheists and agnostics should not work alongside them for a better and more humane society. The central importance which Christianity gives to "loving your neighbour as yourself" must be one of the strongest pillars of a good and humane society for everyone. It also means that atheists, agnostics and their children can enjoy Christian celebrations such as Christmas with their Christian friends. They have nothing at all to fear when they know that all their human rights are safeguarded and that they are living in a democracy within a legal system which exists to defend everyone's human rights. Moreover it is Church teaching that secular society has its own rights: "Give unto Caesar what belongs to Caesar", and its own duties.

De Botton's approach is similar to that of Christian humanism in the modern world. Dialogue can lead to a better understanding and can lead to tolerance and peace in the world. There must be no attempt to enforce religious belief on anyone. Religious teaching must always respect the other person. It insists on freedom of religion and freedom for everyone's informed conscience. It must always respect the other person and his or her position. De Botton is saying that atheists will do well to follow the Christian system of ethics and values, since they have been deduced from the needs of human nature as they have been derived from the best minds of the past.

De Botton's work has been very well received by modern society and different sides of opinion. The "Sunday Telegraph" described it as "a beautiful, inspiring book offering a glimpse of a more enlightened path." The "Times" commented that it is "A serious and optimistic set of practical ideas that could improve and alter the way we live." The "Financial Times" supports it as "A timely and perceptive appreciation of how much wisdom is embodied in religious traditions and how our godless moderns might learn from it"; and the "Church Times" sees it as "surprising and illuminating." We know, from Carl Gustav Jung that all humans are seeking a meaning in life. De Botton shows how many good effects religion has produced in the way we live, love, form relationships, shape our communities and their cultures; and can cope with death, which is really a new birth into another life.

An interesting development has taken place in the new field of neuroscience (the study of the human brain) in very recent times. The "post enlightenment" philosophy of "After Virtue" has attacked "virtue-ethics" because its main tenets take us back inevitably to the existence of a "prime mover" who alone can ultimately define "goodness", rather than the subjective views of fallible human beings. Aristotle, however, believed that "goodness" could be taught and learned from the natural laws set out by the transcendent "prime mover" and reflected in the human nature which He created.

The most advanced findings in neuroscience have discovered that Aristotle was right about this. Brain scanning techniques have shown that the parts of the brain relating to this feature of human behaviour do in fact grow and develop throughout human life and become habit- forming. We become better human beings by actually helping others, because such behaviour becomes habitual; and the opposite vice-versa must also be true.

In the edition of "New Scientist" (19th October, 2013), the front cover is inscribed with "Images of the Mind" and the remark that "The more we probe the brain, the less we understand it." Inside, however, there is a significant section of an interview with the neurosurgeon, James Doty, concerning the scientific discoveries about "human compassion" or love.[1]

"We know that as a species we flourish and thrive when we care for others. Not only do you feel happier, but you live better, you feel better, you live longer. And it's a self-supporting activity in the sense that when you do those activities and they make you feel good, it makes you want to continue it. It's a boon to humanity, but also to one's self . . . we can show that you have the potential to increase your capacity for kindness and caring and that this should result in dramatic improvements in your personal relationships, significant decrease in inflammation, improvement in cardiac function, increase in your telomere length (the DNA) that protects the ends of your chromosomes) which increases longer . . . (So) we can be healthier,

---

1. Doty, *New Scientist*, October 19th, 2013, 28–29.

live longer and make the world a better place by exploring our potential for compassionate behaviour."[2]

It does seem to me that this finding suggests that the development of all the other virtues we read about in Aristotle and later in Christian teaching and its primary command, in the scriptural words of Christ, "love God and love your neighbour as yourselves; "You must love one another as I have loved you", have been designed to help us become more fully human in a more humane society. The opposite procedure, described by Macintyre in his "After Virtue" (1982), as analysis of the new culture in British life, is therefore, unsurprisingly producing the opposite result of a less humane and cohesive society. This is a logical sequence that can be valid for the description of a society or culture, but not of course for that that of individuals within it who have free will and may decide to follow the other way of life guided by "virtue-ethics."

All this chimes well with the teaching of the present Pope Francis who stresses that Christ died for all human beings, including atheists, agnostics and all others; and with his belief that it is the business of the Catholic Church to communicate the supreme love and mercy of God towards all human beings who are his children, in one human family. Indeed, the present Pope, an outstanding Christian Humanist, has insisted in his talks that all human beings come within the scope of Christ's redeeming power. He died to save us all.

Also the proof that we love God is shown by the way we relate to our fellow human beings. We need to "love our neighbours as ourselves." As far as Pope Francis is concerned atheists, agnostics and anyone who is trying to use his or her informed conscience to discover the truth and to work together for the common good, are all people of good will and are capable of working together in pursuit of a better world. I now believe that there is a better climate of thought where all people of good will can work together and exchange views and ideas in tolerance, while pursuing the path of a better world for all. He presents as the epitome of what Arnold Toynbee was hoping for in order to achieve a recovery not only of the Christian faith, but of the culture and civilization of Western Europe.

2. Ibid.

IV

The History of Christian Humanism

CHRISTIAN HUMANISM IS AN essential part of Christian thought and teaching, in which the aspiration is to become fully human in Christ:

"I have come that they may have life and have it to the full." (John 10:10.)

"The Word was made flesh and dwelt amongst us." (John 1:14)

"God in Christ was reconciling the world unto himself." (2 Cor 5:19)

It was expressed succinctly by St. Irenaeus of Lyons, one of the early Christian thinkers, in the second century after Christ:

"The glory of God is man fully alive."[1]

Toynbee proclaimed in his critique of Oswald Spengler's "Decline of the West" ,that there was something unique about Christianity, because it seemed to possess, uniquely, a capacity to renew itself and carry on in spite of several reverses and dangers, from outside and inside the Church, which seemed to be disastrous for its continuation. It seemed to have some sort of dynamo within it which activates into reform and revival when necessary, to renew itself. In this chapter we will look at the history of these challenges and responses which characterise the story of "Christian Humanism."

The first great assault on Christianity came from the Establishment of the Roman Empire under The Emperor, Nero, which persecuted and killed the Christians who lived in Rome, sending them to seek shelter in the Catacombs where they continued to live in fear. The two first great pillars of the Church, St. Peter, the first Pope and St. Paul, the first great missionary, were both crucified in Rome. It looked as if the early Catholic Church

---

1. "Against Heresies," 3:34:5–7, in *Early Church Texts* from the ANF texts series.

might suffer an early death. But in 312, the Emperor Constantine the Great converted to Christianity. It was said that he had seen a vision of Christ on the cross. In 313 A.D., by the Edict of Milan he recognized the Christian Church as one of the legally accepted religions in the Roman Empire. In 324 he invited all the bishops of the Church in Western Europe to the Council of Arles. In 324 he became sole Emperor of the Roman Empire; and in 325 he summoned and presided at the first great Council of the Universal Church at Nicaea. The Church had been revived and saved.

In the words of Pope John Paul, writing to Cardinal Hume, regarding his predecessor, Pope Gregory the Great's sending Augustine to convert England to Christianity in 497:

"Augustine's mission meant the consolidation of Christianity in Britain, giving it strong links with the See of Rome. He and his companions sowed the seed of a Christian people remarkably gifted from the beginning with saintly men and women who spread civilization and learning, provided schools, established libraries and produced a wonderful array of literary and artistic works . . . and quite soon that healthy tree bore fruits beyond England."

The five centuries following Augustine's arrival saw the English play a vitally important part in the creation of European culture and civilization, including the conversion of the Germanic lands to Christianity and their assimilation into Europe. This was largely the work of the English missionary, St. Boniface, a Benedictine monk from Devonshire who had possibly a greater influence on European history than any other Englishman who ever lived.

There were examples of Christian humanism in Britain in the work of the scholar monks, notably the Venerable Bede and his work in the great library, collected from many parts of Christian Europe, in the monastery of Jarrow in the seventh century. His "Ecclesiastical History of the English People" (731) is regarded as the finest work of historical scholarship in the first Millennium; and it provided the theoretical basis for the later emergence of the English nation as a reality.

In the ninth century the reign of the devout scholar, Alfred the Great, inspired the scholarship which further developed the culture of the English people and the move towards a more united English kingdom. Alfred was an outstanding Christian humanist. In an exegetic attached to his translation of Boethius's "De Consolatione Philosophiae" (The Consolations of

Philosophy), he made the ringing statement, that he held, as do all Christians, that it is Divine Providence that rules and not fate.

Boethius was a Christian martyr who had written his work in prison. It was translated again by Chaucer in the medieval period and was one of the most influential books of the medieval period.

The revival of the monastic system by St. Dunstan in the tenth century had important cultural implications for the English people and their development as part of the Benedictine tradition of culture and learning in Europe.

Then in the tenth and eleventh centuries came the next great threat to Christianity, with the Viking invasions into England and other parts of northern and western Europe, causing great destruction and challenging the stability and development of Christian civilization in Europe.

It was in response to this threat, that there emerged in the twelfth and thirteenth centuries the greatest period of Christian Humanism in the first millennium. The distinguished historian, Professor Sir Herbert Butterfield of Cambridge regarded "the recovery and exposition of the medieval world" as "the greatest achievement of historical understanding in the history of historical writing."[2] The outstanding scholar in this recovery and understanding was Professor Sir Richard Southern of Oxford University. In his final work "Scholastic Humanism and the Unification of Europe" (1995), he described the huge contribution of Christian Humanism to the recovery of religious and secular life of Western Europe, contributing largely to the great unification of Western Europe in these two centuries.[3] Indeed, Southern, writing in the twentieth century, wondered whether this recovery could be a "model" of how to recover unity again after the period of destructive internecine warfare which had culminated in two World Wars in the twentieth century:

"The study of scholastic humanism emerged as a model of order at a time of increasing disorder on a world-wide scale in the late nineteenth century. With what results time alone will show."

Southern's work revealed the great framework of principles of faith and rational thought which underpinned the comparative peace, order and creativity restored to Europe during the twelfth and thirteen centuries. In this period of the "high Middle Ages" there were great developments in both the religious and secular aspects of society. The spiritual life was

2. Butterfield, *Man on His Past*, 33.
3. Southern, *Scholastic Humanism*, 1–3, 13, 17–23, 133, 305, 310.

enhanced by the "creativity" exemplified in the life of St. Francis of Assisi whom Toynbee regarded as "the greatest soul that has appeared in the western World" while the greatest of the Christian philosophers of the time was St. Thomas Aquinas. Between them they certainly provided the "spiritual creativity" which Toynbee regarded as the necessary pre-requisite for the recovery and development of a culture and civilization. They were at the centre of the one of the greatest advances of Christian Humanism in the life of the Universal Church.

Conspicuous among the elements of development was the unity of "Faith" and "Reason" in the minds of these people. Man is composed of body and soul or she needs to exercise both facilities to become fully balanced, human They are the concomitant elements which can solve our human problems. Reason is needed to retain "common sense", see things in perspective, and relate to "real" life, as well as to make our scientific and "analytic" inquiries, though it must be exercised equally and even more importantly in using its "holistic" abilities. Faith is necessary in life, to meet the needs of our spiritual or religious access to another type of truth. It supplies the means of achieving "transcendent", spiritual or religious truths which are consistent with, but above and beyond human understanding, something similar to "intuitive" or "instinctive" truths which can work for human beings in a situation of sudden and immediate danger when nothing else is available or beyond human reach.

There was a unity in the thinking of these people which denied any artificial attempt to separate the spiritual, intellectual and physical aspects of humanity. They were not hidebound as much of modern society in the West is, by the analytic view that truth is only available by "scientific" means.

In a narrowly secular society, the residue of the openness to this form of "holistic truth" can be detected in what we are beginning to call again the "intelligence of the feelings" or the truths conveyed by the effects on us of some of the greatest works of the creative arts such as painting, poetry or music which can take us somehow "out of this world" by the "stirring of the feelings" aroused through its sheer beauty. There has been a recent emphasis on the importance of music in particular as being a powerful force for people at large as a transcendent and spiritual experience which can benefit them considerably as human beings.

Many of the most inspired pieces of Music and the Arts have been written or painted in praise of God, such as "The Heavens are telling the glory of God" (Handel); or the transcendent beauty of Verdi's "Requiem"; and who can resist the sublime beauty of Kathleen Ferrier's rendering of "I know that my Redeemer liveth." In a recent broadcast of the popular programme, "Britain's got talent"; a nervous young girl, sang a beautiful rendering of "Ave Maria" and suddenly the whole "ethos" of the very crowded Hall, and the judging panel, changed. There was complete silence and awe-struck wonder and beauty on all their faces, as they all experienced a transcendent moment. Such effects are sometimes regarded as "wonderful" but not "real." We are just beginning to understand that they are "real" and have an important effect on our lives and outlook and mental health. This is a "depth" phenomenon which, I believe, all of us have experienced at some time or other.[4] To the Christian humanists of the medieval period, all this was regarded as a way of seeking and finding an experience of the truth of the supreme "beauty" of God as reflected in these activities.

Southern showed that the great schools of Christian humanist studies such as Paris, Bologna, Oxford and Cambridge produced values in Religion, Theology, Law and Medicine which were to permeate life in Christian Europe, underpinning not only intellectual life, but the culture, government, social and legal structures of Western Europe. They provided an extraordinary sense of social coherence and unity. Christian Humanism declared that the Universe and all its parts were filled with meaning; and it was the business of the theologian, the doctor, the scientist, musician, artist, poet, and lawyer to discover and celebrate this meaning, for the common good, in their professions. The ordinary people were assured, in any case, of their own inestimable and inalienable importance as children of God, the Creator of it all. The aim was to push the boundaries of human inquiry and discovery of the marvels of the World created by God. Theirs was "an attempt to make the created universe and its relationship to the eternal being of God as fully intelligible as the limits of human nature allow."

The Christian Humanism was expressed quite succinctly and accurately in the poetry of Robert Browning, in the nineteenth century, when he made his Fra Lippo Lippi, the medieval Italian painter, say: "The world's no blot for us, nor blank. It means intensely and means good. To find its meaning is my meat and drink"; and he expresses the joy involved in the

---

4. Tillich, *The Theology of Culture*, 143–44.

process: "How good is this life, the mere living. How fit to employ all the heart and the soul and the senses, forever in joy."[5]

Southern refers to the long lasting conception by Protestant writers from the sixteenth century and "almost to the present day" that the Bible was diminished by the schools of Christian humanism"; but in fact, he declared that the Bible was their "sovereign text book." Their teaching in the schools was developed to meet the needs and understanding of the "High Middle Ages," but its chief source was always the Bible.

It was St. Francis of Assisi who had the vision from God, telling him to "rebuild' my Church' and he did this by stressing the need to retain the values of love, simplicity, poverty and mercy to be found in the life of Christ. He established the religious "Franciscan order" which lived on these principles and continued his spiritual tradition in the Church. It still exists. The present Pope Francis has adopted the name of this Saint to show that this is the spirit of the new Papacy, in his own attempt to "rebuild the Church" for the needs of the people of the new Millennium.

Pre-eminent among the humanist scholars was St. Thomas Aquinas (1226-74) who had synthesized all the knowledge of the past, bringing together in a balanced construct, the ideas of Aristotle and Plato from the Greek world, the great heritage of the Jewish tradition, and some of the work of the outstanding Moslem philosopher, Averroes (1126-98), before assimilating all this into the Christian tradition on which the religious and secular civilization of Western Europe was to be based.

It was truly a masterly work, bringing together the greatest of the early "secular" philosophers and the thinking of the three Monotheistic (belief in one God) religions, to develop a "Catholic" or "Universal" religious philosophy, without in any way contradicting the revealed truths of Christian Scripture and the Catholic Church. He, too, was a genius who was not initially understand by the contemporary establishment figures who did not quite understand what he was about and were rather suspicious; but in due time it was to become the official and authoritative expression of the philosophical thinking of the Church, and still is, renewed under the inspiration of Pope Francis.

Several modern theologians have been working on certain developments of "Thomistic" thinking to meet the various needs of life in the new Millennium. Our concepts of democracy, human rights and modern

---

5. Browing, *Men and Women*.

science can all be seen in embryonic form in the "SummaTheologica" and "Summa Contra Gentiles" of St. Thomas.

Another important figure of this period was Gratian, who brought the moral law to bear on legal matters, stemming again from Christian Scripture, showing that it was reflected in the tenets of Roman and Canon Law (Church Law). His "Decretum" (1139) was the "first masterpiece of scholastic humanism"[6] in the legal aspect of life, influencing the work of jurists and artists and demonstrating how these fundamental moral principles, underlying the legal principles, could be applied to "the events of ordinary life and full of human situations."

These Christian humanists created a culture of law, literature and ethics which enveloped the lives of people and created an ethos of meaning, unity and stability, after the chaos and destruction caused by the earlier Viking invasions. Their principles of Christian humanism were also to become the seed-bed of some of the most creative and progressive ideas of the modern world. This is what made Carl Gustav Jung, the greatest psycho-analyst of the twentieth century, say that the answers to modern man's problems lay in the medieval period.

One of the high points of my own stay at Cambridge, were the annual "Dominican Lectures"- given to packed audiences- in which prominent Dominican philosophers and scientists from various parts of the World, demonstrated the inspiration which they had derived from the works of St. Thomas Aquinas and the many ways in which his profound and subtle ideas had been misinterpreted and misunderstood and therefore under-appreciated in the twentieth century world of secular philosophy. One of these – a former student of mine in Port Talbot is Brian Davies, Professor of Philosophy at Fordham University in the U.S.A. and a World authority on the work of St. Thomas Aquinas.

In my opinion one of the outstanding Christian Humanists of the medieval period was one of the "mystics" who had a great influence at the time and whose influence has been recreated in the twentieth century to the benefit of thousands of people living in this very modern period. I refer to the person who we know only as "Julian of Norwich." So concerned was she to make herself anonymous in order to point everyone to Christ, that she never divulged her own name, but simply adopted the name of the small church in Norwich in which she was allowed to have her own cell, with one window into the church and another open to the outside world. It was

---

6. Southern, *Scholastic Humanism*, 310.

to this window that people problems flocked to listen to her comforting advice and spiritual help.

In May, 1373, one of England's great mystical writers, a woman keen intellect, great common sense, and profound spiritual insight, experienced a series of mystical "revelations" which she described in the first book written by an English woman, entitled "The Revelations of Divine Love." She spent the rest of her life as an "anchoress" in prayer and giving advice to all sorts of people who came to her for help. We know nothing about her background, but in the twentieth century there has been a great revival of interest in her book which has helped people from all over the world who find that her spiritual teaching is completely relevant to their own lives and conditions of life; and also a great help to their spiritual needs. She is the one English mystic, to be quoted in the most modern Catechism of the Universal Church after Vatican II.

She summarized succinctly the message of her book, based on her conviction of the wonderful compassionate power of God's love for us all:

"Would you know the Lord's meaning in this thing? Learn it well. Love was His meaning... Our failing is fearful, our falling is full of shame... but the sweet eye of pity and mercy never looks away from us, nor does the working of mercy ever cease... All will be well... live merrily and gladly because of His love."[7]

A woman of courage who had suffered herself, a counsellor who was completely down to earth, she well knew that God is concerned with our physical, emotional and psychological needs, as well as those of the intellect. With the instincts and insights of the artist and psychologist, as well as a mystic, she has been ranked in the twentieth century as one of the greatest of all theologians. She brought a feminine intuition to our understanding of God.

Well acquainted with the evils of the world, she taught the ultimate triumph of love through that great power by which "God can subdue all things to Himself" and consequently she is one of the least neurotic of writers. She is concerned with true penitence rather than remorse and guilt which can be another form of concentration on self. True penitence means looking outwards in joyful recognition of God's power, mercy, love and forgiveness, which had been revealed to her in her mystical revelations. It means that the greatest sinner can become a great saint. Her visions describe the infinite love and compassion of God, and consequently the great

---

7. Llewelyn, *Enfolded in Love*, vii–viii, 15, 59, 64.

hope which exists for us all. She insists that her revelations come within the framework of "Holy Church"; but she is quite prepared to push and extend outwards the boundaries of theological understanding. In my view she is the greatest of the English "mystics" and an outstanding example of Christian humanism. Her "cell" still exists in the little church of St. Julian in Norwich, where thousands of pilgrims from all over the World can visit, as I have myself.

The word "mystery" is usually and rightly associated with the spiritual life and its approach towards transcendental truth, but it sometimes seems that modern science is coming nearer to the same kind of understanding. Noam Chomsky, one of the world's most prominent scientists and philosophers, spoke to a Vatican group concerned with dialogue between science and religion. His lecture was on "Neurosciences, Human Nature and Language" and it turned out to be on common ground with Christian teaching. This 85-year-old emeritus professor of the Massachusetts Institute of Science and Technology discussed the limits of human knowledge and the probability of a fundamental and complete understanding of the world being out of the reach of human science.

His premise was that the innate cognitive abilities of humans provide the grounds for appreciating the wonders of "mystery", even when these are out of the reach of human understanding These fundamental constraints on human intelligence apply equally well to our highest mental faculties. We cannot reach an understanding of many things, even of our own human minds and the phenomenon of consciousness. The mystery deepens as we proceed from Newton to Einstein's view of the world. Neuroscience seems unable to provide a mechanical answer to the deepest questions. Human free will cannot be answered in scientific terms. Newton himself seemed to understand this. He did not throw away the "ghost in the machine", but "exorcised the machine, leaving the ghost intact"; and remained a man fully aware of the transcendent aspect of life. Similarly, Einstein's view of the world proceeded to an even greater mystery as he proceeded into the realms of time and space where human knowledge reached an awareness of its own limitation. Incidentally, Einstein spent much of his time and energy deploring the catastrophic result of the use of the atomic bomb in Japan, which his work had been involved in making.

Some of the greatest and wisest of human minds seem to reach awareness, in the light of their own superior knowledge, that while we can stretch our curiosity to the limits, we must also accept that a greater "mystery" is probably outside our reach because, after all, we are only "human", pitifully small but very precious in the sight of a merciful God.

It will be useful, I think, in understanding the spirit of Christian humanism, to advance to its next startling appearance in the Renaissance of the sixteenth century; and its expression again of a unity between the achievements of modern science, technology and the arts and their relationship to religion. I take as an example the life of one of the most symbolic figures. I speak of Leonardo da Vinci (1452-1519), the truly great Italian painter, sculptor, architect, engineer, anatomist, mathematician, scientist and technologist. He is acclaimed by the world at large as one of the true geniuses in the realm of human achievement.

I visited the house in Northern France where he lived out the last years of his life and which is now a Museum containing original examples off his life's work and the inspiration behind it all. His pioneering and accurate work in establishing the basis for future scientific discoveries in so many areas of life leaves one aghast. His analytic ability was extraordinary; but so was his "holistic" appreciation of the World and its wonders. His own private note books contain many examples of the way in which he anticipated the findings of modern science by working on his own mathematical and scientific premises. His paintings exist to show us the extent of his artistic and anatomical abilities which reached the limits of human powers, by any standard.

What is well less known about him is the way in which he embodies the very spirit of Christian humanism by his obvious attempts to become fully human in Christ, from which he derived his huge humility in the face of God. They reveal the spiritual and transcendental thinking which took him above the realms of human reason, though not at all inconsistent with it. So, for example, this greatest of anatomists of the human body can write, for example, in his notes:

"If this outer carcass of man seems marvellously created, consider that it is nothing compared to the soul which has informed it."

And:

"I leave stand without touching, the crowned letters (Sacred Scriptures) . . . for they are the Supreme Truth."

And again:

"Oh God, you sell all things to men at the cost of their effort . . . if you do not know God, you cannot love Him . . . What is the undefinable thing which would cease to be if it were formulated – the infinite which would be finite if it could be defined... Even more the Spirit in the universe. But the finite cannot be extended into the infinite."[8]

Leonardo, the human genius, stood in humble recognition of his own human limitations, before God, the Creator of the Universe and Mankind. Such genius, if questioned now by a modern critic, would laugh at the idea of ever achieving a complete understanding the mysteries of the Universe. This would be to think that we are gods ourselves; and this would explain the "hubris" or "pride" which is one of the main dangers involved in the outlook of modern man.

We come now to the next great challenge to Christianity; this time from the inside rather than outside. It was called "The Reformation" of the sixteenth century. It happened alongside the Renaissance, the great movement of human development, which the "Reformers" opposed because of its breakaway not only from the Catholic and Universal Church, but also from the precepts of Christian humanism which we have described. It is an intriguing story with faults on both sides – the Church and the new Protestants. Only the Christian humanists come out of it well.

At the turn if the fifteenth and sixteenth centuries, the Catholic Church was suffering from very bad leadership, because the Popes at this time were not fit for their job and did not meet the spiritual standard required. We are reminded that Christ did not promise that all his followers would be good, and that one of the first twelve apostles turned out to be a traitor; though remarkably there was no change in any of the essential teachings of the Church. The fault lay in the lack of sanctity and discipline; and some faults and sins such as the selling of "indulgences" were obvious.

The reaction to this was two- fold. Martin Luther, a German priest was the initiator of one reaction. He protested against these abuses and eventually decided to leave the Church and start another of his own. Incidentally he was also a great opponent of the Renaissance because he believed that human nature was totally corrupt and any expression of it was wrong. One example is that the educational system he established was allowed to use only the Bible as its text book.

The second reaction was from the Christian humanists who believed in the inherent goodness, though warped condition of human nature. They were among the leaders of the Renaissance. Among the leaders were Desiderius Erasmus from the Netherlands and Thomas More and Bishop John

---

8. Sertilages, *The Thoughts of Leonardo Da Vinci*.

Fisher in England. All these wanted Church reform and both Erasmus and Thomas More worked for this in the form of their satirical writings. Erasmus in particular also worked with Luther to get reform, but when Luther took it further and decided to leave the Universal Church and to set up a new one, with him at the head, Erasmus left him. Luther famously attacked his former supporter by calling him "another hog from the Epicurean sty", referring to Epicurus, the ancient Greek philosopher who had taught that soundly based human happiness was the highest good and should be pursued with rational thought.

Erasmus was in fact the first great example of a "pacificist" outlook, because he hated war of any kind, regard it as one of the greatest of human follies as became clear in his satirical book "In Praise of Folly" (1509). He was also the most important representative of the Renaissance in northern Europe. His unforgettable writings on the folly of War are still some of the most impressive examples of their kind in the history of Pacifism.

The real disaster was that Luther was supported by the German princes who wanted to be free of the Hapsburg Emperor, Charles V. Luther supported them by helping them to put down the "Peasants Revolt" (1525), and by advising them, in the most violent language, to use radical force and punishment against them. In other words religion was becoming dangerously involved in politics.

In England Henry VIII decided to leave the Catholic or Universal Church and start his own, because he wanted to be free from his wife, Catherine, to marry his mistress, Anne Boleyn; but the Church could not allow this. Moreover, he decided to kill anyone opposing him and put down the Peasants' Revolt in England (1536), killing over 200 of them after falsely promising to meet them and discuss the situation with them. He also executed his Chancellor, Thomas More, Lord Chancellor, a very distinguished Christian Humanist who wrote the "Utopia" (1516) and Bishop John Fisher, the only English bishop with the courage to oppose Henry, and again a man who has been described very recently as "a neglected giant among Christian humanists and the most distinguished Catholic theologian in the Europe of his day."[9]

Reform soon came in the Catholic Church, with what is called the "Counter-Reformation. It was a good example of the "dynamo" (series of reforms which arrived when needed in the life of this Church) at work. It came with the election of good Popes, such as Paul IV and even more so

---

9. Duffy, *Saints, Sacrilege and Sedition*.

under Pope Sixtus V with whom these reforms reached their apogee. They banished the abuses and started a spiritual revival in the Church, associated with the founding of new religious orders, especially the Jesuits, the new Reforming Council of Trent, and a stream of saints, such as Philip Neri, Charles Borromeo, Ignatius Loyola, Theresa of Avila and many others appearing in the Church which became spiritually revived. The Counter-Reformation had completed its task by the following century and the Universal Church was again at its peak spiritually.

But by now the damage had been done, with the breakdown of Christendom and its Christian unity.[10] The Catholic Church had reformed itself, but the fear which Christian humanists shared turned out to be true. Other breakaway groups, such as those led by Calvin in Geneva and Zwingli in Switzerland formed their own different versions of Christianity. As time went on more splinter groups became apparent within Protestantism, and the Christian religion became increasingly involved in politics. As a result of this, the witness and authenticity of Christianity in Europe and later the World at large was greatly weakened. Christ Himself had emphasized the need for unity among his followers, "so that the World may believe that You (God the Father) hath sent me."

Moreover this was concomitant with the rise of new Nation states, of which England was the first, in which it became the custom that political rulers could decide the religion of their own people. Then these Nation states began a series of internecine wars causing destruction and huge loss of life. The worst was the savage 30 years war (1613-16480) between mainly between Germany and France, but soon involving most of Western Europe. In these internal wars Politics had become mixed up inextricably with religion and Christians of different nations were fighting and killing one another. This was a complete abuse and denigration of the Christian faith. Instead of it becoming a main cause of World peace, it was doing the opposite. The Peace of Westphalia (1648) proclaimed the principle of "cuius regio, eius religio", confirming the fact that political leaders would choose the religion of their own people.

This continual warfare continued through four centuries and led inevitably to the two World Wars of the twentieth century, which both started in Europe before leading to the involvement of other continents.

This was the tragedy which Christian humanists, such as Erasmus, Thomas More and Bishop Fisher, had predicted. They were "holistic"

10. Greengrass, *Christendom Destroyed*.

thinkers who could see the wider and longer picture of these proceedings for the future, which could not have been foreseen or intended by the short-term, intensive and narrow vision of the more analytically minded Luther. With hindsight, and with better understanding and good will on all sides, and if the admixture of politics had been avoided, the break-up of Christendom could have been avoided. The doctrinal differences between the Church and the views of Luther could have been settled.

For example the reformers' idea of "predestination", and "salvation by faith alone", which seemed to offend again the Catholic doctrine of "free will" and the importance of "good works", has now been solved. The Church itself has always taught that pre-destination in the sense that God, for whom time and spaced does not exist, does know what is going to happen, but this does not mean, in the human life span, that free-will does not exist at this lower level. Also, while the Church teaches that we are saved by Faith alone, the proof that we have Faith must be confirmed in the good works that it produces.

The Catholic Church itself was affected adversely because though it had benefitted from the reforms of the Counter-Reformation, it tended from now on to adopt a kind of fortress mentality in opposition to the various Protestant sects that continued to emerge from break-ups within Protestantism itself. The Church developed a negative attitude towards the outside world. It became inward looking rather than outward, reducing greatly its proper role in evangelisation.

This is one problem which the present Pope Francis, "The Great Reformer" and Christian Humanist, is determined to repair as part of his reforms in the outlook and role of the Universal Church, as the teacher and servant of mankind. He is very concerned with bringing Christians together again, emphasizing the all-containing unity of the "Kingdom of God" to which all Christians belong and to strengthen Christian evangelization which benefits from this unity.

Over the next four centuries there is no doubt that the proper witness of Christianity to the World was increasingly weakened by the divisions created which started in the sixteenth century, and from this "fortress" like attitude which this produced in the Church towards the outside world. Protestantism produced its own good work, especially in its emphasis on the importance of the knowledge of the Bible by everyone.

Peace on Earth

The Catholic (Universal) Church always cherished the Bible, but was too concerned, especially after the "Reformation", to teach it through its own authority, rather than expose it to the danger of it being wrongly interpreted by ordinary people who lacked the knowledge and authority to interpret it properly. Pope John XXIII (creator of Vatican II) and Pope Francis, the present applicator of Vatican II, have put this situation right and given every encouragement to everyone to read the Bible, partly because the laity has now become much more educated, but mainly because they have the right to do so. The Universal Church has itself been benefitted greatly by this new emphasis on this confirmation of the Bible as the supreme authority when it is interpreted properly.

Toynbee describes what happened quite pithily:

"Since the Reformation, the Church which had once been the institutional expression of Western Christendom's unity, has only been one among a number of rival Western Christian sects whose rancorous mutual hostility has torn the Western World in pieces, has brought Christianity itself into discredit there, and has thus opened the way for the supplanting of Christianity by nationalism, a post –Christian resuscitation of the pre-Christian worship of collective human power."[11]

This was accentuated by the strange and unfounded belief which started in the Western World, in the seventeenth and eighteenth centuries, that the only possible kind of "proper or realistic truth" was that which could be achieved by man was through science. This notion that man could do without God, was a great temptation to the human predilection towards pride that comes before a fall. Such "hubris" was well known to the philosophers and the writers of "Tragedies" in ancient Greece. It is also writ-large in the history of the Western world in modern times, ending with the real tragedies of the two World Wars in the twentieth century, which represented the lowest point in the history of mankind.

By now when the devastation caused by the scientific advances in military power was bringing the death of millions of people and a life times' misery to many thousands of families , it was striking evidence of man's foolish inhumanity to man, and its consequence which Erasmus in particular had anticipated, four centuries before.

It was in the second half of the twentieth century and now at the start of the twenty first century and the new Millennium, that Christian humanism stepped in again in the form of two Christian humanist Popes, who,

---

11. Toynbee, *A Study of History*, 210.

despite the 50 years between them, worked together. Christians know from their experience that God is frequently surprising us. Working together, yet not known to one another, they seem to have given expression to the mysterious "dynamo" effect, mentioned by Arnold Toynbee. It came into action, unexpectedly, to produce the creative conditions by which a spiritual revival within the Universal Church always seems to come into effect when needed. I shall be coming to a description of what happened next in the following chapters.

Firstly, we can now turn to the first piece of evidence, produced in the second part of the twentieth century that Christian humanism, working in the hands of the Christian laity, is capable of producing practical effects in the political world in which we now live, as an example of what can be done at this important turning point in world history, to make a dramatic and hopeful move towards peace and unity. It is an example, too, of the spiritual principles behind this movement.

V

Robert Schuman and the European Union

AFTER THE CATASTROPHIC EXPERIENCE of the two World Wars in the twentieth century, there was a general feeling that mankind had "gone off the rails." The old Christian values associated with European civilization had been discarded and humanity brutalised across the Continent. At the end of the Second World War a movement was started intent on making sure that such an experience would not happen again. There had been previous attempts to do this before, such as the League of Nations, but these had failed. The new movement was to be different in character and methodology. It was to become one of the most significant movements in European history, though little understood in Britain itself.

It happened because of the quiet but steely determination of a group of Catholic thinkers and statesmen who established Christian-Democratic Governments in France, Germany and Italy immediately after the fall of the Fascist Governments in 1945. These leaders had all suffered imprisonment for their opposition to the fascist regimes during the War. They were determined to establish a lasting peace in Europe for the first time since the sixteenth century.

It was a noble and heroic enterprise, which required great courage, perseverance and will power, to construct and follow a vision, finding its inspiration in Christian humanism, and including a unique and unprecedented combination of ancient wisdom and modern enterprise. Their work had none of the trappings of triumphalism which had been shown by too many European leaders of the warring nation-states during the previous four centuries. It was accomplished so quietly and methodically that its true significance has gone almost unnoticed, especially by the British people who seemed to remain largely unaware of its origins and fundamental purpose.

It was a movement designed to create a union or family of European peoples, using a method which had never been used before. Its intention was to make it practically impossible for any future internecine war between European nations to take place. The first step was taken by Dr. Conrad Adenauer (1876-1967) of Germany. He belonged to a Catholic family of lawyers and had been Mayor of Cologne since 1917. He was an opponent of Hitler and had suffered imprisonment from 1933 because of his opposition to the Nazi Regime. He had witnessed the horrors inflicted on Germany and the wider world from Hitler's ideas and actions. After the collapse of this regime in 1945, he founded the Christian-Democratic Party in West Germany and worked with General de Gaulle of France for reconciliation between their two countries; and in 1949 he became the first Chancellor of the West German Republic.

Adenauer appears to have been the first statesman in European and perhaps World history to have as his first aim, that his own country would never again be able to use its strength and military power for warlike purposes. He went so far as to state publicly in 1949, on being elected as the West German Chancellor and, when the danger of Russian invasion from the east became apparent, that he would never again consider the establishment of German armed forces, even if the Allies were to demand a military contribution to European security.

His aim was idealistic; nothing less than lasting "fraternity", unity and peace in Europe. His aim was devastatingly simple, practical, realistic and unprecedented. He wanted to unite nations in Europe so closely together by economic and political bonding that it would be simply impossible for them to go to war with one another again. He also wanted, in this way, to strengthen Western Europe against the possible menace from Communist Russia. His first step would be to ensure that Germany and France, two of the main perpetrators of past wars, would be brought together in this way.

One of the less well known features of his life, however, was his devoutly Catholic commitment to a spiritual outlook on life, as found in his private note books:

"When I reflect how God created the universe, everything else seems so superfluous."

"There are thoughts which are prayers. These are moments when, whatever the posture (of) the body, the soul is on its knees."[1]

And his reflection, indicating his Christian humanism, indicated that it could have stopped the advance of Nazism in Germany:

"Enlighten the people generally, and tyranny and oppression of body and mind will vanish like evil spirits at the dawn of day."[2]

All this is a complete contrast to the mentality of conquering German leaders of the previous four centuries. To those who would consider his ideas unrealistic, it is good to remember that he initiated the extraordinary rebirth of Germany by its innovatory political, economic and social policies, designed by applying the "fraternity" principle to all these areas of German life. It was to produce an extraordinary re-birth effect in the progress and position of Germany in Europe.

Before the end of the century, Germany was to become the leader of Europe. In 2005, after the results of his policies, continued by his successors such as Helmut Kohl and eventually, the Lutheran Angela Merkel, Adenauer was voted by the German people to be "the greatest German of all time." All this was underlain by a remarkable revival of Christian humanism in Germany, after the War, more than in any other European country, which visitors from Britain witnessed, as we shall see below.

Meanwhile there was a remarkably similar development taking place in France, which was to have an even more remarkable effect on European history through the work of one Christian humanist.

He was Robert Schuman (1881-1963), a most extraordinary man and statesman who had also been imprisoned by the Gestapo, for his opposition to Hitler's occupation of France. After the fall of the Nazi regime, Schuman formed the Christian-Democrat Party in France, where he became Prime Minister in 1947. Politically speaking, his leadership qualities brought him to the premiership of France and later to the first Presidency of the European Movement for Peace and Unity (1955-61).

What makes him truly remarkable, if not unique, however, is the evidence showing that his political life was simply a practical expression of his spiritual life. A very devout Catholic and daily communicant, he had

---

1. This quote was made famous by the French poet and writer, Victor Hugo.
2. Mapp, *Thomas Jefferson*, 266.

chosen politics as his "vocation" and religious apostolate. His own private thoughts are very informative and revelatory:

"I learn to think like God, instead of repeating the slogans of the world."

And, he himself is simply an instrument in the hands of God:

"We are all instruments, even if imperfect, of Providence which uses them for purposes which are above us."

Schuman was a Christian humanist, choosing to serve God and his fellow men, in his work as a politician and statesman. He reveals himself as a neo-scholastic thinker, knowing and applying the principles enunciated by St. Thomas Aquinas in the medieval period. God's grace is completely free to blow where it wills, as the Holy Spirit directs it. There can be no rigid separation between the natural world and the life of the Spirit. The supernatural is built upon the natural, but transcends it. The Spirit of God can bring its power to work in all elements of secular life, such as politics, economics, social work and the creative arts, through the action of human beings in the secular world.

In the search for truth, you start with the known facts exhibited in the nature of man and the Universe and build the theory on them. God had given humans a free will, meant to help them to serve Him and his fellow men by encouraging the development of their innate goodness. Man's pride and selfishness had interfered with this and threatens to imprison him in the cell of his own self-centredness. The strategy of good man-management is to encourage the human virtues of love and fraternity for the common good and to free him from this cell of selfishness.

He might well have been helped by the work of the contemporary French philosopher, Jacques Maritain (1882-1973), a convert from atheism, who had a great influence in France and who built his work on exactly the same principles derived from Aquinas and now applied by him to all aspects of modern life. I know the force of Maritain's work having been influenced in my own field of education at this time, by his "Education at the Cross Roads", which I applied with the same effect in this particular field.

All this had made a great impact on Schuman and his use of his own political power. He set out to apply these ideas to the development of a "fraternity" (brotherhood) of peoples in Europe, willing and able to provide the great benefit of unity and peace in this newly created family. The enterprise would have to be based on concrete facts so that the transcendent power of goodness in man could be freed to express itself. It was to be built upon the strategy of building a new Europe in which the constituent states would be so closely built together in economic and political terms that war would become impossible and the common good would emerge.

The task appeared to be simple and logical, but Schuman was well aware that it was new and revolutionary. The premise of placing politics and economics at the service of the common good would require great human qualities. It would demand good and enduring leadership, assisted by all the "virtues" which Aquinas had imbibed from Aristotle and later strengthened by Christian teaching, such as "Truth", "Justice"," Charity", "Courage", "Prudence", "Moderation", "Wisdom" and great "Patience" and "determination." All this would be required to achieve perhaps the most difficult of all human tasks –to overcome the selfishness and pride in human nature, not only in one individual, but in a whole Continent of nations which had hitherto been individual and independent nation states, continually at war with one another because they had succumbed to these defects in a warped human nature. It was perhaps the most noble of human initiatives; and the most difficult. Moreover if success could be achieved, it might, in showing that it was possible to do so, provide a giant step forward as an example of what could be done in the new global village.

The previous philosophies behind people-management in the twentieth century, Fascism, Marxism, Unbridled Capitalism, had all failed because they did not understand human nature and its needs. It is indeed the fact that no such system in politics or education, can succeed without firstly understanding and establishing this premise of thought, on which it can be built. Schuman's thinking was characteristic of the Christian humanist approach to this human problem, seeing a necessary "transcendent" power, arising from a basis of concrete and rational thought. This was the necessary core element behind the success or failure of the scheme. He was to state later, in his Presidential speech to the European Movement for Peace and Unity, in 1958:

"All the European Countries are permeated by Christian civilization. It is the soul of Europe which must be returned to it."[3]

Nearly a half century later, in 2015, the present Pope Francis warned this Movement, when it had made a mistake, that it exists to serve Christian humanism and can only survive if it remains open to the existence of God and His commandment to "love your neighbour as yourself." Pope Francis

---

3. Said in first Presidential Speech to European Union in 1958.

addressed the Movement's leaders to remember the outlook of the founder of this Movement, and warned that if this was abandoned for any secular reasons, it would flounder, saying that if Europe was no longer open to the transcendent dimension of life, it would slowly risk losing its own soul and the humanistic spirit which it still loves and defends.

In his book, "Pour l' Europe"[4] written a few years before his death, Schuman reminded us of his basic beliefs:

"Democracy owes its existence to Christianity. It was born the day man was called to realize in his daily context the dignity of the human person in his individual freedom, in the respect of the rights of everyone, and in the practise of brotherly love towards all. Never before Christ, had similar concepts been formulated"

And again:

"The togetherness (of peoples) cannot and shall not remain an economic and technical undertaking. It must be given a soul. Europe will not live and will not be saved except to the degree in which its awareness of itself and its responsibilities exists when it returns to the Christian principles of solidarity and fraternity."

Schuman laid down the spiritual basis and value system on which the Movement for European Unity and Peace was based from the start; and although the leadership was changed as time went on, it remains unique as a modern institution based on spiritual values; and these values have remained up to the present. At present, over sixty years later, the leadership in this has been taken over by another Christian humanist, Angela Merkel, the Lutheran leader of Germany, who is very able and worthy to continue in this amazingly difficult role.

This distinguishes it from all other purely secular movements. It is also the reason why some, unfortunately including Britain, have not yet understood it, though they entered the movement for different reasons. From the Christian viewpoint it was based on rock rather than sand. The two great Christian humanist Popes, John XXIII and now Pope Francis have been strong supporters of this institution created by laymen to produce Peace and unity in the Continent of Europe; but have left it to lay Christians, helped by many other people of good will, such as Jean Monnet of France and Henri de Spaak of the Netherlands, who have also wanted to support these aims and joined the Movement. Pope John Paul II said that Schuman was "the ideal European."

4. Schuman, *Pour l'Europe*.

The whole enterprise, starting with two, has ended up with 28 member States of the fraternity. As a result over 500 million people in Europe have lived in peace together for the first time in four centuries of modern history; a quite extraordinary achievement, though I think sometimes taken for granted and under-endorsed by the rest of the world which seem more interested in more materialistic criteria of development. It has had all the spirit of Erasmus of Rotterdam, four hundred years before, about it.

By 1990 a group of French, German and Italian people belonging to the Fraternity of St. Benedict (the Patron Saint of Europe) petitioned the Vatican for the process of beatification and canonisation of Schuman to be started. In 2006 his cause was "validated" by the Vatican which means that he is now in the "pipe-line" for the usual lengthy period of consideration for being proclaimed a Saint of the Universal Church.

On October 12th, 2012, the Movement for European Peace and Unity was awarded the Nobel Prize for its achievement. The citation stated its:

"Achievement of peace and reconciliation, democracy and human rights."

It referred to its expansion to 27 states as representing "the fraternity of nations."

After announcing the prize, which is of course very prestigious in global terms, the Chairman of the Norwegian Prize Committee, Thorbjorn Jagland, warned against the possible return to "extremism" and "nationalism":

"We should do everything we can to safeguard it, not let it disintegrate, if the euro starts falling apart, then I believe the internal market will also start falling apart. And then obviously we get a new nationalism in Europe."[5]

Angela Merkel, the German Chancellor, linked the "wonderful selection" to her Country's determined effort to save the 17 nation euro-zone:

"I often say that the euro is more than a currency . . . at the end of the day it is about the original idea of a union of peace and values."[6]

Herman von Rompuy, the President of the European Council and Jose Manuel Barrosos, the President of the European Commission, said in a joint statement that it was a "tremendous honour":

---

5. Cited in *The Tablet*.
6. Ibid.

"It is a prize not just for the project and the institutions embodying a common interest, but for the 500 million citizens living in our union."[7]

The "common market" in this Union is now the greatest in the World, composed of 500 million people. In February, 2013, President Obama of the United States of America, started negotiations with the European Union, to combine together the trading markets of both these federations, with free trading between them, which would increase the prosperity and strength of them both.

This was the first concrete achievement, in political terms, of the resurgence of Christian humanism in the modern world. Its example holds the greatest sign of hope for the future peace of the World. It shows how effectively the application of Christian principles can be in contributing to the common good of all people in today's secular and pluralistic society. It represents a first step forward to world peace. These principles and values are dynamic and organic in nature and there is no reason why they cannot be used, in due time, to bring peace and "fraternity" to the human family in the World at large, by the process of what Toynbee called "mimesis" or imitation. It creates a "vision" for the peoples of the World in the new Millennium; and there is much truth in the old scriptural statement that "Without a vision, the people perish."[8]

We ought, I think, to add some historical background to show the factual basis on which this human achievement was based, to bring it "down to earth" so to speak. After the Second World War ended in 1945, there appeared immediately a new threat to Europe. Communist Russia, led by the Marxist ideology of Stalin, had refused to leave its occupation of Poland, and had even insisted on remaining in Eastern Germany. It became clear that there was another threat from Stalin's expansionist policy into the West.

From 1945 to 1950, there were a series of continuous talks among the other allies, of how to deal with the situation. The United States wanted to support a united front in Europe, led by Britain, to strengthen a united Europe against the new threat. But Britain was not inclined to take up this role again. After much prevarication over ten years, it became obvious that Britain did not want to do it. There was a complete stalemate and Russia in the meantime was extending its influence in Eastern Europe by establishing

---

7. Ibid.
8. Ibid.

the "Iron Curtain" behind which Marxist Communism was spreading its domination.

It was at this critical moment of European history, that Robert Schuman stepped into the breach by taking the matter into his own hands, knowing that he would have the support of his Christian Humanist colleagues –Adenauer in Germany and de Gasperi in Italy, with whom he had been discussing his own vision of peace and unity in Europe. He knew, too, that there were other leaders in Europe who shared the ambition of creating unity in Europe. Jean Monnet, the French economist who was an influential supra-national figure was a strong supporter who worked alongside Schuman in France; and Paul Henri-Spaak of Belgium, who became leader of the Benelux Countries (Luxembourg. Belgium and Holland), was another enthusiast for peace and unity in Europe.

Schuman decided that the time was ripe for action. On 5th May, 1950, he made what has become known as the "Schuman Declaration" beginning with the following statement:

"It is no longer a time for vain words, but for a bold, constructive act. France has acted and the consequences of her action may be immense. We hope they will be. She has acted essentially in the cause of peace. For peace to have a chance, there must first be a Europe. Almost years to the day since Germany's unconditional surrender, France is taking the first and decisive step to rebuild Europe and is inviting Germany to play a part. This will transform the situation in Europe. It will open the door to other joint activities inconceivable hitherto. Europe will emerge from all this, a Europe which is firmly united and solidly built."[9]

What a difference this was, compared to the action taken after the first World War, when the British Prime Minister, Lloyd George, had said that the allies who had won the War would "squeeze the Germans until the pips squeak", an action which turned out to be one of the main causes of the Second World War later!

After making this "Declaration", and with Adenauer's support, Schuman immediately called for a conference in Paris to which the European state leaders, outside the "Iron Curtain" would be invited. He asked his colleague, Jean Monnet, to chair the Conference. It was at this Conference that Monnet proposed a new principle of political dialogue which was to be, and remains still, hugely important in the history of the European

---

9. Schuman Declaration, 1950.

Union, and could become central to any approach to World peace and union in the future.

Monnet's words were short but unprecedented, dynamic and organic in the sphere of politics in the modern world. They contain the essence of what is needed to overcome the selfish weakness of human nature, by applying a super-natural principle of unselfishness:

"We have here to undertake a common task... not to negotiate for our own advantage, but to each it is the advantage of all. Only if we eliminate from our debates any particularist feelings shall we reach a solution. Insofar as we gathered here, can change our methods, the attitude of all Europeans will likewise gradually change."[10]

It is the same principle being employed now in 2016 as the Movement reaches the final stages of changing the old "sovereign nation-state" approach to that of a united and peaceful Europe. It is the only methodology by which this can be achieved; and the same applies to any fundamental move towards progress and peace in the new "global village. It means the transcendence of the supernatural (unselfishness) over the natural (selfishness), based on the methodology used by Schuman, and derived from the philosophy of Thomas Aquinas.

It was proposed at this meeting that there should be a "High Authority" to guide the Movement to Unity. All agreed and took for granted that it should be constituted by France and Germany who were recognized as the "Founding Fathers." A Council of Ministers representing all involved States would be established, to approve any major decisions. A Parliamentary Assembly would be set up with representatives from all constituent States. All present gave their unanimous consent to all these proceedings.

This established the institutional structure of the new organisation for European Government. All this was legalised by the Treaty of Paris in 1951. This had all Schuman's political skills stamped all over it. He was able to be infinitely patient when necessary, but was also capable of acting quickly and decisively when the opportunity presented itself. He was creating in practise an inspiring vision which would set the States of Europe on an entirely different path from that of the internecine warfare which had caused the destruction of humanity to an unprecedented extent in Europe over the last four centuries.

The vision was simple but its application very difficult and complicated to achieve. It required great and resolute leadership, together with

---

10. Jean Monet's speech to the first Conference of the Union, 1950.

all the old "virtues" which had been admired in humans since the time of Aristotle, such as fortitude, charity, justice, patience, freedom, prudence, moderation, and particularly what we now call "dialogue", instead of war.

Aristotle, in the fourth century before Christ, had taught that "virtue", not competition, was the true basis of the common good in the healthy society, as revealed by the natural law. It is a very salutary thought that this truth was discovered well over two thousand years ago and is now having to be discovered again for the world in the third Millennium. It should certainly dispel any foolish thoughts that we are cleverer than people of the past.

The concrete base, as a first example of the efficacy of Schuman's political theory, was the bringing together of the two largest industries in France and Germany and the two greatest offenders in internecine warfare of the past. The "Schuman Plan" proposed a union of the Coal and Steel industries in both these States, to ensure that War between them would be impossible in future; and other States were invited to join in as well. This was established by the Treaty of Paris (1951), as 'The European Coal and Steel Community (ECSC), representing a single authority for these industries in France, West Germany, Italy, Holland, Belgium and Luxembourg. It eliminated all tariffs and other restrictions on trade between them.

This was the origin of what we now know firstly as the "Common Market", which soon became "The European Community" and finally emerged as the "European Union." The idea soon developed as it was seen to succeed. In 1974, the United Kingdom, Denmark and the Republic of Ireland joined. Greece followed in1981, and then Spain and Portugal in 1985. After the collapse of the Communist system in Eastern Europe in 1989, all the States which had suffered under Communist rule rushed to join the Union. It invoked also the influence and idealism of Christian Humanism, together with skills of ethics and virtues that went back Aristotle and the wisdom of the past. It proclaimed human rights, democracy, tolerance, freedom of religion, the sanctity of the informed conscience; and it required all the classical "virtues" if it was to succeed.

So far it has succeeded. It has shown that extraordinary achievements are possible, having already survived more than a half century in spite of many obstacles and problems which it has had to face which initially had seemed impossible to overcome. Its aims are among the most important in human history and its achievements have been extraordinary, though not always understood and appreciated by those who have not shared the same vision as is adherents.

In 1974 the United Kingdom, Denmark and the Republic of Ireland applied successfully to join. Greece followed in1981; Spain and Portugal in 1985. Then, after the dramatic collapse of Communism behind the "Iron Curtain" in1989, the Easter Europe States rushed to qualify and join in order to enjoy freedom and democracy and peace, together with a better quality of life enjoyed by the Union or family of peoples. By the turn of the century, the Union was composed of 28 states and a population of 500 million people –the largest economy in the World.

The first significant step forward was the Treaty of Rome (1957) in which Schuman was careful to establish a fundamental pillar of the enterprise. It stated that any change in future legislation must satisfy the criterion of bringing the people of Europe closer together in peace and fraternity. This criterion must be built in to any future developments. Political and economic considerations must be considered according to their main purpose of improving the quality of life of the "brotherhood as a whole"; and this has been the case in all succeeding treaties.

In the Treaty of Maastricht (1992), the common need for a single currency, to bring the Union more together as a unit, was accepted by 17 of the states, which then became known as the "Euro-zone", with 10 others, including Britain, outside this zone.

In 2008 the need for a permanent office of "President", to give a more effective and central direction, was accepted and also the office of foreign minister, to provide cohesion in managing relationships with other countries. This was passed at the Treaty of Lisbon (2009). The first President chosen by the whole group of states in the Movement, was Herman Von Rompuy, Prime Minister of Belgium, who was chose unanimously. Significantly enough, he was little known outside the circle of leaders of the Union, except for his quiet but very effective work in bringing cohesion and stability to Belgium in the face of seemingly intractable economic problems and equally difficult and highly charged disputes about solving the problem of diverse groups devoted to using different languages in the Netherlands; and achieving reconciliation and peace. It was his quiet and effective style of negotiation by dialogue which had brought him unexpectedly to the leadership of Belgium.

They could not have chosen anyone more alike to Schuman, the Founder of the Movement, which accounted for his promotion to

President. His mission in life seemed to be the making of peace. He was a devout Catholic and Christian Humanist, a poet, family man and very serious thinker who was also a professional and highly skilled economist. During his long period as President he developed an enviable reputation as quiet negotiator, reconciler and "bridge builder" between different political groups, demonstrating the qualities of patience, prudence, temperance and fortitude. He summarised his stance in political life in the following terms:

"Christian politics will always be a balance between ethical idealism and political realism."[11]

He became an effective adviser to Angela Merkel, the Chancellor of Germany, a Lutheran and Christian Humanist herself. They became a very successful partnership in leading the Movement for Peace and Union in Europe, and ensuring that its heritage of would not be neglected.

When World economic crisis became threatening in 2008, the need for central regular inspection of budgetary and fiscal deficit became apparent and the significantly named Treaty of Solidarity, Co-operation and Fraternity was agreed in 2012, with only Britain and the Czech Republic, refusing to join in closer Union. In the meeting of Euro-zone leaders, in 2013, important steps have been taken towards closer fraternity. Intermediate steps to deal with short-term problems have been agreed.

The European Bank's "bail-out" Fund will give loans directly to banking systems with special and immediate difficulties, such as those of Italy and Spain. Even more significant was the decision that a single supervisory body for all national banks in the euro-zone should be established to regulate budgetary and fiscal spending.

The movement for European Peace and Unity has drawn great strength from its newly integrated economy. It has become the largest economic market of trade and commerce on the world stage. It has played a leading part in aiding under-developed countries such as Africa and Palestine. It exercises a leading influence for good in the development of environmental care in the world. Its principles of solidarity, democracy, religious freedom and human rights, which have all become compulsory requirements for any country joining the Union, have spread and benefitted the world. Its Courts of Justice have provided a final court of appeal for human rights throughout Europe.

---

11. A reply that made to a question put to him by an interviewer as reported in "The Tablet."

Germany has become the main power-house, using these principles of Christian Humanism to lift itself from the ashes of destruction and shame in 1945 to the position of leading power in Europe. It firstly established its own highly successful principles of Christian Humanism, such as fraternity and equality in its domestic spheres of education, social cohesion, and industrial areas; and then brought them into force while leading the continuing movement forward for peace and union in Europe.

Angela Merkel, Chancellor of Germany, has taken on the mantle of Robert Schuman as the leading statesperson in Europe. Herman von Rompuy has now retired; but his role now has been replaced by the new Pope Francis who is much more active in his practical support of the European Union, than his two predecessors who, while supporting the Movement, did not involve themselves in politics as such.

Angela Merkel says that Pope Francis is an "inspiration" to her, adding that she, too, bases her political decisions on Christian values, adding that:

"We need this important ethical-moral compass. Without the Churches, Germany would only be the poorer spiritually, it would be colder socially."

Adding that the engagement of Christian Churches was "indispensable" for German society; and that before making political decisions, she always turns "to ask God if what I am considering is right."[12]

The European Union has produced very beneficial results for the people of Europe part from the primary aim of providing them with and democracy have replaced authoritarian rule in Greece, Spain and Portugal. The eastern European countries which had lived under Communist control behind the "Iron Curtain" from 1945 to 1989 have benefitted greatly in terms of freedom and comparative prosperity. There has been a general increase in the quality of life throughout Europe, especially in poorer countries such as Eire and Portugal which have been helped to develop. The prosperity of everyone in the world has been damaged by the economic and financial collapse of 2008; but there is now a general recovery hopefully taking place.

Critics, particularly in Britain, look for weaknesses in the European Union. No human organisation is perfect. Difficulties, obstacles and weaknesses will arise from time to time, especially when this particular organisation is pursuing a very high ideal of unselfishness and peace. It is a noble

---

12. Ibid.

and praiseworthy path towards a better world for all concerned. It could well be a template for similar developments on a larger global scale.

It could also indicate, as an important sign, that any real progress towards peace in the world will depend on a new and welcome inclusion of that transcendence of the Christian spirit over the warping effects of the selfishness in human nature, which would seem to be a central and essential part of its procedure. It will also depend on the co-operation and support of all people of good will, because they are given the "free will" to decide which path they want to follow, rather than force. Christians would say that such a development will need the grace of God to provide the strength, through prayer and Christian faith for this to happen.

Its most recent and greatest challenge has been the influx of great numbers of persecuted people from outside the Union seeking refuge from war and persecution and to enjoy a much better life by enjoying the 500 million people living in the Union. Angela Merkel is now attempting to solve this latest challenge in terms of all its constituent member states agreeing to share proportionate intakes of these refugees.

From what one viewpoint, this is a credit to the success of the Union in creating such an attraction for the rest of the world in its own unprecedented length of peace for its own family of people. This, however, is now a big test of whether the 28 countries themselves developed sufficiently in unselfishness as to agreeing to take their allocated number. This would be a perfectly rational and charitable solution to the problem. If they agree to do this, it would be a great victory for Christian Humanism against its enemy, the warped aspect of human nature. It would be a great step forward in the pursuit of World peace; and great example to the rest of the world, some of whom have already offered to help. It is significant that it is usually the ordinary people, rather than their governments, who are pressing to do this, confirming our view that human nature is innately good

I believe that this decision of how we, in Europe, can welcome these refugees in a properly planned way, but in a true spirit of solidarity as part of the human family, will be a vitally important part of true human development in the world at the present time; and a vitally important example for the rest of the world to follow

The situation also marks clearly the difference between the two great opponents involved in this argument. There are two outstanding world leaders in the renaissance of Christian Humanism in the present World, representing the two essential ingredients of it. There must be a secular society, advised and respected by an important religious presence. At present the best example of this is the German leader, Angela Merkel, who has already offered to accept a million refugees and more afterwards, though not all at once, because it needs proper preparation. This can be done very well if all the European states will co-operate with accepting their proportional share.

This, too, is the solution advised by Pope Francis as a world religious leader who has taken on world-wide responsibilities in the cause of world peace. But until we reach a future stage of world government, one has to think of the people who could fill these roles in different countries. For example, we might l think of the Archbishop of Canterbury, in Britain, who would be a good representative of the British religious heritage.

Critics and sceptics will say that the Union lacks military "clout" in the World. But this would go against the philosophy of the Movement and the reason for its existence. The unprecedented contribution of its founder was to think in terms precisely opposite to "military clout" and spending of vast sums of money on military armaments. Certainly, however, an increasing number of new and progressive thinkers in the secular world of economics and politics, would now approve of the policy of spending money on human security, such as the development of the "Third World" and the more just distribution of the World's great resources, rather than military security. Certainly, too, history shows that mankind has not been well served in the past, by the philosophy of "military clout"; and it is difficult to understand anyone who would wish to take the risk of another World War. The "signs of the times" suggest that the present time might be ripe now for a global consideration by the World's leaders and for all people of good will to support a new approach to one of their greatest problems. This has been the achievement of the laity within a secular society, led by their visionary adoption of Christian Humanism as the way forward.

The great truism that the modern world needs to learn together is that the only real way forward is to recognize that we are moving towards a "one-world" existence in which we must learn to live together as a great human family. The great principle that we must learn is that to achieve this, and all the wonderful human developments which would result, is quite simple that we must "love our neighbour as ourselves." It is essential that we all abandon the old "nationalisms" which feed the weaknesses of human nature (selfishness and "me first") and have caused so much disasters in the past; and learn to accept the principle that we must live together unselfishly to help one another.

This is the rational and moral aim which will lead to World peace and human development. This is what the European Union is all about, no more and no less. It is difficult to deny the rationality and moral nobility of this aim. I do hope that we in Britain can understand and accept this before the Referendum concerning it takes place, and can follow this positive vision in helping Europe and the World to become what destiny is meant to be. This would be a much more "glorious" role in the World than was ever achieved by the old Empire which has gone and will never come back.

We proceed now to an even more important development in the religious, cultural, and moral development which can be the real power house behind the European and World development of humanity.

VI

Pope John XXIII
and his Encyclical, "Pacem in Terris"

THERE IS NO DOUBT that the Movement for Peace and Unity in Europe was profoundly strengthened by the fact that Pope John XXIII was unexpectedly, to himself and to everybody else, elected by the Vatican in 1958, being regarded as a "caretaker" Pope in the event of the lack of any obviously outstanding candidate and of his advanced age. There is no doubt, also, that his election was to become considered by most Christians, as one of the most recognizable actions of the Holy Spirit in the life of mankind. Pope John's death in 1963, at the end of a very brief but sensational part in the life of the Universal Church, was mourned by a worldwide reaction. I remember personally being surprised by the number of non-Catholic friends and even strangers, who were experiencing such an emotional response. This Pope was the very embodiment of Catholic Humanism. One non-Catholic historian, John Julius Norwich, has described the reaction in a very few words: "It would be impossible for anyone not to love him."

Angelo Giuiseppe Roncalli (1881-1963) was of peasant origin in the North of Italy; and never forgot this. His renowned friendliness and simplicity was sometimes misread as a lack of intelligence, but this simplicity was of a kind, often remarked upon of geniuses in other walks of life, which indicates wisdom and spiritual insight of the highest order. He never failed to see the wood for the trees in the religious life. He believed absolutely in the Fatherhood of God over the Family of all human beings; and he really did believe in and act towards all other people, as his brothers and sisters. He also had a great belief and trust in the guidance of the Holy Spirit.

Roncalli had worked as diplomat in the Balkans, including Greece, Rumania and Bulgaria, where he had supported and served the needs of the Jewish people of these areas who were suffering from Nazi persecution, saving the lives of several thousand Jewish children, by contriving to get them out of the country into safety. In 1944 he was moved Paris where he proved to be a strong supporter of the "Worker- Priest" Movement in which priests were chosen to work in various industries to become more aware of the lives of the people they served.

He was an early supporter of Schuman's work for establishing Peace and Unity in Europe and was an admirer of his religious outlook and philosophy. In 1962, just after Schuman's Presidency of that Movement, and a month before his own 77th birthday, he was elected as Pope, in a rather unusual fashion. After 12 failures to get a unanimous decision, he was elected as "caretaker" Pope who would not be there for long. Instead, in 5 years he changed the outlook and image of the Catholic Church and became perhaps the most important Pope of modern times, with the exception of Pope Francis. He seems to have decided straightaway to do this on his own, against the advice of the Roman Curia. Like other notable Christian humanists such as St. Francis of Assisi his actions could sometimes seem alarming to the "establishment." Having been surprised by his election, he stared with the utmost simplicity of mind at the present state and outlook of the Church and decided that it needed to be reformed in order to serve and care for the human family in the name of Christ.

The Church had been on the defensive against the waning of religious belief which had started with the divisions caused by the "Reformation" in the sixteenth century and the rise of warring nation States. It had started to regard itself as a kind of spiritual "fortress, looking out at a hostile world with suspicion. Pope John decided to change all this. For him the Church needed to look outward to the needs of the modern world in order to serve mankind. He said that he wanted to "open the windows of the Church and let in the fresh air" of God's love and care for all mankind. He recognized fully the need to distinguish between the essentials of Church teaching and the "accidentals", meaning the "baggage" of man-made accretions which had accrued to it. This had to be done by a process of self-examination, leading to the "Good News" of God's love for mankind and the vocation of the Church to demonstrate this to the whole World.

He wanted to establish an "aggiornamento" or updating of the Church to open its face and mind, with confidence in God, to serve the secular world and its poor people who were suffering and deprived in many ways. His wish was to stress its role as Christ's teacher of mankind and also its servant. He meditated on the symbolic action of Christ in His insistence on washing of the feet of the apostles at the "last supper" before His own Crucifixion, to show what they must do as the servants of mankind. He had introduced a new rule from Jesus Himself, that "You must love others in the same way that l have loved you." This was an important development from the past when the religious rule had been "to love your neighbour as yourself." This new rule is the basis of Christian humanism. It means the need to love others as Christ Himself loves us.

Pope John followed this rule conscientiously and put it into practise by his symbolic words and that he loved everyone. It was not surprising, then, that he regarded all others as His brothers and sisters in the family of God. He began by improving relations with the Soviet Union, reforming the Church liturgy so that everyone could understand it in his or her own language, to improve and establish "fraternal" relationships with the Jews, and to encourage the ecumenical movement for unity among all Christians. He would amaze any visitor, even previous opponents of the Church by advancing towards them with the welcoming words of "my brothers and sisters," and had such an inherent and obvious sincerity, that they believed him.

His first great statement to the World was his remarkable Encyclical, "Peace in the World", the first papal encyclical (letter) which was written not only for Catholics, but to "All people of Good Will." Published in 1963, it is a letter "on establishing Universal Peace in Truth, Justice, Charity and Liberty", based on the first principles established by Scripture, Church teaching and Thomistic philosophy; a combination of the wisdom of the ages, the findings of modern learning, Catholic humanism, and Catholic Social teaching. It is a vast amount of learning, contained within a simply stated and expressed document of just over fifty pages; and one of the most impressive documents I have read. It would be very difficult, I think, for anyone of good will to disagree with it. In fact, I find it difficult to comment on it without thinking it would be better for any reader to read it him or herself; but I must try to convey a flavour of it.

There is a paragraph which seems to me to distil the essence of Christian humanism and certainly identifies the personality of Pope John who, incidentally, has now been proclaimed as a Saint of the Church, something which most people thought of him anyway during his life:

"May Christ inflame the desire of all men to break through the barriers which divide them, to strengthen the bonds of mutual love, to learn to understand one another, and to pardon those who have done them wrong. Through His power and inspiration may all people welcome each other to their hearts as brothers, and may the peace they long for ever flower and ever reign among them."[1]

It is a wonderfully clear and rational statement of developed thinking, related to the basic needs and hopes of every human being, and proclaiming on several occasions for the first time the developed teachings of the Universal Church on important principles for the modern world, such as human rights which are universal and inalienable, democracy, freedom of religion, freedom of the informed conscience of all men, the equal value and dignity of all human beings; and special insights on social teaching such as "solidarity" and "subsidiarity" .

It starts with the premise of a divinely established "order" in the Universe:

"That a marvellous order predominates in the work of living human beings and in the forces of nature, is the plain lesson which the progress of modern research and of technology teaches us. And it is part of the greatness of man that he can appreciate that order, and devise means of harnessing those forces for his own benefit."

It goes on to stress that there are also natural laws inscribed in the nature of human beings, by their Creator and:

"that (the natural law) is where we must look for them; there and nowhere else."[2]

Also "men's common interests make it imperative that at long last a world-wide community of nations is established" based on this "order", for human development. It predicates that Peace on Earth is a basic desire of all right-thinking human beings; but it can be realized only by the acceptance of this "order" and on the inalienable human rights and duties which are embedded in human nature and in the conscience of every individual. The word "order" here is used in terms of the scholastic sense employed by the medieval philosophy, as fulfilling the requirements of 'justice, reason, and ethical consideration for all parties.

1. Cited in *Peace on Earth*.
2. Cited in *The Tablet*.

The principles behind this "order" are discerned from a fundamental understanding of what it means to be human. They are capable of meeting the needs of human beings, not only in terms of nations and states, but also of continents and a global world. They are now to be seen especially pertinent in terms of the new global world, arising from the great advances in the technologies of human communication, leading to the concept of the "global village."

This was the first clear and official statement on the matter of human rights by the Universal Church. This has always been implicit and latent in Church teaching on the innate dignity and infinite value of each and every human being born in the image of God, with the promise of eternal life. Thomas Aquinas had stipulated it in his philosophy; and it was his philosophy which was largely responsible for the phrasing of the inalienable nature of human rights in the statement made by the United Nations in 1945, as we shall see below.

This is a perfect example of the principle of "development of Church doctrine", giving it, in Cardinal Newman's terms "a more immediate apprehension and more lucid enunciation of the original dogma" . It was, too, an example of the Church learning from "the signs of the times", that such a development was needed, after the terrible devastation of the Second World War. It was authoritatively stated by Pope John in his encyclical only one year after his election as Pope, indicating the urgency that he felt for initiating world peace for his "family of mankind":

"Men's common interests makes it imperative that at long last a worldwide community of nations be established."[3]

The Encyclical then concerns itself with "order" in the relationship between individuals and the state; between individual states; and between the individual states or continents and the world community. John XXIII was, in a sense up-dating and re-enacting the work of Thomas Aquinas, to provide a coherent system of values and beliefs which could give meaning and purpose and direction to the people of today, in the pursuit of world peace and progress.

Here we find for the first time developmental phrases being brought to the forefront of Church teaching. Prominence is given to such phrases as "the common good", "democracy", "human rights", "religious freedom", "the sanctity of informed conscience", "collaboration between all men of good will", "solidarity" and "subsidiarity." All these concepts were soon to

3. See Toynbee, *A Study of History* Foreword, 10.

be found again in the "Second Vatican Council" which John had already called into being in 1962.

To give an example of the way in which the moral "order" works, we can turn to the Encyclical's treatment of the rights of minority groups in the face of political moves towards "political autonomy and national integration." It sets out the principles to be applied:

"Truth calls for the elimination of racial prejudice . . . One thing is clear and beyond dispute; any attempt to check the vitality of these racial minorities is a flagrant violation of justice; the more so if exertions are aimed at its very extinction."[4]

But, to achieve balance and perspective, such minority groups should not "magnify unduly their own racial characteristics . . . or rate them above those human values which are common to all mankind, as though the good of the entire human family should subserve the interests of their own particular race."

Ways of achieving positive and fruitful results for people naturally wanting to retain their racial characteristics without losing their identity are discussed. So, for example:

"They should realize that their constant association with a people steeped in a different civilization from their own has no small part to play in the development of their own particular genius and spirit."[5]

This recognizes that benefit by mutual attraction within the family of cultures, to the benefit of all, if truth, reason, justice and prudence, are applied.

Again, in working matters, it is emphasized that all people have the right "to the means for maintaining a decent standard of living" and to wages which allow "a standard of living consistent with human dignity." Workers have the right to meet together and to form association with their fellows." Also "the common good is something which affects the needs of the whole man." Such rights are balanced with personal responsibilities and duties to other members of society and the state.

Other sections deal, for example, with "the proper balance between population, land and capital, and the rights of refugees. The vital importance of disarmament throughout the world is emphasized, together with the rights of ordinary citizens in the processes towards world peace. A

---

4. Cited in Peace on Earth.
5. Ibid.

recital of some of the main headings will give some idea of the width and range of the Encyclical's concerns.

Order in the Universe; Order in Human beings; Order between men –Rights pertaining to moral and cultural values; the right to worship God according to one's conscience; the right to choose freely one's state of life; economic rights; the right of meetings and association; the right to emigrate and immigrate; political rights and duties; right to social life lived in truth, justice, charity and freedom; equality of men; the rights of refugees; attainment of the common good; the treatment of minorities; active solidarity.

Other sections deal with: causes of the arms race; need for disarmament; the evolution of economically under-developed countries; signs of the times; inadequacy of modern states to ensure the universal common good; connection between the common good and political authority; political authority instituted by common consent and not imposed by force; relationship of men and political communities with world community; the universal common good and human rights; and the principle of subsidiarity (that all decisions should be made at the lowest appropriate level of appropriate and interested parties).

Modern developments towards world peace are examined; pastoral exhortations; scientific competence; technical capacity professional experience; apostolate of a trained laity; an immense task; integration of faith and action; integral education; constant endeavour; little by little; philosophies and historical movements towards world peace; and Christ as the "Prince of Peace."

The Encyclical makes clear the ways in which age-old truths, going as far back as Aristotle, have been developed in ways to serve the needs of individuals, society and the world community in the new millennium. The various human rights of man are now to be found in the official and authoritative teaching of the Universal Church which is the oldest institution in the world and contains over a billion of the World's population.

Many of these principles were present in the minds of the founders of the European Union when working towards Peace and Unity, discussed in the previous chapter, which gives an example of the way in which progress in this direction can be made by the adoption of the principles involved. The Encyclical's influence on this development is palpable.

It would be counter-productive to try to describe the Encyclical in greater detail in this essay. I could not describe it as simply and clearly as it is shown in the text itself. I would not want to deter any one from reading it in the original. I think it may be helpful, however, to quote at length its treatment of the causes of the Arms Race and the need for Disarmament, as an example of its quality, on this vitally important part of the movement for peace in the World at the beginning of this new Millennium:

Causes of the Arms Race:

We are deeply distressed to see the enormous stocks of armaments that have been and continues to be, manufactured in the economically developed countries. This policy is involving a vast outlay of intellectual and material resources, with the result that the people of these countries are saddled with a great burden, while other countries lack the help they need for their economic and social development.

There is a common belief that under modern conditions peace cannot be assured except on the basis of an equal balance of armaments and that this factor is the probable cause of this stocking of armaments. Thus if one country increases its military strength, others are immediately roused by a competitive spirit to augment their own supply of armaments. And if one country is equipped with atomic weapons, others consider themselves justified in producing such weapons themselves, equal in destructive force.

Consequently people are living in the grip of constant fear. They are afraid that at any moment the impending storm may break upon them of horrific violence. And they have a good reason for their fear, for there is certainly no lack of such weapons. While it is difficult to believe that anyone would dare to assume responsibility for initiating the appalling slaughter and destruction that war would bring in its wake, there is no denying that the conflagration could be started by chance and some unforeseen circumstances.

More, even though the monstrous power of modern weapons does indeed act as a deterrent, there is reason to fear that the very testing of nuclear devices for war purposes can, if continued, lead to a serious danger for various forms of life on earth.

Need for Disarmament:

Hence justice, right reason and the recognition of man's dignity cry out insistently for a cessation to the arms race. The stock piles of armaments which have been built up in various countries must be reduced all round and simultaneously by the parties concerned. Nuclear weapons must be banned. A general agreement must be reached on a suitable disarmament program, with an effective system of mutual control. In the words of Pope

Pius XII: "The calamity of a world war, with the economic and social ruin and the moral excesses and dissolution that accompany it, must not on any account be permitted to engulf the human race for a third time."

Everyone, however, must realize that, unless this process of disarmament is thoroughgoing and complete, and reach men's very souls, it is impossible to stop the arms race, or to reduce armaments, or to abolish them entirely. Everyone must sincerely co-operate in the effort to banish fear and the anxious expectation of war from men's minds. But this requires that the fundamental principles upon which peace is based in to-day's world be replaced by an altogether different one, namely in mutual trust. And we are confident that this can be achieved, for it is a thing which not only is dictated by common sense, but is in itself most desirable and most fruitful of good . . . it is an objective which is rich with possibilities for good. Its advantage will be felt everywhere, by individuals, by families, by nations, by the whole human race. The warning of Pope Pius still rings in our ears: "Nothing is lost by peace, everything may be lost by war."

This plea from Pope John reveals his heart-felt love for all human beings whom he regards as his own family under God, the father of us all.

"We therefore consider it our duty as the vicar on earth of Jesus Christ –the saviour of the world, the Author of peace –and as the interpreter of the ardent wishes of the whole human family, in the fatherly love We bear all mankind, to beg and beseech mankind, and above all the rulers of States, to be unsparing of their labour and efforts to ensure that human affairs follow a rational and dignified course."[6]

Should not this statement be the most urgent subject of a world-wide meeting of the World's powers as they consider the way forward for mankind in the new Millennium?

We know that the Soviet leader, Mikhail Gorbachev, had read this Encyclical before he became leader of Russia in 1985; and he was very much influenced by this "exceptional document" as he referred to it. Its call for the abolition of nuclear weapons must have played a part in his unexpected act in deciding to inaugurate an 18 month long unilateral ban on nuclear bomb tests in Russia. This in turn was the most important act in bringing about the end of the "Cold War" between Russia and the West. This sort of action and re-action could be repeated as steps towards the eventual end of nuclear weapons, which would be a definite step towards "Peace on Earth."

---

6. Cited in *The Tablet*.

VII

Pope John XXIII and the Second Vatican Council. (1962-65)

During his first year as Pope, John had opened the Second Vatican Council and had indicated his intention to the entire assembly:

"Voicing his regret that so many of the human race do not know or do not accept what the Church brings to them. The great purpose of the council is to ensure that from the side of the teaching Church, nothing shall be left undone to make that acceptance easier; that whatever has come down from the past in the trappings and modes of action that is today not a help but an obstacle shall be discreetly but thoroughly replaced by a style and form better suited to the new age and the whole wide world in which the Church is free to operate."[1]

The Council, when it met, was the greatest ever assembly of Catholic bishops and heads of religious orders throughout the world, 2,540 in all. Representative from other Churches were invited as observers; and there were "periti" or special advisers, to help. Its documents would provide the most authoritative and conclusive teaching of the Catholic (Universal) Church. It was an individual action of Pope John, himself, which caused surprise and even opposition from those who did not want to disturb or develop Church teaching in any way. To John, it was a special inspiration from the Holy Spirit in whom he always had great devotion and trust, which explains why he acted so quickly on becoming Pope. Some officials of the

---

1. Cited in *The Tablet*.

Church were frightened by what was happening. But, after all, he was a Saint, as the Church has since proclaimed him.

He gave his opening address to the Council:

"The Council now beginning will rise in the Church like daybreak, the forerunner of a splendid light. It is now only the dawn . . . The great desire, therefore of the Catholic Church is raising aloft at this Council the torch of truth, to show herself as loving mother of mankind; gentle, patient, and full of tenderness and sympathy for her separated children . . . Everywhere through her children, she extends the frontiers of Christian love, the most powerful means of eradicating the seeds of discord, the most effective means of promoting concord, peace with justice and universal brotherhood. To the human race oppressed by so many difficulties, she says what Peter once said to the poor man who begged for alms: "Silver and gold I have none; but what I have, that I give Thee." In the name of Jesus it is no corruptible wealth, nor the promise of earthly happiness, that the Church offers the world today, but the gifts of divine grace which, since they raise men up to the dignity of being sons of God, are powerful assistance and support for the living of a more fully human life."[2]

The Council was to change the attitude of many who attended it in an extraordinary way. Many surprised themselves be coming from it with a completely unexpected new frame of mind. This was no longer to be fortress Church on the defensive and exclusive against a hostile world. It was to be a humble but confident teacher, servant and saviour of humanity, continuing the role of Christ Himself in the world. Its work would be to offer the secular state the culture of Christian humanism to enable that state to become more fully human and humane. The Church has no desire to rule the secular state. Christ Himself had proclaimed: "My Kingdom is not of this World . . . Give unto Caesar what is Caesar's and to God what is God's" (Mark 12:17). The Council document "Evangelii Nuntiandi", makes it clear that the Church has no objection to a secularized and pluralistic society in itself. In fact it commends a "just and legitimate secularisation which is in no way incompatible with faith or religion." It would object, however, to a militant and intolerant atheism, such as that of a Marxist state, which attacked the idea and existence of religion.

Another important attitude of the Council was that the Church was there for the people, not the people for the Church. Christ had made clear to the apostles during the "Last Supper", when He had insisted on washing

2. Ibid.

the feet of the apostles, to teach them that they were essentially servants to the people, not to be served by them. Any Christian given authority in Church or State must regard this authority as an adjunct of service, not power. This is why the early Pope, St. Gregory, who had sent St. Augustine to take the Christian faith to Britain, had described himself as "The servant of the servants of God." Indeed that is precisely why he became known afterwards as "Gregory the Great." God's idea of greatness was connected with humility and service, not pomp, ceremony and power.

At the beginning of the Second Session of the Council, Pope Paul VI, newly elected after the death of Pope John in 1963, opened it by re-stating its main aims, to clarify more fully the nature of the Church and the position of its bishops.

1. To renew the Church in its life and ministry.
2. To seek to restore unity among Christians, asking pardon for the part the Church had played in their becoming separate.
3. To begin a dialogue or "aggiornamento" with the modern world.

The document, "Dignitatis Humanae" (the dignity of the human being) provided a new emphasis on the important principle, always present and latent in the original dogma, of religious freedom in the modern world, and also the sanctity of the human informed conscience. In the modern world of the "global village" and pluralistic society, it is essential to know that all human beings are able to live their lives in freedom from any form of religious persecution. The failure to discern this religious truth had been a sorrowful feature of human society in the past, and needed now to be stated emphatically as one of the most important "sign posts" for the new millennium. This is another example of the Council's development seen as "a more intimate apprehension and more lucid enunciation" of original Christian truths based on Scripture and Christian dogma. This is an important development, indicating strongly that the Church is now speaking to the whole human family, openly and authoritatively, in its protection and promotion of human dignity.

The great English theologian, John Henry Newman, was an Anglican who formed a central part of the "Oxford Movement" in the 1840's.

Pope John XXIII and the Second Vatican Council. (1962-65)

He converted to Catholicism and played an essential part in preparing the ground for the Second Vatican Council which came into being a century later. He became a Cardinal of the Universal Church and is recognized by both Anglicans and Catholics as one of the outstanding theologians in modern history. Some of his reforming ideas became the seed-bed for later developments, a century and more later.

Newman's "Essay on the Development of Christian Doctrine" (1845) showed that Christian teaching is live, organic and "developing"; and therefore a dynamic body of thought. The fundamental dogma can never change because it is revealed truth concerning our relationship with God and with our fellow human beings; but it must "develop" because it is "alive" and "dynamic." It is evolving in relation and reaction to new situations, new knowledge and new insights. The original truths do not change, but in Newman's own words "development" means "the more intimate apprehension and the more lucid enunciation of the original dogma" which takes place as we become aware of its implications and relevance to new circumstances and cultures.

In fact Newman's aim was to preserve the authenticity of the original dogma rather than change it. A revealed truth, in a live and changing situation had to develop in order to preserve its validity. It could not remain static. It was Lord Acton, the Catholic historian, who saw clearly what Newman was saying:

"The development of doctrine is essential to the preservation of its purity; hence its preservation implies its development."[3]

Newman had written to Acton in answer to his question: "What is meant by development? Is it more intimate apprehension and more lucid enunciation of the original dogma? For myself I think it is and nothing more."[4]

This principle of "development" became a very important part of the thinking behind the Second Vatican Council, a century later, in the mind of Pope John. Newman himself was beatified, a step towards sainthood, by Pope Benedict XV who visited Britain in 2010 for this specific purpose.

Newman, like Popes John and Francis was undoubtedly a Christian humanist. He wrote in his "Idea of a University" 1873:

"I say that a cultivated intellect, because it is good in itself, brings with it a power and grace to every work and occupation which it undertakes,

3. MacDougall, *The Acton-Newman Relations*, 58.
4. Ibid., 162.

and enables us to be more useful and to a greater number. There is a duty we owe to human society as such, to the state to which we belong, to the sphere in which we move."[5]

Again, Newman's thinking about the human conscience was a development in itself, which provided an important step in the preparation for Vatican 11. When Cardinal Ratzinger (the future Pope Benedict XVI) spoke to a synod of bishops on "conscience" in 1991, he named Socrates and Newman as precursors of the developed nature and interpretation of conscience. Socrates had spoken of "his confidence in man's capacity for truth", instilled in all human beings by their very nature; and so this pagan philosopher "could become in certain respects the prophet of Jesus Christ." It was this same belief in man's human ability to discover the truth which provided the basis for Newman's teaching on the subject.

In fact Cardinal Ratzinger went on to say that, in Newman, "conscience received an attention in Catholic theology it had not received since Augustine."[6] He went on to distinguish between two types of conscience. One is concerned with the practical decision on a moral course of action. This is ultimately dependent, however, on another and deeper level of conscience which he termed "anamnesis", which had been innately instilled into all human beings by their Creator:

"We could never judge that one thing is better than another if a basic understanding of the good had not already been instilled in us."[7]

Such developed thinking was to be the basis on which the teaching of the freedom of the informed conscience was proclaimed in Vatican II; and this remains a prime element in the tradition of Christian Humanism and the teaching of the Catholic (Universal) Church.

It is significant to recall the similarity of outlook on this matter between Newman and Pope John himself. Newman in his "An Essay on the Development of Christian Doctrine" (1845) wrote:

"If Christianity be a universal religion, suited not simply to one locality, but to all times and places, it cannot but vary in its relations and dealings towards the world around it, that is, it will develop."[8]

And Pope John said on his death-bed concerning "development":

---

5. Dessain, *The Mind of Cardinal Newman*, 167.
6. Ibid.
7. Ibid.
8. Ibid.

Pope John XXIII and the Second Vatican Council. (1962-65)

"It is not that the gospel has changed. It is that we have begun to understand it better. Those who have lived as long as I have ... were enabled to compare different cultures and traditions, and know that the moment has come to discern the signs of the times, to seize the opportunity, and to look ahead."[9]

The importance of the laity and its full participation in the life and mission of the Church was another theme introduced by Newman a century before, which was taken up and introduced into the documents of Vatican II. This has been implemented very recently by the present Pope Francis who had demonstrated this in practise, by seeking the opinion of all lay Catholics concerning certain matters.

Another important theologian and Christian Humanist who had a great influence on Vatican II, was the German. Karl Rahner, whose "incarnationist" theology taught that when God became Man in the form of Christ, human nature had become even more exalted and enhanced in the sacred image of God. This increased the innate and inalienable dignity and status of all human beings. It gave a renewed strength to the basis of Catholic thinking about the rights and responsibilities of the human being. This spiritual status of the human being stands as the most powerful argument for human dignity, and all human rights which flow from it, including democracy, freedom of the informed conscience, freedom of religion, which were clearly built into the documents of Vatican II. These documents also form the basis of the principles involved in the formation, and development of the Movement for Peace and Union in Europe.

This development is reflected in the document entitled, "Gaudium et Spes" (1965), of Vatican 11. (Pastoral Council document on "The Church in the Modern World"):

"Christians are convinced that the triumphs of the human race are a sign of God's grace and the flowering of His own mysterious design. For the greater man's power becomes, the farther his individual and community responsibility extends. Hence it is clear that men are not deterred by the Christian message from building up for the world, or impelled to neglect the welfare of their fellows, but they are rather more stringently bound to do these very things."[10]

This, incidentally, is the answer to those who mistakenly, have believed that Christianity is another other-worldly religion which ignores

---

9. Ibid.
10. Heffernan, "Outlines," 38.

the problems of this world in its concentration on the next life. We are reminded here, too, of a statement made by the foreign correspondent of the "Sunday Times", Tom Stacey, who made a heart-felt remark, describing, from his experience:

"the honour in which the essential Western ethic . . . is secretly held throughout the world. The secret spiritual muscle and objective authority of the West's stubbornly Christ-informed core- that ethic which does defend human rights, feed the poor, protect the weak, spread healing medicine, challenge its own shibboleths and question itself with daring . . .(no opposition) can logically prevail, or indeed seek to prevail."[11]

Of course the Christian humanism of Pope John himself inevitably exudes itself into the background behind the documents of Vatican II. A marked feature of his personality was his belief in the brotherhood of man under the Fatherhood of God, together with his trust in the guidance of the Holy Spirit of God, active in all people of good will. His humility was the basis of his strength. He was able to accept that he could not depend on himself, but on the Holy Spirit Who was in charge. An amusing but revealing section of his reaction to his totally unexpected election to the Papacy is characteristic. He later described how he woke up one night in a panic about the heavy responsibility he had incurred; then quickly pulled himself together by talking to himself: "Giovanni, why don't you sleep? Is it the Pope or the Holy Spirit who governs the Church? It's the Holy Spirit is it not? Well, then, go to sleep, Giovanni!"[12]

It was very fitting that at the very opening of the Second Vatican Council, on 11th October, 1962, the whole proceedings began by Pope John intoning the" Veni Creator Spiritus" (Come Holy Spirit Creator come . . .), followed by the 2,500 patriarchs, archbishops, bishops and cardinals, all singing this hymn together as the procession moved by way of the "Scala Regia" and the bronze doors to St. Peter's Square and through the central door into St.Peter's Basilica. The Council itself has been called by John O'Malley "quite possibly the biggest meeting in the history of the world."

One very important change at the very commencement of the Council was that the drafts of the Council documents prepared, as usual, by officials of the Roman Curia for approval, were put aside, with the approval of Pope John, and the bishops from 116 countries settled down to prepare their own. The extraordinary outcome was that it changed the minds and

---

11. Stacey, The Tablet, April 19th, 508–509.
12. Fesquet, *Wit and Wisdom of Good Pope John*, 38.

attitudes of many of the people who were often surprised at the change in themselves and by the way in which they voted.

Pope John himself died in 1963, calmly announcing that "my bags are packed and L was ready to go", but to the consternation of many people, Catholics and many others throughout the world who loved him, having come to recognize in him the sheer, unmistakable qualities of goodness, spirituality, humility, wisdom, gentleness and humanity.

The document, "Nostra Aetate" came as something of a surprise because it had not appeared in any of the preparatory work for the Council. It came there mainly because of Pope John's determination that the Council should make a statement on the part of the Catholic Church against any form of anti-Semitism (anti-Jewish feeling}, and it was later widened to include a new and welcoming approach to Moslems and people of any other religion. This document spoke in the language of the whole brotherhood of man and the family of God. It was a great development in relations with other faith groups in the World. Indeed its inclusivity goes well beyond this, for it has no end. John XXIII had no problem about including all human beings in this brotherhood of man in the family of God the Father of this great family. The last paragraph of this document is very significant in this respect:

"We cannot pray to God the Father of all if we treat any other people in other than brotherly fashion, for all men are created in God's image. Man's relations to God the Father and man's relation to his fellow men are so dependent on each other that the Scripture says "'Whoever does not love, does not know God'" (1 John 4:8).

It was not surprising that, just before his death, John greeted some Jewish visitors in public, advancing towards them and proclaiming enthusiastically:

"I am John, your brother."

Widespread notice was taken of this unprecedented action. Relations between Catholics and Jews had not been good in the past. This action had a tremendous effect and prepared the way for the document which completely transformed this relationship, with the Church proclaiming its own debt to its Jewish heritage. Meanwhile of course, John had quickly removed from one of the prayers in the old Catholic liturgy which included praying for the "perfidious Jews."

The Vatican Council took giant steps forward to have the dialogue and "aggiornamento" with the modern world, which John said was so badly needed. In its role as Servant and Teacher of mankind, it stated:

"The basic equality of all men must receive increasingly greater recognition . . . every type of discrimination, whether social or cultural, whether based on sex, colour, condition, language or religion, is to be overcome and eradicated as contrary to God's intent."[13]

It points to some areas of life where human rights, including those of women are not being properly served:

"Some fundamental rights are still not honoured, such as the right of a woman to choose a husband, choose a state of life, and acquire an education or cultural benefits equal to those of men."[14]

The human being is the centre and purpose of all life, cultural, social, political and economic:

"Therefore all these activities have to pursue a humane purpose. They have to be undertaken with the purpose of helping human beings to become more fully human; and to be working for a more human society and the common good."[15]

Another later development of this process of interfaith dialogue has been the work of Cardinal Angelo Scola in establishing the cultural foundation of "Oasis", to improve understanding between the different faiths of the Middle East. There is only one true God and three faiths, Christians, Jews, and Moslems, are praying separately to Him; a fact which "fundamentalists" and extremists on all sides, should take into account and which can lead to better inter-faith dialogue, if all sides are prepared to listen. In Vienna a new centre for inter-faith dialogue is being established, supported by Saudi money, the United Nations representatives of the Catholic Church and Jewish representatives, revealing the important truth that peace in the Middle East can be achieved only by a listening and understanding stance on all sides of the religious divide. Cardinal Scola has commented:

"Pope John Paul II and Cardinal Ratzinger (future Pope Benedict) said we are not here to pray together. We have to make a necessary distinction. There is the one God, but how we look at God is different."[16]

---

13. Heffernan, *Outlines*, 42.
14. Ibid.
15. Ibid., 49.
16. Ibid.

Similarly, there was a great emphasis given now to the importance of healing the long rift with the Christian Eastern Orthodox Church. The Council was expressing and implementing in all its fullness the great plea of Christ in his scriptural prayer:

"That they may all be one, as Thou Father in Me and I in Thee, that the World may believe that Thou has sent Me" (John 17:21).

It will be helpful here to relate some statements from the Council's documents, taken as example of Catholic or Universal teachings now echoing around the World on this matter. So, for example, Catholics are told that they should co-operate with their separated brethren and with all who are seeking true peace; again the Church encourages Christians to live in peace and good fellowship, will all men.

Or, again, the Church respects and esteems non-Christian religions because they are living expression of the souls of vast groups people. They possess an impressive patrimony of deeply religious texts. They have taught generations of people how to pray. They are all impregnated with innumerable 'seeds of the Word' and constitute a true preparation for the Gospel.

The Council took giant steps forward in its bid to have dialogue with the modern World, in representing Christ as Servant, Teacher, and Saviour of all human beings. These include the basic equality and dignity of all men and women, which should receive greater recognition.

In its section on "The Fostering of Peace and the Promotion of Peace and the Promotion of a Community of Nations", we are told that:

"In our generation with its wars and threats of war the while human family faces an hour of crisis. It cannot construct a more human world unless each person devotes himself to the cause of peace. The Council points out the meaning of peace and condemns the frightfulness of war, asking all Christians to cooperate with all men in securing peace based on justice and love."[17]

Pope John had shown the priority which he gave to the cause of "ecumenism" (unity among Christians) from the start of his Papacy; and even before this. Just before the Second World War, the French ecumenist, Yves de Congar suggested principles of Catholic ecumenism in his "Chretiens desunis" (Christians disunited) in 1937; and in 1938 the German priest, Max Metzger started the "Una Sancta", an ecumenical fellowship which spread in Germany among the laity, which was to bring a strong solidarity between Christians in Germany who opposed Hitler and the Nazi party.

---

17. Ibid., 50–53.

Metzger was executed in 1944, but his work had a continuing influence, leading eventually to the establishment of the Pope's Secretariat for Christian Unity in 1960, on the eve of the Great Council.

The decree on the Bishop's Pastoral Office reminds us that the Bishops are the apostolic successors of Christ's first apostles, who worked under the leadership of St. Peter, the first Pope. The bishops work under the authority of the Pope, in a "collegiate of Episcopal governance, with the Roman Curia being a type of administrative group helping the collegiate in its work of government:

"All are united in a college or body with respect to teaching the universal Church of God and governing as shepherds . . . To bishops, in their dioceses, belong all the ordinary, proper and immediate exercise of their pastoral office . . . not infringing on the Pope's authority . . . in the exercise of his authority the Pope makes use of the departments of the Roman Curia, which acts in his name."[18]

There is an interesting development here, however, in which the Council is obviously concerned to create a culture of greater participation, responsibility and "belonging" which should spread throughout the Church:

"This Council desires that these departments (of the Roman Curia) be reorganised (to show that they are administrators, not decision makers) and that the office of Papal legate be clearly defined. It is also desirable that papal officials (in the Curia) come from different parts of the world, that some diocesan bishops be made department members, and that these departments listen more attentively to lay people."[19]

This very important reform, enshrining the principle of "collegiality" was not to be implemented, however, for another sixty years, although all these reforms were totally affirmed and agreed by Pope John himself. Pope John died in 1963 before the Council ended; and these reforms were not fully implemented until the unexpected election of another Christian Humanist in the shape of the present Pope Francis.

The Council addressed itself to the Laity in the following terms. The layman or woman derives their apostolate from their vocation through baptism; and the Church can never do without it. They work in areas of life where there is often no clerical presence and where the Church could

---

18. Ibid., 67–68.
19. Ibid., 68.

hardly exist without the help of the laity who represent the "leaven in the world":

"The Lay person is assigned to the apostolate by the Lord Himself, through baptism and confirmation, in exercising this apostolate"[20]:

"The Holy Spirit gives the faithful special gifts, called charisms. Each believer has the right and duty to use them in the Church and in the world... in the freedom of the Holy Spirit. This should be done by the laity in communion with their brothers in Christ, especially their pastors, who are not to extinguish the Spirit but to test all things and hold for what is good... Christ's redemptive work, while essentially concerned with the salvation of men, includes also the renewal of the whole temporal order. The Christian laity fulfils this mission both in the Church, the spiritual order, and in the world, the temporal order."[21]

In its Document, "Lumen Gentium", the Council states:

"The whole body of the faithful who have an anointing which comes from the Holy One (Holy Spirit) cannot be mistaken in belief. It shows this characteristic through the entire people's supernatural sense of the faith (sensum fidei) . . . from the bishops to the last of the faithful . . . By this sense of faith, aroused by the Spirit of truth, the people of God, guided by the sacred Magisterium (guiding authority of the Church) which it faithfully obeys, receives not the word of human beings, but truly the word of God."

This is saying that the Holy Spirit works in all baptised people, not only the Pope and bishops of the Church. This teaching was to be developed into the principle of "ecclesiastical reception", which means that Christian faith was not only to be "received" but handed on. So that it is never forgotten, it has to be perpetuated.

This principle was to be implemented for the first time, over fifty years later, when the present Pope Francis, in preparation for the Synod of bishops which he called for in the Autumn of 2014, wanted to consult the views of all Catholics on the personal challenges of the family, as part of his plan for "evangelisation" (spreading the faith) in the modern world. He wanted to know the opinion of the faithful on difficult matters which may present obstacles in family life, such as divorce, second marriages, and contraception, which may be obscuring or preventing the process of "evangelisation."

---

20. Ibid., 77.
21. Ibid.

Pope Francis wanted everyone to savour the joy of living with the knowledge of God's infinite love and mercy.

He therefore arranged to send a questionnaire to all Catholics throughout the world, asking for their views and opinions on these matters, so that they could be considered at the next Synod of bishops. This had never happened before in the history of the Church.

In the same spirit, he set out to give more opportunities to give women a greater role in Church government; and also formed a Vatican commission on child protection, focusing on the protection of minors and giving pastoral care for helping anyone who had suffered from abuse by church personnel. This was to ensure that the new guidance given by the Church on the prevention of abuse, will be properly implemented throughout the world, by giving this Commission the powers to intervene and enforce the guidelines where necessary.

In its "Declaration on Religious Freedom", the Council declares that:

"The fact is that all men of the present day want to be able freely to profess their religion in private and public. This is among the signs of the times . . . In view of the greater unit of mankind, it is necessary that religious freedom is everywhere provided with effective constitutional decrees. May all the human family be brought to the "glory of the sons of God."[22]

This is an interesting example of "development." Religious freedom stems ultimately from the teaching of the freedom of he informed conscience of all human beings, the sacred dignity of humans, and the Church's condemnation of any attempt by the State or any other body, to force or deny anyone the freedom to adopt or deny his or her own religion. This constituted a "more intimate apprehension and more lucid expression" of the original teaching. Its timing was helped by the "signs of the times" emerging from the development of a global and more pluralistic society. It relates to, but is not dependent on, the contemporary rise in the pluralistic community in the modern world. The same would apply to the "Declaration of the Relationship of the Church to Non-Christian Religions.

One of the most important developmental aspects of the Council was its "Pastoral Constitution on The Church in the Modern World" which contains advice on the matter of working alongside all human beings of good will:

---

22. Ibid., 109.

"all men, believers and unbelievers alike, ought to work for the rightful betterment of this world in which all men alike live; such an ideal cannot be realized, however, apart from sincere and prudent dialogue."

"What does the most to reveal God's presence, is charity and unity."

"That the Church may stand as assign of brotherhood, there must be respect, harmony, the recognition of diversity and dialogue within her unity, freedom and charity. Christians cannot yearn for anything more ardently than to serve the men of the modern world ever more generously and effectively."

"The Council looks to all men, believers and non believers, to promote the aims here expressed."[23]

One of the most evident examples of the Church learning from the "signs of the times" in the modern world is the way in which the secular world led the way in its authoritative assertion of human rights. The first clear assertion of this to a global world was in the important Declaration of Human Rights by the United Nations in 1948 after the dreadful atrocities committed by human beings in World War II, revealed by the War Crimes Commission and followed by the Nuremberg Trials. It was not until Pope John's "Pacem in Terris" and Vatican II that the Church caught up, so to speak, by an equally authoritative statement on human rights.

It was perhaps the "signs of the times" again which provided the occasion for these rights to be asserted. It remains true that the basis of the argument for human rights was an inevitable development in continuity with Scriptural and Church teaching on the sanctity and dignity of the human person, created in the image of God, but now interpreted with "a more intimate apprehension and more lucid expression of the original dogma."

However, there is an interesting qualification to be made here on the basis of comments discovered later in the Memoirs of Eleanor Roosevelt, the Chair of the UN Commission on Human Rights (1946-51). She reveals that it was a little-known representative from Latvia who spoke so knowledgeably, eloquently, impressively, influentially, and at such great length, on the philosophy of St. Thomas Aquinas, that the Commission decided to base their argument for human rights on it. It explains especially why these arguments concerning the universal and inalienable nature of these rights, were so powerful in the "Declaration of Human Rights." It is doubtful whether Mr. Cameron was acquainted with these rights, when he argued

---

23. Ibid., 39–53.

recently against the European Union's Court of Justice's decision that Britain could not deprive prisoners in British Jails of their right to vote.

It is a sign of Aquinas's genius that he is still keeping "in the picture" so often today after two thousand years. There are still developments and extensions emanating from the inspiration of his work. There are seemingly endless branches of "Thomism" growing from the original tree. Thomists or neo-Thomists are still working on fresh insights developed from his original ideas as they are applied to all aspects of human life and learning in the modern world, as well as in theology and philosophy. To take one example of this, the novelist Flannery O'Connor names the main theme behind her various novels, as "hillbilly Thomism."

It is made clear in the Decree on the Liturgy in the Church, that it should present opportunities for full participation by the laity. So, the reasons for the reforms suggested include: "to give vigour to the Christian life of the faithful" and to adapt what is changeable to the needs of today. The use of vernacular languages, instead of Latin, in the celebration of the Mass, for example, is now introduced for this purpose. In areas such as the creative arts, where paintings or music may be used in churches, competent professional experts should be used in deciding matters of artistic or musical merit.

There is no doubt that Christian humanism comes fully into being in both "Pacem in Terris" and the work of Vatican 11. The service of human beings and the purpose of helping them to become more fully human made central to its teachings. In the foreword of the "Pastoral Constitution on the Church in the Modern World", we read that:

"The focal point of our total presentation will be man."[24]

And again, in its various sections on human life:

"Man is the source, centre and purpose of all economic and social life."

"Technical progress and production must be promoted, for the service of the whole man."

"Human labour is superior to the other elements of economic life which are tools."

"Justice and equity demand the removal a quickly as possible of the immense economic inequalities which now exist."

And, in the realm of political life, we find:

---

24. Ibid., 38.

"The political community exists... for the sake of the common good, in which it finds its full justification and significance and the source of its legitimacy."[25]

Pope Benedict XVI encouraged the Church to commemorate the fiftieth anniversary of the Council by studying anew the actual documents which emerged from it. These show that Vatican II went back to its patristic and scriptural roots by a process of "ressourcement" (studying the original sources), showing how the original truths are organic and dynamic in nature, ever revealing new implications and discoveries of the depths of their richness. Their teachings are an on-going process of refreshment and wonderfully new and evolutionary developments. The Church is in fact on a pilgrimage of discovery of their implications for the human family. The Council used for phrase "semper purificanda" (always purifying), just as Newman had talked of continual development as being necessary to retain the full significance or "purity" of the original truths.

It is clear that Vatican II was very much a proclamation of Christian humanism and a sign-post for humanity, pointing the way forward in the new millennium for the progress and full development of the human family in all its humaneness. This now appears more clearly in the "signs of the times" which reveal, by the development of globalisation and the new technologies of communication, the fact that we are really beginning to live in the "global village." The inter-dependence of this human family has also become clear as a reality and it is a challenge to humanity to harmonize with this fact of life and "sign of the times."

Pope John's belief in the "Brotherhood of man under the fatherhood of God", inspired by the power and guidance of the Holy Spirit, achieved its full fruition in the Second Vatican Council which, in turn represented the renaissance of Christian humanism. The challenge to humanity to respond to all this is proclaimed. Its response will decide its future, because human beings have a God-given free will to decide.

The documents of Vatican II contained all that was necessary to reform the Catholic Church and renew it to meet the needs of the modern world; but John XXIII died before the Council ended. It took another half century until another Christian Humanist was elected as Pope and he proved to be the "Great Reformer" who changed the whole outlook, direction and image of the Universal Church, making it more capable of serving the needs of the modern World. He completed the work which Pope John XXIII had started

25. Ibid., 38–53.

VIII

Pope Francis, "The Great Reformer"

"The World's greatest Communicator and a wonderful human being"
(LORD CHRISTOPHER PATTEN ON POPE FRANCIS, ON BBC, 29/05/2015)

"'The Great Reformer'-Pope Francis"
(AUSTEN IVEREIGH, *THE GREAT REFORMER*, 2015)

"The saintly Pope John XXIII's large-hearted policy may prevail, and if it does, this will benefit the whole of Western society by giving a special inspiration to the oldest of the Churches"
(ARNOLD TOYNBEE, "A STUDY OF HISTORY", 1972, P.210)

TOYNBEE PREDICTED THAT IF the work of Pope John XXIII in reforming the Catholic Church succeeded, this would be of great benefit to Western civilization as well. This did not happen exactly as he predicted, but it did come about 50 years later as a result of the work of two great Christian humanist Popes, John XXIII and his later successor, Francis, who built on and completed his work. Our task in this chapter is two-fold. We need to examine the ways in which Francis has changed the image and reformed the outlook of the Universal Church, while implementing the documents of Vatican II; but we will also be examining whether the second part of Toynbee's prediction has come about –that the whole of Western society will benefit, from the resulting renaissance of Christian Humanism which has reached a peak in the form of this extraordinary world figure.

Since the death of Pope John XXIII in 1963, there have been good Popes who have contributed largely to the Church and the world in the realms of theology and philosophy, with various contributions to the values of secular society; but no one of the same stature in thought and symbolic words and actions in the field of what we have called "Christian Humanism", as Pope Francis, who is at present engaged in implementing in full the principles of Vatican II and also seeking Peace on Earth.

He has appeared on the scene, precisely 50 years after John left it; and immediately he is distinctive in his insistence on giving priority in his position to the pastoral role of the Church as Christ's representative on Earth, as Father of the Human family. The Church needed a man who could appeal to the world as a human being, as John had done, as well as a "creative" and "spiritual" person, capable of providing a new spiritual revival in the Church and in the World as we enter the new era of the "global village." Above all it needed a Pastoral Pope, who could be recognized by the world as a shepherd of the worldwide flock; or in other words a "Father figure" to the people of the World.

There had been a period of some disquiet and waiting, as so many people looked forward to the implementation of the great projects remaining from Vatican II which would be needed to demonstrate a renewal and reform of the Church, changing its image and direction in the World to its true role as a loving teacher and servant, contributing a significant religious element to the secular global community, and responding to the needs and longings of that transcendent and spiritual aspect of all human beings, which we call the "soul", without which humanity as such cannot live or survive for long without falling into a sub-human or even lower state of existence.

People like the Swiss Catholic theologian, Hans Kung, who had helped as a "periti "(special adviser) at the Council, found it extremely difficult to wait for a half century to pass after Vatican 11, without the implementation of those developments which he had received with great joy at the Council. Kung, like many others, had seen the Council as a great and literal

"God-send" and yet very little had actually happened to put them into practise since Pope John, who had prepared the way so well, had died. Kung wrote a critical book, expressing his anxiety and disappointment, called "Can We Save the Catholic Church?" which presented him with problems in the Church.

True enough, Kung was hardly speaking as a Catholic by putting the position like this; after all, the confidence in the survival of the Universal Church is based on Christ's promise that He would be with it to the end of the World, and there is already over two millennia of experience to prove this. But, his fellow colleague among the "peritii" in Vatican 11, the French Dominican, Yves Congar, described him as a man who "charges; he goes straight ahead like an arrow"; and many more like him were impatient with the delay taking place.

But then and "out of the blue", Pope Benedict XVI, that fine theologian and philosopher, retired because he felt too old and ill to be able to meet his obligations, the first pope to do this for many centuries; and in the ensuing election, the same unexpected result happened as when Pope John was elected –a complete surprise. A new Pope was unexpectedly elected; this time and for the very first time, a quite extraordinary Catholic Humanist from South America, entered the scene and completely changed the situation, as we shall see.

When Pope Francis was elected to the Papacy in March of 2013, Hans Kung, who knew something of him, was delighted. He immediately re-published his book and gave it a new title: "Can We Save the Catholic Church? Yes We Can Save the Catholic Church." Kung sent a copy of his book to Pope Francis who replied with a handwritten note of thanks, indicating his interest and signed "Fraternamentel, (Your brother), Francisco."

From the first moment of his arrival on the scene, it became clear that Francis was intent on re-building the Church on the foundations established by the documents of Vatican II, fifty years before. Pope John XXIII was the architect who had created the plans behind the foundations; Pope Francis was the builder, equipped in the most extraordinary and gifted way to complete this re- building, based on his predecessor's ideas with which he completely agreed. This was perhaps the best and most dramatic example of the "dynamo" effect for recovery and renewal in the Church, when needed, which Toynbee had already discovered in his epic survey of previous civilizations.

Pope Francis, "The Great Reformer"

This analysis becomes obviously true when we survey the working life of Francis as Pope, in which he has proclaimed his new approaches and dialogue with the world more by his symbolic actions than by his words, though both forms of evangelisation have been highly effective. He has been continually relating his reforming actions with their origins in Vatican II, from his first contact with the people after his election in2013. His first step after receiving the welcome of the cheering crowd was to change the usual etiquette completely. He simply asked the thousands before him to pray for him, expressing the fact that he was their servant who needed their support. Only after this did he bless them. After which there was even cheering because they knew he was one of them, there to help them.

He has made use of such symbolic actions as a form of preaching, without words, right through his life as Pope. In 2016 he unexpectedly and unofficially, opened the Cathedral in door in Africa in 2016, instead of at the Vatican, to initiate the establishment of his Jubilee year of Mercy (2016) for all mankind. He showed in this way that Africa and its poor people were especially important to him giving the people a sense of the unconditional and unfathomable mercy of their God, instead of concentrating on the fear of God's judgment which would always be lightened by his mercy in any case. The African people were delighted and cheered loudly and at great length.

Who and what was this new Pope? He had been Archbishop and then Cardinal in Buenos Aires, first of all trained by the Jesuits in their order, but after his experience in the slums of Buenos Aires, had become a devoted follower of St. Francis of Assisi, the legendary Saint of the medieval period whose personality had changed the life of the Church and society during that time, after he had experienced in a vision a request by God to "rebuild my Church."

Francis of Assisi had done this by a lifetime of simplicity, poverty, humility and concern for the poor, destitute and marginalised in society. That is why this new Pope had chosen the name of "Francis", which was the first time that any Pope had done so. He wanted to symbolise the fact that he had adopted a "spirituality" based on Franciscan principles. This has been a constant mark of his pontificate right up to the present moment, when he published his great Encyclical "Laudate Si" (2015).

From the very moment of his election, his words and gestures have been symbolic of this outlook. He, too, felt a call from God to "rebuild my Church." One of his first actions happened when, for the very first time in history, he was the very first pope to astonish everyone by saying that he did not want to live in the splendour of the Vatican, but would prefer to live in the visiting priests' guest house lodging where he had been before his election; and, by the way, he did not want to have special transport, but to travel by bus like everyone else; and he had an ordinary, small second-hand Ford Focus car in case he needed it.

When Maundy Thursday arrived, it was the custom from time immemorial for the Pope to wash the feet of people in the Vatican, as a reminder of Christ's action in showing He was the servant of the apostles, as they must now be for the people. Francis decided on another venue for this symbolic action and chose instead to go to the local jail and wash the feet of prisoners, including those of two women, one of whom was a Moslem. In this action, he not only re-enacted the lesson given by Jesus, but he took the opportunity of doing two other things. He demonstrated his dismissal of the age old but completely unnecessary and damaging practise of omitting women from this part of the liturgy and at the same time showed his intention of bringing religions together by choosing Moslem women. He has since changed the old man-made practise officially and authoritatively.

None of this was artificial display,, as people soon learned. It became known that he had faced death in Buenos Aires in "facing down" gangsters who had already murdered Archbishop Oscar Romero; because they were exploiting poor people by selling them obnoxious forms of drugs. He spoke directly and with complete authenticity when this was needed. Respect for him grew among all kinds of people, including the world's political leaders who visited him and learned to value, trust and respect his unselfish authenticity. He had come to save and rebuild not only the Church, but the lives and values of all people of goodwill; and they all seem to have responded to his remarkable and extraordinary charisma.

He makes clear to everyone his belief that God came as Man in the form of Christ, to save all human beings, out of his unimaginable love for all of them; and that he sees Christ in all those whom he meets. This, because of its authenticity, results in them all loving and respecting him, so that he undoubtedly holds a special role of spiritual authority in the world. He has proved to be an extraordinarily good communicator to and with the modern world. Those who study these things, say that his "tweets" are the most effective and most quoted in the world. Certainly, his knowledge of and facility with all the advances of modern communications technology, make his views apparent throughout the world; and so he is well equipped for his immense task.

He speaks regularly and simply to all kinds of people. Like Pope John, who is now a Saint of the Church, he believes strongly in the brotherhood of man under the fatherhood of God; and so all he meets are regarded as brothers in whom he sees Christ Who made them all in his own image. He speaks to all age groups and comes out with short phrases of extempore remarks which are striking and memorable, such as:

"We want a Church big enough to accommodate all humanity."

"I believe that this is the time of mercy, a change of epoch."

"If you have erred, do not fear."

"If a gay person is in search of God, who am I to judge them."

"We need to create a theology of women."

"Never tire of working for a more just world."

"I think the Curia's gone a bit downhill."

"The Eucharist, although it is the fullness of sacramental life, is not a prize for the perfect, but a powerful medicine and nourishment for the weak."[1]

His first important act of reform at the Vatican was to replace the previous holder of a key role in Church management by a fellow Christian humanist, Archbishop Pietro Parolin, who will play an extremely important part in necessary forms of Church government. Parolin is a renowned peace-maker in diplomacy. One former ambassador to the Vatican said of him: "He is a man of great humility, whose diplomatic skills do not trump his priesthood."[2] His doctorate as a young man had been based on a special study of Episcopal collegiality and its essential role in Church government. He had greeted the news of Francis's election with great joy, regarding it as a "wonderful miracle." As a result, the "Holy See", the world's oldest diplomatic body, is now expected to play a major role in the part of peace-making, human rights and support of the poor throughout the world.

Other reforms have quickly followed, such as the reform of Church structures and attitudes, such as clericalism and the exclusion of the laity from decision-making, the reduction in excessive centralisation of Church government, the increase of authority for national Episcopal conferences; and a revised understanding of papal primacy. He has taken extraordinary

1. Cited in *The Tablet*.
2. Ibid.

action to change the management and structure of the Vatican Bank, a notoriously, badly managed organisation, into an efficient and "fit for purpose" support for the Vatican's purpose of serving the Church and the World it serves. He has replaced incapable heads of different aspects of the Curia by people whom he judged to the capable and worthy of these positions.

Francis has criticised Catholics who have "ostentatious preoccupation for liturgy, doctrine and the Church's prestige", instead of preaching the main message of God's unimaginable mercy, compassion, and love for all people. He has a particular distaste for "clericalism" and has made it clear that he does not want to see any Catholic priest or Bishop of whatever position in the Church, "strutting about, declaring "I'm the boss", over the ordinary people whom they exist to serve.

He likes to be known as the Bishop of Rome rather than the "Pope", regarding himself as being there to serve rather than to be served. He lives a simple life, aiming to speak and act as a witness of Christ in the world. He wants his priests to be pastoral figures, giving short but "heart to heart" sermons.

He has continually surprised Catholics and non-Catholics by his unconventional use of words and gestures which are symbolic of his aims and values. They have become what is popularly known as the "Papa Francesco style." He is determined to keep in touch with ordinary people and their problems, which is not so as easy as when he roamed the slums in Buenos Aires. So he has taken to telephoning people in distress who have written to him from various parts of the world, giving them consolation and confidence in the mercy and compassion of God.

He does not take the usual papal holiday from Rome, but just appears in various parts of the City. On one of these he met a group of 200 Japanese secondary school children and spoke to them about meeting people of all sorts in the world and the importance of dialogue and listening. He spoke of such meetings as a "beautiful adventure" of being able to converse with other cultures and other religions:

"And if you don't think like me ... we are friends just the same, because you've learned how I think; and I have learned how you think. This is the dialogue which makes for peace. You can't have peace without dialogue. I hope this trip for you will be fruitful, because getting to know other persons and cultures is also very good for us and helps us to grow."[3]

3. Ibid.

Pope Francis, "The Great Reformer"

In its edition following Francis's visit to Rio de Janeiro, in August, 2013, the "Tablet", the foremost Catholic Journal in Britain, announced in its headline that "Francis defines a new epoch," adding that:

"Mercy is clearly one of Pope Francis' favourite words. He uses it most often to describe a personal encounter with Christ. It is his term for a loving embrace that conveys acceptance and forgiveness, not dwelling on people's faults, but looking for the good in them. It was a powerfully on display during his extraordinary visit to World Youth Day in Rio de Janeiro, which brought three million young people on the beach at Copacabana to join him at Mass, "to meet Jesus and the warmth of His mercy and his love."[4]

It remarks that:

"This is the language of mercy and love, not judgementalism and condemnation, though supplied within an orthodox Catholic framework . . . Pope Francis can change all that . . . The response of ordinary Catholics everywhere, Brazil not least, suggests the "sensus fidelium" (intuitive sense of the faithful) is behind him. It is a defining moment in the life of the Church, when the ice starts to melt."[5]

An interesting feature of all this is that Francis's career is fulfilling another of Toynbee's "laws" of how a culture and civilization can be saved by a "creative spiritual." Toynbee described as the laws of "withdrawal and return" and "challenge and response." The first law was fulfilled in Francis's case by his withdrawal for a time from the work as a bishop and "Master of the Jesuit Order", to work in the slums of Buenos Aires, after which he returned as a changed man, with a new and dynamic vision of the role of the Universal and oldest Church. The second "law" was the amazing "response" he has received in the Universal Church and the world at large to the new "challenge" which he is setting before it.

This was the "great reformer" of the Church, implementing his "aggiornamento" (up-dating) with the modern world, and at the same time leading the secular world in the right direction and creating a new outlook on religion, whom Toynbee had been patiently waiting for to activate the mysterious "dynamo" effect which he had discovered in the various revivals of the ancient "Universal Church" throughout its history, though by now Toynbee had died before he could enjoy another example of his predicted happening.

4. Ibid.
5. Ibid.

The immediate problem facing Francis as Pope was three-fold. He needed to reform the Roman Curia which had been acting in a role which did not belong to it and had been preventing the completion of Vatican II's requirement for a "Collegiate" form of Church government. This means government by the Pope, together with the bishops of the world-wide Church, rather than the Curia which should be concerned with simply administering the decisions made by the "Collegiate." Secondly, the Vatican Bank needed to be reformed, so that the money involved should be spent properly in service to the needs of the world which it is meant to serve. Both these reforms have already been introduced. Francis had made clear in both cases what the proper roles should be for these groups. The Vatican Bank has been restructured, with a change of personnel. New appointments are being made of bishops throughout the world, so that those who have the local responsibility will be able to follow the guidelines of making truly "pastoral" figures as bishops and priests.

There remains the task of seeing that the necessary reforms indicated by the Vatican II documents are properly implemented. Francis has started by appointing 8 cardinals who will be responsible for representing different parts of the world, at a second Synod of Bishops, to meet in Rome in August of 2015. They will gather all the advice and information needed for decisions to be made concerning the global implementing of the necessary reforms involved in the implementation of Vatican II documents which have been in abeyance since the Council, over fifty years before. The likelihood is that after this session of the Synod of Bishops in October of 2015, Pope Francis will dwell on the suggestions and advice given from the whole Catholic world, before making his final decisions on the matter in 2016. These decisions will be of huge importance in the life of the Church, and will decide how the Universal Church can best serve the people of the World in the new Millennium.

Another significant reform Francis has achieved is the new attitude adopted by the Church towards "liberation theology." There had been suspicion in the Vatican about this new movement in South America, striving for the rights of the poor against their exploitation by the Government. This suspicion had been caused because Catholic priests had been working for the same cause but for different and non-political reasons and by different, peaceful means. Marxist ideology advocated class conflict against the Government and the wealthy. Oscar Romero, Archbishop of San Salvador, was martyred because of his defence of the poor and the common good in peaceful protest against the Government. Its agents shot him as he was saying Mass. He saw them entering the Church, but continued saying the Mass as he was shot and killed.

Some in the Vatican had striven successfully to block his cause for martyrdom, because of a traditional view that he been murdered for his work for social justice, rather than hatred against his Christian faith. Francis immediately cleared this blockage and allowed the cause for his beatification to go forward, which thrilled the people of South America who have so much devotion to Romero whom they recognize as a Saint in any case. The cause went forward and led finally to the beatification of Oscar Romero on 23rd May, 2015.

This in fact was a great step forward for the development of Church doctrine to meet the needs of the modern world and the "signs of the times" as Vatican II had proclaimed. Once again, Newman's description of "development", that it was "a more intimate apprehension and the more lucid enunciation of the original dogma", and, vitally important at the same time, was rooted in the truths of the Gospel, was implemented. For example, in the Gospels, the description of the "last judgment" was based on Christ's reminder that what we do for others is regarded as what we are doing to and for Him; or again it is clear from the same vital source that Christ said that all the commandments could be contained in the first two, love for God and love for one's neighbour, and also that the extent of this love was the gauge for one's holiness; and also "Greater love hath no man, than to lay down his life for his friends."

Therefore, to die, as Romero did, for the poor, who were being exploited and abused in South America, was to die for Christ. Of course, thousands of the people suffering there already knew this. They intuitively knew that their hero was a saint, before the Church in the West had worked it out. Nevertheless it was a clear example of what is meant by a "development in doctrine" and Francis was delighted to reveal this.

The great advance here was to show that Romero had died for the Christian Faith because his action was part of Christian faith. Francis was the "reformer" who had opened the way for the development of Christian doctrine; and his role as a Christian Humanist had played an important part. Oscar Romeo was now the great exemplar for this development of Church doctrine in the modern world.

The Beatification of Romero was attended by and hailed by vast crowds in El Salvador, including many heads of state and the presidents of Ecuador and Panama. The current Government was helping in the organisation of this great occasion.

Francis has emphasized the important role of the laity, the ordinary people whose work and experience of life in the world can be of critical importance. He says that:

"Lay people with an authentic Christian formation should not need a bishop-guide, or a "monsignor-pilot" or clerical input to assume their responsibilities at all levels...(part of bishops' role) is reinforcing the indispensable role of the laity willing to take on the responsibilities that belong to them."[6]

This is implementing an important part of the thinking of Vatican II.

Another example of his intent on bringing Christians closer to unity was his meeting and praying together with Pentecostal preachers who were visiting Rome. He has long supported the charismatic aspect of the Christian form of evangelisation.

Now we can turn to the impact of Francis on the World from the moment of his election up to the present moment. One obvious quality which he obviously has in abundance is the ability to speak in a heart to heart manner to all types of people, including world political leaders. He seems to appeal in an extraordinary way to their common humanity, and in such a manner as to evoke their trust in, and respect for, what he has to say. It has a great deal to do with the spiritual nature of his authority and authenticity and produces the most remarkable results.

One very recent example which summarises the impression he makes occurred very recently at the end of May, 2015. He had already made a great impression by his reform of the Vatican Bank which had been in a dreadful state of disorganisation for many years; and this has been admired by economists. The Bank's profits soared by 20% in 2014 as a result of Francis's clean-up of mal-practices.

Then he has set about reforming the Vatican department of Mass-Media, a very important factor in his policy of evangelisation. When the eminent Lord Chris Patten, former ruler of Hong Kong and now Chancellor of Oxford University heard of this and was asked if he could help, he enthusiastically agreed. He seemed to feel a personal calling to do it because he regards Francis as "a beacon of hope and guidance for the Church

---

6. Ibid.

and for the world, unencumbered by a distant formality, or ecclesiastical pomposity . . . Assisting in any way, however modestly, with the reform process initiated by Pope Francis seemed to me a task which should not be turned down."[7]

When interviewed by the BBC recently about this, Patten was asked finally what he thought about Pope Francis. He suddenly paused, taken aback, but said as if he was surprised that they did not know:

"Oh! He is the World's greatest communicator and a wonderful human being."[8]

Perhaps these two qualities are among those which make Pope Francis so suitable for the great task which he is undertaking in the Church and in the World of today. This reform, is now well in hand, with the whole enterprise being brought up to date in expert manner. It also shows the type of enthusiasm which Francis's personality and integrity seems to evoke in people he meets throughout the world.

One extraordinary feature of Francis's Papacy, has been the immediate welcome given him by the world. In the December of 2014, after his election in the previous spring, it was announced that "The Times" an International, prestigious, and secular Journal, based in the United States, named him as its "Person of the Year." A Vatican spokesman stated:

"It's a positive sign that one of the most prestigious honours from the international press should go to someone who proclaims spiritual, religious and moral values to the world and speaks effectively in favour of peace and greater justice."[9]

Adding, that Francis "does not seek fame or success, but only "to proclaim the Gospel of God's love for all people" and give them hope; and that Francis is happy if so many people 'even implicitly' understand this."[10]

The editors of "Times" said that they had chosen Francis because "he has given people so much hope and inspiration in the last nine months." They called him "The septuagenarian super-star" but Francis was not pleased with such terms:

---

7. Ibid.
8. Ibid.
9. Ibid.
10. Ibid.

"Depicting the Pope as a sort of superman, a star, is offensive to me. The Pope is a man who laughs, cries, sleeps calmly, and has friends like everyone else."[11]

He has a way of depicting himself as one of the ordinary people, which is one reason for his universal popularity. He remarked recently that:

"The perfect family does not exist, nor is there a perfect husband or a perfect wife, and let's not talk of a perfect mother-in law! It's just us sinners."

And:

"I prefer a Church which is bruised, dirty and hurting because it has been out on the streets, rather than a Church which is unhealthy for being confined and for clinging to its own security."[12]

We know that he starts his day at 4:30 am, with an hour for prayer, before he begins his full day's work.

Andrea Riccardi, founder and head of the "Sant Egidio Community" in Rome, commented on the early "Exhortation" by Francis in his "Evangeli Gaudium" (the joy of the gospel), that it:

"marks out a path ... a vast spiritual and existential orientation for the whole Church."[13]

On New Year's Eve, 2013, Justin Welby, the recently appointed Archbishop of Canterbury and leader of the Anglican Church, spoke on the BBC and chose Pope Francis as his "Man of the Year." He said that, "this extraordinary man has done quite extraordinary things in his 9 months in the Papacy, to change the direction of the Universal Church and its impact on the World."

They have become friends who have together particularly in their work in opposition to "people trafficking" (the modern form of slavery). Both are determined to create a universal opposition to this form of "modern slavery."

There were many noticeable effects of his teachings in the Catholic Church and other religions. On 3rd September, 2013 a report appeared quite suddenly and unexpectedly on the BBC news, that Catholic churches in Britain had experienced a sudden and dramatic rise in the number of Catholics going to confession, and attributed this to "the spiritual bounce" or revival produced by the new Pope's attractive personality, conveyed by

---

11. Ibid.
12. Ibid.
13. Ibid.

his symbolic words and actions; and the same type of reaction among ordinary people has been seen throughout the world.

In September, 2013, it was reported that Ronald S. Lauder, President of the World Jewish Congress, who had met the Pope recently, stated that:

"Pope Francis's leadership has not only reinvigorated the Catholic Church but also given a new momentum to relations with Judaism. Never in the past two thousand years have relations with the Catholic Church and the Jewish people been so good."[14]

Again, Francis had written to Ahmed et-Tayyib, the sheikh of Al-Azhar University and the highest religious authority in Egypt, calling for a greater understanding between Muslims and Christians. A spokesman for el-Tayyib said that the letter contained "a strong message regarding the normalisation of Al-Azhar –Vatican relations" which had been frozen since January, 2011.

Meanwhile Francis is concerned to bring as much union as he can between the Catholic Church and all other Christian bodies. He is intending to undo the harm done by the break up Christianity at the time of the Reformation. He wants to increase this unity once again as a witness to the whole World. He wrote the "Evangeli de Gaudium", the "Joy of the Gospel", which can be dispensed only by Jesus, the "Light of the World" and Saviour of mankind. This is why he keeps on stressing that the main aim of his Papacy is to "evangelise" the World, by guiding it to the end for which it was created –a great family or "brotherhood" of man under the fatherhood of God, its Creator.

Francis had brought with him from his experience in Buenos Aires, a strong condemnation of "human-trafficking" which is the abuse of human beings who are treated as commodities for gaining money and are treated like slaves. This modern-day slavery has been acute in Britain and it is to the credit of the British government, guided by the Christian MP, Frank Field and his assistant Tim Weedon, that it has changed its position, from originally denying the need for such a Bill, to actually passing the first " Modern Slavery Bill' to counter such human trafficking.

Field(a non-Catholic) had attended Pope Francis' first anti-slavery "summit" in November, 2013, at which had appealed for a universal approach to stopping this crime which was threatening humanity, while being the second most profitable illicit activity. He wanted to create a united and effective strategy to oppose it. He welcomed the British Bill against it which

14. Ibid.

represented a world-leadership in this field. Now Field and Weedon saw that Pope Francis wanted to widen the British contribution to become part of a global strategy. They wrote that, "For two key British campaigners there is only one person who can lead a truly global fight to free modern-day slaves: Pope Francis."[15]

It is worth perhaps noting their comments in their article in the International Journal:

"In leading a truly worldwide effort, Pope Francis is the only player in town. No one can be in any doubt of the Pope's commitment to help eliminate the global evil. He demonstrated incredible determination in fighting modern slavery during his time as Archbishop of Buenos Aires and over the last ten months he has constantly returned to the issue in public addresses and his writings . . . By encouraging Churches around the world to adopt 8th February as a day of prayer for the victims of modern slavery, Pope Francis has begun what could become that world-wide campaign."[16]

They concluded that Francis' action in this matter represented a "huge and important note of hope to all too many of our fellow citizens who are oppressed by modern slavery." It was Francis who gave new names to "people trafficking." He frequently calls it "modern slavery" and a "crime against humanity." When the Pontifical Academy of Social Sciences met to decide on the topics to be given priority, it sent a message to Pope Francis to ask his advice. He sent a note back on the back of an envelope immediately, saying:

"I think that it would be good to examine human trafficking and modern slavery. Organ trafficking could be examined in connection with human trafficking. Many thanks." Francis. May 13th, 2013 (translated from the Spanish).[17]

Margaret Archer, President of the Academy, said that, "this short note contained explicit guidance that we have tried to follow and develop ever since."[18] It formed "the catalyst for a major initiative by the Pontifical Academy of Social Sciences that sets out the social and humanitarian needs of those trafficked." It led to a workshop with chiefs of police and leaders of other religious bodies and then an Ecumenical Declaration of Religious Leaders against Modern Slavery, signed by these leaders who wanted quick

---

15. Ibid.
16. Frrom *The Tablet*, Jan 11th 2014, 12–13.
17. From *The Tablet*.
18. Ibid.

action to eradicate these crimes by 2020. The Declaration specified the target point of action as:

"Opposition to trafficking for forced labour and prostitution, as well as organ trafficking; and any relationship that fails to respect the fundamental conviction that all people are equal and have the same freedom and dignity."

This is another good example, I think, of the way in which Francis can get things going along the lines of Christian humanism.

Francis has exhorted the Church not to be "self-absorbed", but to look outwards to serve God in all our neighbours in the human family. He has upset some people by his complete disinterest and dislike for ecclesiastical and archaic titles and honours. He prefers to be called the bishop of Rome. When he appointed some Cardinals recently, he took some time on telling them to live simple and humble lives as God's servants to mankind and he lives up to this image himself.

He stands out among all popes, with the exception of John XXIII, in the way that he becomes personally involved in the life of the secular world, because this is the world that he is meant to serve. He likes people to say what they mean and is always keen to stress the importance- particularly in his frequent talks with world leaders that it is essential that they put fine words and promises into action, especially when they are talking about critically important issues such as world poverty, climate change, and peace in the world. Tolerance, dialogue and respect for all human beings are part of his life style at all times.

His sight is unswervingly fixed on the example of Christ as portrayed in the Gospels. He has a deep and strong inclination to contribute to World peace for God's family; and a deep and heartfelt sorrow for the inhumanities of war. He has produced his first book, entitled "The Mercy of the Church" and has decided that the year, 2016, will be concentrating in the Church's Calendar, on "The Mercy of God." The inspired leadership of Francis is intent on bringing the joy of the Gospel to the world. He ended his proclamation of the "Jubilee of Mercy" with the words:

"May the Church echo the word of God that resounds strong and clear as a message and sign of pardon, strength, aid and love."

Francis also sees mankind's abuse of the environment of the world a clear threat to their own "God-given Home" and has published a new Encyclical concerning our treatment of the natural world and its environment and its huge importance for the human family. He is re-enacting the attitude of St. Francis of Assisi, the first great lover of the natural world, as well as mankind. We shall be returning to this major contribution in the eyes of the World, below.

He seems to have a quite extraordinary effect on all people of good will who meet or listen to him. We know, for example, that Angela Merkel of Germany, the most powerful political leader in Europe, has been greatly affected by him. A devout Lutheran, she told a Pietist meeting that Pope Francis had been an inspiration for her. The priorities he had expressed in his public meetings were exactly what she felt they ought to be for all Christians; and for all people of good will. She had been deeply impressed by one of his first acts, to make a visit of compassion for the illegal immigrants from North and sub-Saharan Africa who had landed on the island of Lampedusa, just off the southern coast of Italy. She, like him, wants to make political decisions on Christian values.

An interesting feature here, in support of Toynbee's statement that religion and culture are closely inter-related, is that just at the time when Britain, who had won the War, was undergoing the change in culture from "virtue ethics" to "after virtue", Germany who had lost everything in the War and was on its knees was, under the leadership of Christian Humanists such as Chancellor Adenauer and his successor Helmut Kohl, going in the opposite direction. They began to follow a destiny which was quite quickly to take it to the leadership of Europe, but this time to a completely opposite type of leadership in which Christian Humanism played the central part.

In an issue of the British International, Catholic Journal, "The Tablet" (17th August, 1963), there was a comment on the religious situation in Germany at this time. The author who had visited Germany wrote:

"The practise of the faith in Germany today is noticeably more intense than in most of Western Europe. This might be a surprise to many people who, perhaps, might have vivid memories of two world wars. Nevertheless, it is probably true that German Catholics, led by their bishops, are pursuing the practise of religion with as much Teutonic energy and thoroughness as their imperial and Nazi compatriots used to gain very different ends. How is it, then, that this Catholic revival –for this is what it is- has come about?"

And he goes on comment:

"It is sad, but true that I have rarely known such wholehearted response in English congregations as are normal here. It is moving to hear a whole congregation, including a 100 or so young men at the back of the church, sing "Hellig, Hellig, Hellig", at the Sanctus, for example."

It was at this very same time that the "Renaissance of Christian Humanism" was starting on the Continent.

Shortly after Angela Merkel's words of acclamation for the new Pope, the two parties in Germany's coalition government, the Christian-Democratic led by her, and the Social Democratic Party, have combined to underline the essential importance of the German-Christian heritage and the role of the Churches in their country. In the "Accord" binding them together in partnership, entitled "Shaping Germany's Future", both these parties signed this 185 page agreement. Its preamble emphasized that:

"We will intensively foster dialogue with the Christian Churches . . . They enhance the life of society and provide values which contribute to the social cohesion of our society . . . On the basis of our Country's Christian heritage, we espouse equitable cooperation in diversity."[19]

It also adds that the Churches' contribution to their society is "indispensable." Angela Merkel won an overall majority in the earlier election and was sworn in as Chancellor for a third time in December, 2013.

The culture of German society has become a model of what I mean as a secular and tolerant society, in which the religious aspect of life is taken seriously and has become a central, accepted and important part of human life. Religious discussions are held frequently, attended by Church representatives and also important representatives from all other aspects of society. For example, the "Kirchentag", started by a group of lay Protestants, started in 1949, and is held every two years in a different German city. Last year (2015), it was held in Stuttgart.

The German President, explained that "Kirchentags are an encounter between the worlds of faith and life"; and said that "political Germany looks on the event with respect and joy." 100,000, delegates attended, including the German Chancellor Angela Merkel and the former UN secretary-general Kofi Annan. A journalist said that "Kirchentag shows the soul of the Church." Important figures from all religions and state representatives were attending and gave talks on the religious and ethical standards which should be applied to various political and secular problems. Angela Merkel's talk was entitled "Digital and Wise" and was concerned with the need to set ethical standards for the use of online data."

19. Ibid.

Some important resolutions were passed during the 5 days of this "Kirchentag." The topics included items such as:

a. Reduction in the use of antibiotics and of coal.
b. Demands for safer routes for migrants to reach Europe
c. More action to protect Christians, Yedizis and other minorities being driven out of their homes by the "IS" (Islamic State).
d. Urging the establishment of A World day of co-existence.
e. Greater data protection.
f. For investment fund managers to be forced to comply with the regulations.

There were interesting comments made by Anglican representatives who were visitors. The Venerable Robert Jones, Archdeacon of Worcester, reported on, a significant difference in the culture of the two countries:

"Kirchentag shows a Church taking its Bible seriously, A Church taking its politicians seriously, and politicians taking the Church seriously."

Bishop Nick Baines of Leeds, co-chairman of the Meissen Commission, the dialogue body between the Anglican Church and the German Protestant Churches is a fluent speaker of German. He doubted whether all this could happen in England:

"Where in England would you get the Interior Minister and the Foreign Minister, and the Federal President doing a Bible study –and not using it as a political platform? . . . In England we tend to polarize very quickly. People go to the thing that is their part of the Church –Greenbelt, New Wine or a Catholic Festival."

The Catholics send their own representatives to the Kirchentag. On this occasion Cardinal Reinhart Marx, President of the Catholic Conference of bishops did his Bible study, saying that the Kirchentag good for all the Churches in Germany. Bishop Furst of Rottenburg-Stuttgart also delivered a Bible study, saying:

"I'm of the opinion that we have to live out our beliefs. Our faith is not only in listening and speaking, but also in action."

Another Catholic visitor was Winifred Kretschumann, the President of Baden-Wurttemberg, of which Stuttgart is the State Capital.

The Catholic Church has its own "The Katholicentag" or "Catholics Day" as well, which has been going on in Germany even longer and with the same purpose of bringing religious ethics and the secular society together for the benefit of both.

I should add that Germany's cultural, economic, political and sporting achievements have taken it to a position of leadership in the continent of Europe in the period since the last World War; which would seem to me to be some more interesting evidence of Toynbee's argument that the role of religion {I add, such as Christian Humanism} is necessary for the development of culture and society in all their aspects. Also it shows that his argument that a decline in this area can still be corrected by a spiritual and creative response to the challenge, if it is guided by a spiritual leader of a religious revival {such as Conrad Adenauer, Robert Schuman and Angela Merkel). If Germany could experience this after its horrific experience under a Nazi Government and yet respond to it so quickly afterwards by a "spiritual or religious" uplift and a joint initiative of Church and secular government working together, then we know it can be done. It is up to the people to use their free will in this way to show what they want.

It also shows, I think, that sometimes the experience of savouring terrible disaster can make people more prepared to respond strongly to the chance of striving hard to react positively to the prospect of creating a better future.

Meanwhile the Social-Democrat Party leader in Germany, Sigmar Gabriel had been so impressed with Pope Frances' criticism of unbridled capitalism in his "Exhortation" document, "Evangelii Gaudium", that he said:

"If I had a wish, I'd ask Pope Francis to hold an address in the Willy Brandt House (the SPD Centre in Berlin), but that, no doubt, would seem presumptuous on my part. No Social Democrat could have formulated a better criticism of capitalism than Pope Francis has done."

Pope Francis had written on this matter:

"Some people continue to defend the "trickle- down" theories which assume that economic growth, encouraged by a free market, will inevitably succeed in bringing about a greater justice and inclusiveness . . . This opinion which has never been confirmed, expresses a crude and naïve trust in the goodness of those wielding economic power . . . The excluded are still waiting"; and added that the increasing gap between rich and poor in the world was the result of "ideologies which defend the absolute autonomy of the marketplace."

For Francis, unbridled capitalism and the "free market" which results from it, is simply another version, in economic terms, of the "survival of the fittest" and has no place in Christian teaching or in the attempt to produce a more just distribution of the world's resources, to give a decent standard of life for everyone.

Toynbee put great emphasis on the importance of reform in the Catholic Church as a means of stopping the waning of religion in the culture of the West. He warned that to avoid the breakdown of a civilization which is already waning, there needs to be a spiritual renaissance, arising from a "creative individual" who can inspire a religious revival to meet the needs of a global world. He writes:

"The saintly Pope John XXIII's large-hearted policy may prevail, and if it does, this will benefit the whole of Western society by giving a special inspiration to the oldest of its Churches."[20]

Toynbee's aspiration was for a "Universal" Church to fill the spiritual needs of a global world, on the pathway of humanity to becoming a single family in the new "global village":

"Mankind is surely going to destroy itself unless it succeeds in growing together into something like a single family."[21]

This will probably take a long time to achieve; though events may well shorten it. It is likely to be a case of step by step along the pathway. But this is the "vision without which the people perish" and it would give a sense of purpose and direction to the way in which humanity should be heading if it is to save itself from self destruction.

Such a new society would also include toleration and freedom for all other faiths and for those who had no faith. It could provide the best system of protecting the spiritual and ethical values which coincide with human rights and are similar in most respects to those of the other authentic religions. This could meet the needs of a new, democratic, secular, pluralistic and tolerant society. The secular Governments would ensure that the survival of all human rights for everyone is safe under an accepted legal system to ensure justice and peace for all. It was Arnold Toynbee deduction from his close examination of Human History, that this continuing religious inspiration would be needed to keep alive the awareness of the essential spiritual needs of mankind, within a secular society which itself needs this help to survive, but can also contribute enormously to the dual Universal Church/Global World establishment.

20. Toynbee, *A Study of History*, 210.
21. Ibid., 10.

Pope Francis, "The Great Reformer"

It would also enshrine the "memory" of the past which is as essential for humanity as it is for each human being. We know that a human who loses his or her own memory, has to be hospitalised, because he or she could not cope with life in these circumstances. The same is true of all communities which are led into a cultural life without meaning. In short, all human beings need a sense of identity in which religion plays a vital part in providing a coherent sense of meaning, purpose and direction in their lives.

In the August, 2015 edition of the American, very well known and world-wide popular "National Geographic Magazine", based in Washington, the front cover is taken up completely by a picture of Pope Francis with the title "Pope Francis remakes the Vatican." The editor in chief, Susan Goldberg, has a preface to this edition, entitled "Getting close to the Pope", which in itself seems to summarise how many people seem to react to him. It is something which usually happens when we instinctively feel and appreciate the sheer goodness of some human beings. Dave Yoder the magazine's photographer was chosen to take pictures of the Pope. He turned up and found Francis surrounded by bishops. He turned up and stood hesitantly against a wall on his own. Francis noticed him "came right up to me, extended his hand and just waited. He looked me in the eye with an expression, like are you not going to greet me? And all went well."

Inside the Magazine there is the main theme article of this edition, concerned with Pope Francis's effect on the World since his election to the Papacy in March, 2013. It says that he is known "in every corner of the world, as a figure of radiance and charisma."[22] Again: "His impact thus far is as impossible to miss as it is to measure. Francis has kindled a spiritual spark among not only Catholics but also other Christians, those of other faiths, and even non-believers . . . He is changing religiosity throughout the world."

And again: "to the outside world Pope Francis seemed to have exploded out of the skies like a meteor shower . . . He wanted the Church to make a lasting difference in people's lives, a hospital on the battlefield, taking in all who were wounded, regardless of which side they fought on."[23]

And: "Now if you ask people (What's the Catholic Church for and against), they'll say, "Oh, the Pope- he's the guy who loves the poor and doesn't live in a palace." That's an extraordinary achievement for such an old institution.

22. Draper, "Will the Pope Change the Vatican?" 36.
23. Ibid., 38.

It also headlines a significant quote from of one of Francis's public speeches of 2014, indicating Francis's concern for updating the outlook and direction of the Catholic Church in the new Millennium:

"GOD IS NOT AFRAID OF NEW THINGS! That is why He is continually surprising us, opening our hearts, and guiding us in unexpected ways."

But perhaps among all the noteworthy and world-wide reactions to him, the most significant may be the words of an unknown man who happened to be passing when the camera men were on the spot. They asked this stranger what he thought of Pope Francis; and he just said: "All I can say is that he seems to me to be like I imagine Christ to be", and shuffled off into the darkness before anyone could enquire farther.

Francis would not be at all aware of this, but it struck me that this was a perfect summary of what the world sees in this new Pope. It too, is the short answer to his effect on the world outside and its secular leaders. His themes and his symbolic actions are constantly expressing the infinite love, mercy, compassion and forgiveness of Jesus for all his people, rather than on rules, regulations and ideologies. He is intent on teaching his own Church and the World, that God knows and understands the difficulties which many people are facing in the new conditions of this new world. He knows them and He loves them and His Mercy is much greater than our weaknesses. The living truths and teachings of the Gospel do not change, but they do develop and express themselves in different ways over the centuries. Christ died willingly so that we are enabled to live, according to God' plan for human redemption. It was this which Francis is teaching, that now it is in the love, pastoral care and service of people that the Church can best teach these primal qualities of "loving God and loving my neighbour as I (God) loves you", stressing that bishops and priests should focus more on being "pastors", relating to people and meeting them where they are, rather than preaching on "complex doctrine." This is what "Christian Humanism.

There are several examples we can call upon to demonstrate how Francis is able to use his spiritual authority and authenticity to affect global issues with unprecedented effect. The first instance happened only a few months after his becoming Pope, when he was largely unknown in the West.

In early September, 2013, the long-lasting political crisis in Syria came to a head when the West, led by President Obama had evidence that President Assad of Syria had allowed chemical weapons to be used, illegally against his own rebellious people. This caused President Obama of the USA, the most powerful of all the world leaders, by threatening armed military intervention which could have led to global warfare since Russia was on the side of Assad. It was a frightening moment for the whole world.

Pope Francis immediately called a huge peace vigil to be held in Rome. In a couple of days, 100,000 people packed into St. Peter's Square for a four-hour vigil of prayer, fasting and litanies. Punctuated by periods of profound silence, Francis proclaimed that:

"Violence is no answer to violence; and death is no answer to death."

His call to the people of good will in the World was immediately taken up and millions of Catholics were joined by people of other religions and none, to conduct their own vigils and joint prayer-groups in all parts of the World, including the Holy Land in the Middle East, Jerusalem, the West Bank town of Ramallaha where Moslems and Christians gathered together in candle-lit procession.

At the same time, in Turkey, the Ecumenical Patriarch Bartholomew I of Constantinople welcomed the call of his "brother in Christ, Francis Pope." In Istanbul, a Moslem preacher was invited to read parts of the Qur'an in the Catholic Church. In Pakistan at Lahore the Muslims joined in a prayer vigil with the Catholic Church. In India the Catholic Archbishop was called by Hindu leaders to "express solidarity . . . fasting and prayers in Hindu temples." In South Africa, Argentina and Venezuela there were similar expressions of support for the Pope's appeal.

Other faith leaders then also responded. In Rome the Chief Rabbi said that the "Jewish Community was in harmony" with the Pope's Vigil. In Iran, followers of Shia Islam, people of the Bah'faith, and members of the Iran Rights Watch, joined together in fasting and praying in response to the Pope's call. Vigils were held throughout the United States and in Australia 500 of Sydney's Syrian Catholic community fasted through the night. In Paris, hundreds attended a Vigil, and in Lourdes thousands took part in a torchlight procession. At the trade fare in Austria, the Catholic bishop was joined by a Protestant, a Serb-Orthodox priest, two Imams and a Buddhist monk, in reciting prayers together.

Francis followed this up immediately by making arrangements by which 180 Vatican ambassadors would express the Pope's views on the situation to the various nations of the world. He wanted:

"The use of chemical weapons to be immediately stopped and condemned."

The resumption of dialogue between the warring factions.

"An emphasis on respect for humanitarian law; assistance for innocent citizens and refugees; protection for minority groups such as Christians and Alamites; and respect for Syria's integrity."[24]

In the same day, 4th September, Francis had also written a letter to Russian President, Vladimir Putin, who was hosting a meeting in Russia of all the leaders of the G8 major world economies, urging him to read it to the assembled leaders and asking them to "set aside the futile pursuit of a military solution." He added in the letter to Putin:

"It is regrettable, from the beginning of the conflict in Syria, that one-sided interests had prevailed and, in fact, have hindered the search for a solution which would have stopped the senseless massacre now unfolding."[25]

Putin read and relayed the message to all the economic leaders. He changed his mind. He was Assad's chief supporter. He prevailed on Assad and his Government to allow all their chemical weapons to be investigated and destroyed by agents of the United Nations Security Commission. Previously Putin had been the main obstacle in the United Nations to getting this crisis solved and had shown no sign of changing his position. The immediate crisis had been solved.

The USA and other Western Countries were astonished and then delighted by this sudden and unexpected change in events which enabled real progress to take place, not only in Syria but in other parts in the Middle East. It suddenly created a different atmosphere among all the interested parties.

> The President of Iran, Houssan Rouhani, another supporter of Assad, then telephoned Obama to suggest that they could meet to arrange a peaceful settlement on the question of Iran's nuclear capability, a remarkable happening since there had been a 30 year "cold war" between the two Countries. True enough, Iran was suffering economically from the sanctions imposed by the USA on Iran, which they may well have wanted to alleviate but the President of Iran, Rouhani, went on to make the sensible suggestion that the long term aim of World peace would be best served by a general ban on all nations from holding nuclear weapons.

24. Ibid.
25. Ibid.

It does appear that Francis's moves had played a big part in producing a totally unexpected string of positive moves and attitudes which until then had been considered as impossible and unthinkable. They were now appearing as rational and sensible discussion between the contending parties.

This was the first time that Francis had become known to the group of world leaders involved with the Middle East; and it was from this time onwards, that they began to make a habit of calling on him from time to time. These events in 2013 solved the immediate danger of global warfare stemming from the use of chemical weapons, but they were also the forerunners of later meetings –involving all interested parties including both parties in the Syrian civil war (between Government and "rebels"), Assad, Putin, Obama, Rouhani, and the leaders of France and Britain They are all meeting together for the first time, in February 2016, to hopefully find a final solution to the Middle Eastern problem. Beforehand Rouhani went to Rome to meet Pope They talked about the life of the Church in Iran and inter-religious dialogue and ended with Francis saying that he had "high hopes for peace." Rouhani gave Francis a "Persian rug" and the Pope gave Rouhani a medal of St. Martin of Tours, a bishop who had cut his cloak into two, to give half to a beggar, commenting that this was "a sign of brotherhood."

Meanwhile Putin went to Rome after the events of 2013, to meet Francis and discuss further the "Middle East question. They agreed that any eventual peace should involve all the interested parties including all Syria's "various ethnic and religious groups, recognizing their essential role in society; "the need to promote concrete initiatives for a peaceful solution to the conflict"; "the defence and promotion of values which involve the dignity of the person and the protection of human life and family"; and "the defence of Christian groups throughout the Middle East."

Putin finally presented Francis with an icon of Our Lady of Vladimir, his own birth place. Francis said he liked it. Putin made the sign of the cross, bowed and kissed the Icon, while Francis followed suit. Since then, too, Putin has issued a pardon to the "green-peace" activists who had been imprisoned by Russia for their activities in the Antarctic (claimed by Russia).

There are several examples of Francis being involved quietly in big conflicts and producing remarkable results. Recently, in 2015, for example, Francis visited Cuba and received a warm and excited welcome from the people and their leader, Raul Castro, whom Francis had come to see. Cuba had a long history of confrontation with the United States, because of its Communist past, when it was seen as a dangerous ground for a possible attack by Communist Russia. Obama, the USA President, and Raul Castro were invited to a private meeting with Francis in Rome. He wanted to bring the two sides together in peace.

The next surprising move of which the world became aware was that the two leaders had made contact and Obama was actually visiting Cuba, for the first time, to speak to Castro. Finally Obama went back home to announce that the two countries had made peace and were going to work together for the benefit of both peoples. Obama has identified the key part played by Pope Francis in bringing about this change. The intervention of Francis had worked again on the international stage, to bring peace and a better life to this part of the World, which had once been, in the first half of the twentieth century, at the peak point of a possible new World War between the USA and Russia.

All this was done very quietly and without revelation of what lay behind this truly unexpected and surprising change for the better. Recently the first tourist buses from the USA have been authorised to be free to take Americans on holidays to Cuba; and the old enmities have been left in the past as they have come to know each other better. The USA and Cuba have now installed their respective foreign embassies in each country, proclaiming their acceptance of one another as friends. This is, too, already having very beneficial effects on trade between the two which is especially benefitting the development of the standard of life in Cuba. The US embassy was officially opened on 14th August, 2015, after 54 years of hostilities. In his speech at the ceremony, the US Secretary of State, John Kerry thanked Pope Francis "for promoting new start in relations between our two countries", referring to his pivotal role in healing the disputes between them.

After his audience with Pope Francis on 10th May, 2015, Raul Castro said "I read all the speeches of the Pope, his commentaries, and if the Pope continues in this way, I will go back to praying and go back to the Church, and I'm not joking" When Francis visited Cuba again, on his way to the United States, he celebrated Mass in Havana with tens of thousands of Cubans who gave him a great welcome on 20th September, 2015; and Raul was at the Mass, with the message that his elder brother, Fidel Castro, the earlier and more famous leader of Cuba, now old and ailing, asking if the Pope could come to see him as well. Of course Francis was only too pleased to oblige. He went to the home of the old and infirm, but still famous "revolutionary." They exchanged gifts, and I can only guess, but would love to know what they said to one another. I know that Francis' pastoral gifts would have been put to great use.

The "Sunday Telegraph" had a main headline on 20th September, stating that:

"Pope holds the key to open up Cuba."

In fact Cuba had been "closed" from the rest of the world because of its alliance with Communist and Marxist Russia in 1961 which could have resulted in a world-war at one stage. It was a great advance when Cuba was again open to the world and vice versa. It was vital to the proper social and economic development of Cuba; and also beneficial to the United States' sense of security, after years of a "cold war" policy with its close neighbour.

Francis was greeted as a "liberating hero" who had started a new future for Cuba and its relationship with the USA. He wanted to help Cuba establish a new form of Government after its Marxist past and to build a better future based on restoring "the soul of the Cuban people", with its own religious values and human solidarity. Raul Castro met him at the airport, declaring that he wanted to rebuild the country on the values which Francis had preached and particularly to "exercise religious freedom as a right consecrated in our constitution." At every Mass for the people which he celebrated, there were hundreds of thousands of welcoming people, for example, 150,000 in the eastern city of Holguin where he preached on Jesus recruiting St. Matthew by his merciful gaze upon him who had been banished to the outreaches if society. Again, he called for a Church "which goes forth to break down walls, to sow seeds of reconciliation." In Revolution Square, he spoke to 200,000 people on the theme that "Service is never ideological, for we do not serve ideas, we serve people."

Then Francis left Cuba for the USA where there was anticipated trouble to be expected from the right wing politicians. It did not happen. In the first place he was given a wonderful welcome by the working class people. Fr. Kiley, the priest who had founded the "labour-priest" initiative, explained:

"When I am with ordinary working people, they tell me all the time, "I love this pope, he speaks to us, he is with us." It is not about teaching, it is about effect. I've been a priest for 40 years and I have never seen anything like it. They look at the Pope and they see their champion."

Francis went on, insisting on meeting the ordinary people, especially those on the margins of society- the poor, the destitute, the sick and those in prison- in his usual style of spreading the good news of God's love for them. Then he proceeded on to meeting the "establishment figures" of America as the first Pope ever to be invited to speak to the combined forces of the two houses of Congress, perhaps the most contentious group of politicians in the world. Typically, he stopped his small fiat car, swamped by the limousines in the procession around him on the way from Philadelphia airport, to embrace a boy suffering from a severe condition of cerebral palsy, but was waving to him, and after speaking to him, allowing the procession to proceed. By now he was being greeted by large crowds and widespread admiration.

Perhaps the best commentator on his speech to the combined houses of Congress, was Sir Ivor Roberts, a former British ambassador to Ireland, Italy and Yugoslavia, and now President of Trinity College, Oxford, who was clearly impressed by his "subtle art of friendly persuasion." He writes:

"Getting both Republicans and Democrats in Congress to agree on their admiration for what you have said is little short of miraculous. In his visit to the US and in his thoughtful and ground-breaking speeches to both the UN and Congress, Pope Francis achieved just that. "Uplifting, majestic" from the Republican side; "philosophical, dignified, non-partisan" from the Democrats were just some of the comments from senators and congressmen after hearing his speech to a joint session of the Senate and the House of Representatives." Even Donald Trump, the right-wing Republican presidential contender, who was opposed to immigration, staggered out after the Pope's speech, muttering that Francis's words about immigration were "Beautiful." Previously, at the White House, Francis had used his own immigration background to establish a link with his hosts, establishing himself as a "son of immigrants"; and at the Congress he said that: "We, the people of this Continent, are not fearful of immigrants, because most of us were once immigrants."

Francis spoke to the united Congress about climate change and responsibility for the environment, abolition for the death penalty, compassion for the poor, abortion, the abhorrence of war and the arms trade, love of the family and the refugee crisis; but all through there was the philosophical emphasis on mercy and compassion for all human beings and on the words of St. Francis of Assisi: "Where there is hatred, let me sow love, where there is injury, pardon." He said that business and economics could be noble professions when dedicated to the creation and distribution of wealth and jobs to help eliminate poverty and restore dignity to the excluded; and talked about how we could become better people intrinsically.

Francis also made opportunities to meet, listen to, and talk to various groups of people on the margins of society, including the homeless in Washington ("I need your support, your closeness"), the inmates in Philadelphia prison ("everyone needs to be "cleansed""), the religious sisters in New York who had been inspected for their orthodoxy by the Vatican and the US bishops ("I love you very much"), to sex abuse victims ("God weeps" at your experience; and those who failed to protect children will be held to account"). At the New York Memorial for 9/11 victims, he met families of those killed, he called for peace "for those faces which had known nothing but pain." Here, too, he attended a prayer service with faith leaders from five religions where an imam and a rabbi alternated words of peace. Speaking to Catholic bishops, he said that "a Christianity which does little in practise, while incessantly explained its teachings, is dangerously unbalanced"; and to beware of laying down the law on what the Church teaches all the time, instead of discovering the deepest riches of the Universal faith contained in the unlimited mercy, compassion and love of Jesus.

In speaking to the United Nations, his emphasis was on championing the poor, and inviting all world leaders to eliminate poverty, protect the environment and find ways of removing conflict without resorting to the idea of mutually ensured destruction by possessing nuclear weapons which were an insult to the whole philosophy and framework of the UN. He chose the examples of conflict in Ukraine, Syria, Iraq, Libya and Sudan; and lamented that some had used the UN not to solve problems but "as a means of masking spurious intentions." Here was an obvious rebuke to those leaders who destroyed the effect of the UN by stopping international efforts to stop these conflicts, by continually threatening or using the threat of vetoing their proposals.

In my view, it was no accident that days after Francis made this speech, Presidents Putin and Obama were both busy, having their first formal talks to discover a political solution in Syria, which could lead to effective action to bring peace there, and to combine action to stop the threat of the "Islamic State" to all sections of humanity. Francis is probably the only world leader who could bring these two other world leaders together, to make a huge effort towards establishing peace in the Middle East; and indeed in the World at large. In establishing the concept of making no distinction between nations and religions in this fashion, Francis was pointing the way to world peace; but he made it very clear that he was also aware that this would require not simply words, but effective and courageous action by the world leaders to achieve positive

He made this same distinction between the use of words and effective action when he said that, while he was confident, he would still be watching closely, to see that in the imminent meeting of the UN in Paris in December, on climate change, there would be "fundamental and effective agreements", not just fine words and doubtful promises.

On the flight back to Rome, Francis was asked whether his celebrity status was of any use to the Catholic Church. His answer was that he had no wish to be a "star", because they quickly fall from grace, but only to remain what he really tries to be: "a servant of the servants of God" to the human family.

Sir Ivor Roberts ended his commentary with the statement that "Certainly, this Pope's luminosity shows no sign of dimming."

It occurs to me at this stage that this kind of agenda of activity is quite extraordinary and perhaps unprecedented for any world leader. It certainly meets the kind of spiritual creativity and inspiration, which Toynbee predicted might happen if the "Universal Church" was in fact reformed; and that this would have a beneficial effect not only on the Church, but on the whole of secular society in Western Europe, thus reversing the disastrous "decline of the West."

The only addition we can make is that his influence is global, rather than simply affecting Western Europe. Only recently I have photographs showing private visits being made to Francis by both President Putin of Russia, who has great influence in Syria and the Middle East, and President Obama who is the most powerful secular leader in the world. Both have a great respect for him as a truly unprejudiced and reliable adviser. There were two interesting events immediately associated with his arrival. Very unusually, as was reported on the BBC News today, 23rd September, 2015, President Obama came to greet him on his arrival at the airport in Maryland, as a friend would do; in spite of them having arranged a special official meeting between themselves later. Secondly, it stated that there was a limousine commandeered to drive him from the airport, but he chose instead to travel in a small fiat. There was an official welcome to the Pope, before a huge welcoming crowd of enthusiastic people. Obama spoke of his great respect for Francis, as:

"A great moral force in the world, not only by what he says, but by what he does."

When the USA Labour Party learnt that Francis was coming to the USA, the President Richard Trumka, announced after their June meeting that:

"The Americ Labour Party: is at the disposal of the Pope" and that they would make every effort to support and help him.

Francis was the first Pope in history to be invited to address the joint meeting of the whole Congress of the United States.

It may also be the case that when President Obama came out strongly and surprisingly at the beginning of August, 2015, in support of placing the USA to the forefront of World support for action against climate change, at the risk of creating strong opposition from certain vested interests in the USA, he may well have been encouraged to do so by Pope Francis's strong appeal to the World's leaders to do so in his very recent Encyclical, giving the moral as well as secular reasons why mankind should take action to save the World from catastrophe. The two men have obviously made a supportive friendship.

In 2015, Francis has met President Abbas of Palestine and recognized Palestinian statehood. His deputy foreign minister commented that:

"The accord could, even in an indirect way, help the Palestinians in the establishment and recognition of an independent, sovereign and democratic state of Palestine."

Also the two Palestinian nuns have been canonised as the first Palestinian saints to be proclaimed in the modern age. This has helped the feeling of solidarity and encouragement that Francis feels for the other faith groups, including Christians in the Middle East who have been displaced or persecuted because of their faith. Francis has made a courageous but considered decision in this case. He has already shown by other actions, that he highly respects the Jews; but has judged that the ongoing struggle between Palestinians and Israel can only be solved by a "two-state" division of the area involved.

Israel has already been accepted as an independent State. Francis has shown his wish to be friends with both sides, but to be fair to Palestinians they need to assured of their own separate statehood as well. Most of the rest of the world would agree with this, but Francis is the only person to have come forward to assert what he thinks is right; and in this he is leading the way to a solution of this long-lasting and highly injurious and dangerous conflict. Certainly no one could accuse him of partiality; but he, I believe, has already played an important part in the eventual solution of this problem, by bringing Palestine in from its previously marginalised position.

Putin visited Pope Francis in June 2015. Francis has been to the forefront, in the debates concerning the Middle East, in defending the rights of those Christians who are being persecuted because of their faith. Putin has become an important champion of this cause as well, and has been described as "the last hope for Christians in Syria." He has given his explicit support for their defence; and Putin has more influence in Middle Eastern politics than do the Western powers. Putin is also a strong supporter of the Russian Orthodox Church and this has given Pope Francis a chance to bridge the antipathy which has existed between it and the Catholic Church in the West; and to establish ecumenical relationships between the East and the West in this respect.

Putin sees himself as being against the "secularism and relativism" of the West and supporting Christian values, while the West has relinquished them. It seems that Francis is the only world leader whom Putin trusts and respects. There might well come a time when this meeting will have played an important part, behind the scenes, in bringing about peace between Russia and the West when an opportunity presents itself. Putin may yet be in a position to be a peacemaker in Syria as he did before.

While, they remain friends, we know that there is a significant obligation on the part of Putin to respond to the important questions raised by Francis. The main one concerned the "Minsk accord." In the Belarus capital, Minsk, in February, 2015, Russia, Ukraine, France and Germany made an agreement on a cease-fire in the Ukraine. This had specified the withdrawal of heavy weapons from eastern Ukraine, withdrawal of all foreign militia, together with "decentralisation" for rebel regions and Ukrainian control of the border with Russia, by the end of 2015. The EU sanctions against Russia arose because it accuses Russia of not having kept to these conditions.

Francis advised that Putin must seek another dialogue with the EU. The Ukraine could become a useful "bridge" between East and West, but he "would have to withdraw his weapons from the east." It will be interesting to see what develops in the future.

After this meeting with Francis, Putin presented him with a gift which was very significant. It was a representation of the Cathedral of Christ the Saviour which had been destroyed by Stalin but now restored, costing £230 million pounds; this was meant to shows that he is a supporter of Christianity. It may be surprising to many that he appears as a defender of the Christian faith and particularly concerned with defending religious minority groups in the Middle East, but at least he is doing something which Western powers have significantly failed to do.

Then on 25th September, the "Daily Telegraph" reported that Putin has informed Obama that he is willing to lead a military, self-defensive, attack on "Isis" to bring peace and safety back to Syria, but that it would involve supporting President Assad. It is another surprise move on the part of Russia, which Obama and the West will need to consider. What is very important is that both Putin and Obama know that Francis takes people as he personally knows them, not as various types of propaganda on both sides describe them. This explains the extraordinary influence which Francis exercises in his role of peace-making.

Indeed, Francis made his last great impassioned appeal to the International Community to bring peace to Syria by organising a meeting of world leaders to achieve a peaceful settlement for Syria, in February 2016; and shortly afterwards we received sudden and unexpected news that this had happened as Putin, Obama, with other leaders arranged a successful meeting to enforce a complete cessation of fighting by all parties, so that a negotiated political settlement could be decided.

There appears to be so much respect for Francis in Russia that they seem to attribute to him honours that he has not yet received. It is amusing to find that "Pravda" recently reported that:

"Pope Francis joined seven other Nobel Prize winners in a campaign calling for dialogue between Argentina and the UK to find a peaceful solution to the Falklands."

It does seem to me that the solution of the problem in the Middle East can only be found in an alliance between Russia and the US which might just be possible through sensible dialogue between them; and I think that Pope Francis thinks likewise. What if Putin is really thinking in terms of self-defence rather than aggrandisement which the West takes for granted? Putin may well want to assert his place as one of the global players involved in the problem; but this is the fact of the matter. He wants to retain hold of a foothold in Syria in his only naval facility at Tartous, which he inherited from the old Soviet Union. Parts of Syria are very near to dangerous and volatile regions such as Chechnya as far as he is concerned. He needs to keep stability in Syria.

Assad is no hero, but as far as Putin is concerned, he is the only chance to avoid anarchy –for he can point at the examples of Afghanistan, Iraq and Libya where the interference of western powers have left chaos behind them. A further break down in Syria would Jeopardise Russia's only naval base in the eastern Mediterranean. Similarly any expansion of the "Islamic State" into Syria would have the same effect. It would seem that Putin's main end here is to safeguard the stability of Syria. I think that Pope Francis will have an important part to play in bringing both of them into a dialogue, in using his influence to bring peace to the whole area. He is the only person who knows both Obama and Putin and is trusted and respected by both of them.

The most recent news on this matter is that on late October, a President Assad left Syria for the first time since the revolution started there in 2013, to visit President Putin in Russia and discuss the future. It does seem that the Western leaders are perhaps becoming less demanding in their attitudes and that some progress is being made which pleases both the Pope and Angela Merkel of Gemany. The main aim of all, it seems, is to fulfil the original needs stated by Pope Francis initially to ensure peace in Syria, together with proper defence against terrorism in all its forms, which should bring an agreement soon.

Whatever our view on all this, there is no doubt that Christians in Syria, together with other minority groups have suffered greatly in recent years from persecution, killings and having to flee from their homes in which Christian families have lived for centuries from the beginnings of Christianity, in peace with others including Muslims and other minority groups. The West has witnessed all this and lamented much but has deigned it unwise to get involved. Putin has decided to break the deadlock and defend these Christians and other such groups, against all terrorists, and to attempt to stabilise the position in Syria, inviting the US to join him.

This is certainly the view of religious leaders in Russia itself. The Inter-Religious Council of Russia, including Orthodox Christians, Muslims, Jewish and Buddhist leaders, are strongly behind, proclaiming:

"While strictly observing international law, Russia is again ready to support people whose life, health and freedom are now in real danger."

The Council, chaired by Russia's Christian Orthodox Patriarch, Kirill 1,it hoped that Putin's air strikes against all terrorists, including "Isis" (Islamic State) would:

"Remove the threat of terrorism from Syria and promote dialogue and concord between ethnic, religious and ideological groups across the Middle East."

The Christian chairman added separately that he had seen the extreme violence adopted towards both Christians and peaceful Muslims in the Middle East "with pain in his heart"; which reflected what all other Christians in the world were feeling. During his press conference with President Bashar al-Assad, he added again that:

"Russia has taken a responsible decision to use its military forces to protect the Syrian people from woes brought on by the tyranny of terrorists."

Nato, however, replied to Putin's successful attacks on the terrorists, by warning him that "his irresponsible behaviour risked extreme danger." Time alone will tell. It is interesting to recall, however, that just after his becoming Pope in 2013, Pope Francis had made his first contact with Putin, sending him a letter which contained his advice on bringing peace to Syria, when it was on the verge of war with the US and began a friendship which was to continue.

It is interesting that Francis made an impassioned plea to the international community and its leaders to work for a negotiated settlement to bring peace to Syria in February, 2016, and it happened within days that sudden news came unexpectedly that world leaders, led by Putin and Obama, agreed to come together in such a meeting to stop all fighting and to agree on a negotiated settlement. This could be the first step towards solving the Syrian problem.

At the same time Francis was making further progress towards reforming the Curia, discussing with chosen Cardinals the need to proceed with the policy of making what Francis called " a sound de-centralisation" of administration in the Universal Church.

And just before this, Francis initiated a meeting of historic importance in the airport at Havana, during his visit to Mexico, when Patriarch Kirill, the reigning pontiff of the Russian Orthodox Church, was visiting Cuba. This was typical of Francis's extraordinary method of quickly seeing an opportunity to do something of major importance by actually having a "heart-to heart" (as he calls it) with the leader of a group of Christians who had separated from the Universal Church and had not been able to get together again since 1054. This meeting was occasioned to help both groups of Christians to work together to help and protect Christians who were suffering persecution in Syria and the Middle East. It ended, however, with the joint statement that this alliance would "mark an important stage" in Catholic-Orthodox relations. I am fairly sure that this will be the first step towards bringing these Churches together again after 1000 years separation. This would be a major achievement in bringing all Christians together again in the "Universal Church."

Francis believes that it is through "dialogue" and personal consultations with one another, rather than central directives, that progress can be made, both within and without the Universal Church. He says that:

"Christian faith is not only knowledge to be committed to memory, but also truth to live in love," adding that "unity and plurality" should be the approach of the Universal Church. These words also indicates that the reason for the existence of the old Vatican "Congregation for the Doctrine of the Faith" and its personnel, which used to be regarded as "the doctrinal watch dog" will be changing radically. The latest enterprise of this Congregation was to investigate and warn the religious sisters of the United States for certain work which they were doing, which occasioned the need for Francis to go to and see for himself and to congratulate and thank them for the great work they were doing.

These important initiatives, taken by Francis, in a short time, shows the extraordinary vitality, life style and inspiration which flows from the 78 year old "Great Reformer."

A key member in the great problem of the Middle East is Iran's role. Iran is mainly "Shia" Moslem and an ally of Assad, President of Syria. Western countries have been mainly supporters of the "Sunni" Moslem opponents of Assad in Syria's civil war. Pope Francis wants to bring peace to the Middle East. Therefore he is keen to avoid all propaganda from both sides and to bring peace by adopting a detached approach and bringing both Moslem sides together. He avoids appearing as an "enemy" of either of them. Iran contains a small Catholic community from the time of the early Church which has existed in harmony with the Moslems around them.

One good result of this tragedy in the Middle East, especially in Syria and Iraq, however, is that it is bringing all Christians together again what Pope Francis has repeatedly called "an ecumenism of martyrdom", with reference to the fact that the many Christians who have been persecuted, killed or driven out of their country. This has certainly brought all Christian groups together in "solidarity" within this area. This has been shown by the recent meeting in 2015 of all Christian leaders from different churches, in "solidarity" to discuss the problem which is vitally important to their own communities and to the region as a whole. This situation was giving a bad name to Islam itself. It needs the help of the international community, and especially the involvement of Russia, which, which could play an important part in producing peace in the Middle East. This shows the need for a sense of "solidarity" and support from among the European States as a whole. Pope Francis has shown his own open-hearted approach of friendship to all people of good will. This was shown again in June, 2015 in his speech to an American Pentecostal conference, emphasizing the unity that must exist amongst all denominations of Christians; and indeed among all people of good will in the world. He recorded this particular speech in a video message produced by the Vatican Television Centre, for a conference arranged by an ecumenical meeting which included Evangelicals and Catholics. He noted in this speech a "budding unity" among Christians and added:

"There is someone (the force of evil) who "knows" that, despite our differences, we are one. He knows that Christians are disciples of Christ: that they are one, that they are brothers! He doesn't care if they are Evangelicals, or Orthodox, Lutherans, Catholics or Apostolic... They are Christians. And that blood (of martyrdom, in the Middle East) unites."

Pope Francis's foreign minister, Archbishop Paul Gallagher, brought an important message of the need for "solidarity" in the matter, to indicate that a longer and wider view needs to be undertaken:

"It has to be underlined that Christians do not want simply to be tolerated, but want to be full citizens in those lands where they have been present since the beginnings Christianity, long before the arrival of Islam. It is important that this citizenship is promoted more and more as a point of reference for social life, guaranteeing the rights of all, including those of the minorities, with appropriate juridical means."

And Andrea Riccardi, founder of the Catholic Community of Sant' Egidio, which engages itself in conflict resolution and interfaith and ecumenical dialogue reminded the sme meeting that an attempt to eliminate the Christian minority groups would be a tragedy for the Muslim world since they had acted as "a dam against the totalitarian impulses of (some) in the Muslim world."

However, it does show that Francis is deeply involved in helping to produce peace in the world, by his spiritual and secular interventions in world affairs. It is becoming increasingly obvious that Francis is earning increasing respect among the world's major secular leaders who appear to go out of their way to seek his advice on contemporary world problems. They know that he is the one world leader who can be trusted to give unprejudiced advice in his aim for the common good of all. They know that they can trust him; and this seems to have strengthened the process of dialogue and mutual trust between men of good will, rather than the disaster of war making.

One of Francis's great aims is to bring all people of good will together within the brotherhood of the human family under the Fatherhood of God. So he reaches out to find unexpected examples of common ground between people of all traditions and beliefs; and to discover and express the common good which is inherent in human nature and can bring out the best in them. His course of action is to reach out in friendship to all his brothers and sisters in the family of God, rather than to look for heretical menaces. His attitude towards other Christians and to other faiths is always to have respectful and friendly dialogue with them; and the same with those who claim to be atheists, agnostics or nothing in particular. He wants to cut through old antagonisms in his belief that all people of good will have important contributions to make towards world peace.

The rise of the extremist "Islamic State" in the Middle East has been a major problem for all other Countries and Religions. There are signs now, however, of the joint realisation that only a united front from all the other countries and religions can resolve this problem. It is another reason, or pressure which makes it more likely that such a united front will be established and the need for a peaceful solution for other problems will also be addressed.

Francis, soon after he became Pope had showed his compassion for refugees fleeing from North Africa, via Libya and risking their lives by the various dangers involved in crossing the Mediterranean to Italy, to escape from the instability and breaches of human rights in their own Country. The European Union had originally established a "mission" to help such refugees, by which its member states were all involved in helping "to seek, find and protect any refugees who were in trouble on the seas.

In 2014 the Union had withdrawn this wide support and had left it to Italy to protect them. Francis had shown his compassion with these refugees just after his election by going down to the island of Lampedusa, to comfort and support those who had suffered a disaster and lost many lives on their way. He was quick to point out to the Union's leaders their mistake in withdrawing their mission. In his speech, he warned the European

Parliament that they were straying from their Christian principles, putting political and economic interests before Christian humanism.

"A Europe which is no longer open to the transcendent dimension of life is a Europe which risks slowly losing its own soul and that 'humanistic spirit' which it still loves and defends."

The Union had apparently withdrawn the mission because they felt that it was encouraging greater numbers of refugees to attempt the crossing the Mediterranean from Libya. Francis could see, I think, that they may have inadvertently fallen into the moral trap of forgetting that "the end does not justify the means."

There were soon repercussions to Francis's warning. In April, 2015, there was a catastrophic loss of nearly two thousand lives of refugees on the Mediterranean from two shipwrecks in two weeks, which shook the hearts and minds of all people of good will. There was widespread criticism of the Union in Europe for "abandoning its common humanity for economic or political expediency." There was an immediate response from the Union, setting up an emergency meeting to put things right and take up their human responsibilities again.

It had been a mistake on its part. Now the Union has announced that it will spend treble the amount of money in making sure that there is a properly combined policy to "seek and save" these refugees and to welcome them to a safe haven.

The result has been dramatic. With the increased help of the European Union, literally thousands of fleeing refugees have been saved in the Mediterranean within a week, as reported in the beginning of May, 2015. Some commentators, including parts of the British press, wrongly saw this as Francis discrediting the Union; but this was far from the truth. He simply wanted to strengthen it by reminding it of its own principles. He was obviously very successful. I believe that Francis's statement that "these (the refugees) are people like us" went around the world and produced a worldwide sense of shame and produced an outcry and an appropriately positive response by all European and other states. We can be proud in Britain of the conspicuous part which has been taken by a British ship in saving many lives in recent weeks.

For the last ten years, the Special Representative of the United Nations Secretary General for International Migration, Koffi Annan, has been Peter Sutherland, an Irish lawyer and economist of distinction. He has been largely responsible for the Global Forum on Migration and Development, which is a very important group of NGOs and governments. His central idea is that migration actually promotes the global development of mankind.

It was as a result of this that Pope Francis appointed Sutherland as President of the International Catholic Migration Commission in 2014. His reaction was to register his pride in Francis's work for the suffering, needy and marginalised, explaining that he "finds Francis an inspiration; so this appointment is of great importance to me."

This question of helping refugees from Syria and the Middle East came to be seen as a European wide problem, as the numbers increased. The different reactions in Europe were significant. Angela Merkel's reaction as a Christian humanist was immediate and the same as that of Pope Francis, that "We must treat the refugees with the utmost respect for their dignity and humanity." She agreed to take 800 thousand of them in Germany." Unfortunately, in my view, Mr. Cameron did not want to take part in this, arguing that Britain had given a lot of money to help their cause in Syria

From its very beginning, the founder of the European Union who was the Catholic statesman, Robert Schuman, was determined, as we have seen to build it upon the rock of Christian humanism. In political terms this meant the principles which expressed Christian values. We have also seen how the doctrine of "solidarity" (the dignity and equality of all human beings in terms of their human rights) was emphasized in the documents of Vatican 11, as an essential part of everyone's social, human rights. We have seen how Pope Francis has advised on the continuation of this teaching in the political and economic policies and actions of the European Union.

Pope Francis and Angela Merkel are both Christian humanists. When the Pope heard of the terrible difficulties facing the fleeing refugees, his reply was typical. The Guardian newspaper reported the call of the Pope, during his "Angelus" address in Rome, for:

"Every Catholic parish, convent, monastery and sanctuary in Europe to shelter a family."

Angela Merkel, the Chancellor of Germany, is a Lutheran who continues to insist on this aspect of the European Union in which she is the most powerful political figure. In fact she has earned for herself the compliment of being perhaps the most powerful Christian humanist political leader in the world. It is no accident then, that when Europe has recently been faced with perhaps the greatest challenge, socially and politically, of its modern history –the unprecedented number of refugees fleeing from persecution and war in the Middle East- that Angela Merkel, like Pope Francis, asserts positively and calmly the dignity and human rights of all these refugees, who must be actually welcomed by all members of the European Union in just and appropriate numbers (though Britain has opted out). She then states calmly (September, 2015) that Germany will talk the lead by taking the greatest number, 800 thousand this year and 500,000 every year for the next 5 years. She has said that, because of the number of people, who are not refugees, applying from the Balkans, these will be identified and returned to their country. Also there must be proper preparation so that they cannot all come at the same time, but in stages ensuring that they are properly treated. So far this has been applauded and accepted by the majority of her people.

This action is probably the greatest example of Christian Humanism and its principle of "solidarity", expressed readily by any political leader in the modern world; and in my opinion is of such stature and importance as to be described as one of the most politically important exemplary steps towards global peace and "solidarity" so far in the new Millennium. To her refugees are not burdens, but our brothers and sisters, as they are to Pope Francis.

In his earlier speech to the European Parliament, Francis had spoken of the two elements which should always be present in their thinking –the spiritual or transcendent and the other, the earthly reality, for "the future of Europe depends on the recovery of the vital connection between these two elements. He had warned that the great spiritual vision (peace and unity of peoples) of those who had founded the European Union, should never give way to "the bureaucratic technicalities of its institutions . . . laying down rules perceived as insensitive to individual peoples, if not downright harmful.

Francis visited Turkey recently but annoyed the Turkish Government by saying that it was important to acknowledge that there had been an attempt to obliterate the Armenian minority there in 1915, leading to a loss of life of about 2 million Armenians. This has been a "festering sore" in the Armenian culture since then, because of the failure of the world to recognize this, for political reasons. Now it seems that the world, too, is acknowledging its failure in this respect; and sees an apology and admission as a necessary step towards a new start and reconciliation in this matter. This is another example of Francis's willingness to make the truth known as a necessary part of progress towards reconciliation and peace in the area between the Armenians and the Turkish Government.

Even more recently Francis visited Bosnia-Herzegovina, which has had a history of sad warfare between religious factions. Hundreds of thousands of people attended his open-air Mass; and Francis spoke of the need for forgiveness and reconciliation. His great influence was apparent as the people listened in silence and he seems to have sowed the seeds for a much better and more peaceful future for the peoples of these regions. The latest examples of Francis's obvious wish to visit all the peoples of the World if possible, to make friends of them all, is clear. The most recent will be his planned visit to go for a five day visit to Mexico which is suffering huge problems of internal violence and misery for its people. The Archdiocese of Mexico's leading newspaper says: "His Holiness will be in violent, poor and miserable places and the (state) governors cannot try to cover the sun with their finger." A priest there has welcomed his coming:

"In the Year of Mercy, we are all eager to listen to his message of God's mercy to all peoples, particularly in a city where mercy has been notably absent in recent years."

Preparations are being made for him to speak to nearly half a million people in Juarez.

He is also trying to raise hope of improving relationships with China. He has expressed his hopes for visiting China where there is a fast growing Catholic minority. He spoke to the "Asia Times" in February, 2016:

"For me, China has always been a reference point of greatness. A great country. But more than a great country, a great culture with an inexhaustible wisdom. It is necessary to recognize the greatness of the Chinese people, who have always maintained their culture. And their culture –I am not speaking about ideologies that there may have been in the past- their culture was not imposed."

In his interview with the "Asia Times" he spoke openly of Europe's need to accept the contribution of the eastern world and to "run the risk of balancing this exchange for peace:

"The western world, the eastern world and China all have the capacity to maintain the balance of peace and strength to do so. We must find a way, always through dialogue; there is no other way."

For the very first time, Francis sent Chinese New Year Greetings to President Xi Jinping and his people:

"The world looks to this great wisdom of yours."

In the meanwhile the Vatican's Secretariat of State, led by Francis's chief diplomat, Cardinal Pietro Parolin who was already making close contacts with China between 2002-2009, has led a delegation to meet Beijing officials in ongoing talks for a breakthrough in normalising Sino-Vatican relationships.

One of the most indicative actions taken by Francis as both a spiritual and world leader is his new Encyclical,'Laudato si (Praise be to You), in which he is reviving the teaching of the Church to make it more relevant and up-to-date with the needs of the modern world. He shows that there is an inextricable link between the spiritual and the secular needs of the world. He restates Catholic teaching showing that the biblical statement that God has given man "dominion" over the world does not mean that nature is there to be exploited and abused by man. Man has been given stewardship to care for and love the wonderful home which God has provided for him to live in, and he must care for it, just as man must love and care for all his neighbours in God's great family. So the Church has a duty to become a player in global, environmental politics. Francis is speaking like another Francis of Assisi, bringing his spirituality up to date with the circumstances of the modern world.

He integrates care for nature, with care for people, bringing it into Catholic social teaching to: "integrate questions of justice in debates on the environment, so as to hear both the cry of the earth, and the cry of the poor."

And it indicates the breadth of the implications: "a global problem with grave implications, environmental, social, economic, political and for the distribution of goods. It represents one of the principal challenges facing humanity in our day."

Francis refers to the lack of global leadership in this critical matter for mankind; and the Encyclical is obviously meant to fill the vacuum. He is confident enough to step into the breach and accept the role. In the autumn of 2015, as we have seen, he visited the USA which is a major atmospheric polluter, and spoke by invitation to the US Congress and the United Nations General Assembly. Even more significant is the timing of the Encyclical in preparation for the summit meeting of World leaders in Paris at the end of this year, to attempt a new settlement. Its aim is to achieve a manageable level of limiting global warming, with a fair sharing of the costs involved among the world's nations. The Encyclical should make a considerable contribution to this meeting, stressing the religious, moral and secular duty to save the future of mankind.

This is the first papal encyclical devoted entirely to the question of caring for planet earth; and it is not surprising in that this Pope is the only one who has chosen the name "Francis", because he specifically chose to follow in the footsteps of the medieval St. Francis of Assisi, known for his love of the physical world and all its inhabitants. He has also made it known that he wants the world to take careful note of its contents before the crucial climate change summit meeting in Paris next December, 2015. Already in his "Evangelii Gaudium", he had shown his deeply-felt feelings for the planet created by God for the benefit of His children:

"Thanks to our bodies, God has joined us so closely to the world around us to feel the desertification of the soil almost as a physical ailment, and the extinction of a species as a painful disfigurement."

Francis's new Encyclical, "Laudate si" (In praise of the planet) was published in June, 2015. Its sub-title is "Sulla cura della casa commune" (On the care of our common home). In Genesis we read that "God saw all that he had made and that it was very good" and after the flood we are told that "God made his covenant, not only with men and women, but with "every living creature on the face of the earth." At this time, we are rapidly destroying the very home that God has created for us.

Francis is fulfilling the essential role in this Encyclical of the religious leader who is showing mankind how to save our home. Mark Dowd, former strategist for Operation Noah, an ecumenical campaign to respond to the threat of climate change, believes that "tackling climate change, caused by man, is not only an issue of justice and human survival, but an act of faith in God's creation of the world." He also believes that "Francis's Encyclical on the Environment will be a game-changer" in this process, happening at what may be "humanity's eleventh hour."

It is indeed possible that this Encyclical will mark a turning point in persuading humanity to take responsibility for saving itself from the danger of destroying itself, by ignoring that which is keeping it alive. There is no world leader in a better position than Francis to succeed in this, because of the trust and respect that he is given across the World. (See Appendix 2, below).

George Lean in his column in "The Daily Telegraph" wrote that:

"Environmentalists believe that the intervention of the world's most popular and respected leader will have a major, possibly decisive, impact."

Nicholas Stern, one of the world's foremost environmental scientists, regards it as a "compelling document":

"Francis", eagerly awaited encyclical subtitled "Care for Our Common Home" shows deep scholarship as well as great wisdom both in recognising the scale of risks humanity faces from environmental degradation, and in identifying ways to make progress.

The encyclical is grounded in analysis of how human activities are creating a range of acute environmental problems, including climate change, deforestation, air pollution and loss of biodiversity.

"These are not just damaging the natural environment, but also harming humanity. While we are all facing immense risks of our own creation, it is, in particular poor people in both rich and developing countries who are often the most exposed, for instance to extreme weather conditions due to climate change.

As a result, these environmental problems present profound ethical and moral challenges. Many of the products of economic progress that have created wealth and prosperity also threaten lives and livelihoods, particularly of the most vulnerable members of society. And the kind of world that our children, grandchildren and future generations will inherit from us depends on our ability and willingness to manage better the unintended adverse side effects of scientific and technological advances."[26]

In "The Sunday Times", Paul Vallely comments:

"The Pope feels that the indifference of the rich to both the environment and to the poor has its roots in the same spiritual malaise."

John Vidal, in "The Observer", predicted that the encyclical would "address the root causes of poverty and the threats facing nature, or "creation."

And Catherine Pepinster, the Editor of "The Tablet", comments that "Francis is willing to intervene in quite a deliberate way in the global political process."

This Encyclical been awaited for a long time; and in the event it was leaked by some days before its due publication on Thursday, 18th June. Its message resonates most in poor countries, such as Malawi where there are several initiatives in progress to deal with the effects of climate change. The UN Climate Change Conference to be held in Paris in December, 2015. Francis is well aware of the ineffectiveness of earlier conferences and warns that this must change:

---

26. Nicholas Stern, *The Tablet*, June 27th 2015, quoting the Encyclical.

"International negotiations cannot make significant progress due to positions taken by countries which place their national interests above the global common good. Those who will have to suffer the consequences of what we are trying to hide will not forget this failure of conscience and responsibility" and, "change is impossible without motivation and a process of education . . ."

The "Independent" newspaper reported immediately on 16th June, 2015, from two reporters:

"Pope Francis warned that the world is heading for "unprecedented destruction" unless mankind confronts climate change and reforms the way it treats the planet, as the most eagerly anticipated papal document in living memory was leaked last night. In a 192-page encyclical warming that looks set to define his tenure, the Pope paints an apocalyptic picture in which the world's poorest are caught up in a web of environmental, human, financial and ethical degradation that puts the entire planet at risk. In an extraordinarily frank document, the Pope lambasts rich countries for "looting" the world and takes aim at bankers and climate sceptics for accelerating its decline. He warns that the world is facing widespread crop failures, economic ruin, mass migration and the destruction of entire eco-systems. Although he accepts that there may be some natural causes of global warming, he lays most of the blame squarely at the feet of mankind. If the current trend continues this century, we could witness climate change unlike anything seen before and the unprecedented destruction of eco-systems, with serious consequences for all of us."

The "Independent" says that this Encyclical has been awaited with fevered anticipation and claims that it is the first encyclical to be addressed to everyone in the world, regardless of religion:

"Climate change is a problem with serious implications for the global environmental, social and economics, distribution systems and policies, and constitutes one of the main current challenges for humanity."

Then, there is another feature in the same newspaper by another reporter, under the heading of "Another Review." This points out that:

"The word momentous is over-used, but we can apply it with justice to the pronouncement by Pope Francis about poverty, the environment and climate change which was leaked last night . . .(it) is expected to be a dramatic intervention in the international political process insisting that the fight against global warming is a moral issue which must be addressed by the whole world. The timing is remarkable. In essence the 78 year old

Argentine pontiff is throwing the moral force of the Church into the negotiations for a new climate treaty to be concluded—as is is hoped—at the UN Climate Conference in Paris in December. There has never in modern times been such a decisive involvement of the spiritual with the political- and certainly not with regards to the environment . . . it is Francis, the former Jorge Bergoglio of Buenos Aires who may come to be the long-term bearer of that title ("The Green Pope"). . .

"He took Francis as his papal title after Saint Francis of Assisi, the thirteenth century Italian saint who was devoted not only to the poor but- almost uniquely for a Catholic prelate in the past- to the natural world. The Encyclical's title, meaning "Be Praised" is not in the normal Latin, but in medieval Italian, and comes from "The Canticle of the Sun", St. Francis's famous poem in which he refers us to Mother Earth who feeds us."

This is "an ethic of stewardship, the stewardship of God's creation . . .(this is) likely to move the Church decisively into line with environmental thinking. But it is the direct effect it will have in the outside world, the real world of international politics which is likely to be the explosive aspect of Laudato Si. It will throw the Church's moral endorsement behind the longstanding claim of climate scientists that global warming is a real, urgent and terrible problem for the world . . . If the Encyclical is as trailed, it may prove to be the tipping point in international opinion about climate change, and be a powerful force for the conclusion of a climate treaty in December."

"This is an unprecedented and unusual aspect of life for the Church to have an effect on international politics and decisions, but the stature and respect for, and trust in, Francis is obviously something which is now of real significance in the contemporary world. On this occasion, of course, it is exercised against the opinion of the opponents of action of climate change, "those determined pretenders that the whole thing is a huge left wing hoax, America's republicans."

Francis has decided to establish a "World Day of Prayer for the Care of Creation", to be celebrated annually on the 1st of September" by all Christians in the World. He was:

"Sharing with my beloved brother the Ecumenical Patriarch Bartholomew, his concerns for the future of creation . . . taking up the suggestion by his representative, the Metropolitan Ioannis of Pergamon (John

Zizioulas) who took part in the presentation of the encyclical "Laudate si" on the care of our common home."

In a letter, dated 6th August, to Cardinals Peter Turkson and Kurt Koch, he emphasized the ecumenical aspect of the announcement:

"The celebration of the Day on the same date as the Orthodox Church will be a valuable opportunity to bear witness to our growing communion with our Orthodox brothers. We live in a time where all Christians are faced with identical and important challenges and we must give common replies to these in order to appear more credible and effective. Therefore it is my hope that this Day can involve, in some way, other Churches and ecclesial Communities and be celebrated in union with the initiatives that the World Council of Churches is promoting on this issue:

"I ask you, Cardinal Turkson, as President of the Pontifical Council for Justice and Peace, in collaboration with the Episcopal Conferences to set up this Day, so that this annual celebration becomes a powerful moment of prayer, reflection, conversion and the adoption of appropriate life-styles."

Francis also wants to bring together all Christians as part of an ecumenical movement to support the movement for caring for our common home and working to deal with the problem of climate change. He asked Cardinal Koch, President of the Pontifical Council for the Promotion of Christian Unity:

"to make the necessary contacts with the Ecumenical Patriarchate and with the other ecumenical organisations so that this World Day can become the sign of a path along which all believers in Christ can work together."[27]

It shows how active Pope Francis is to produce that sense of Unity among all Christians, which Christ Himself prayed for: "So that the World may believe that Thou has sent Me"; and which has been sadly lost over the last four centuries, dominated by nationalistic and internecine in Europe and the World.

We are now able to say that, at the great meeting of 195 of the World's political leaders in Paris (December, 2015) they have committed themselves, in an unprecedented manner, to the task of supporting the positive decisions made concerning action on the necessity for achieving climate change and activating the necessary procedures required. There was a new and enthusiastic ethos of understanding the global truth that the whole world was in danger of annihilation unless it came together as united mankind to abandon the selfish "particularism" of the past and devoting itself

---

27. From *The Tablet*, August 15th, 2015, page 25.

to the "solidarity" of the one-world approach of united and determined action.

President Obama proclaimed this as a moment of global change of direction achieved by the whole of humanity. The world's leaders proclaimed their work as "a huge step forward for mankind." I believe that Pope Francis's Encyclical had played a very important part in achieving this end and, on its own, was important evidence of the great need for spiritual guidance from an accepted source of altruistic authority in the affairs of a secular and temporal world.

Pope Francis has become, undoubtedly, a figure of respect and of world renown; but he is facing a task of great difficulty and of immense importance for world development. He does need the support of all people of good will if his task is to be successful in guiding humanity along the right path to a better world in the new Millennium. This is obvious from his Easter Message to the world in 2015. This was his "Urbi et Orbi" (to the City and the World) blessing to 50,000 pilgrims, braving the rain in St. Peter's Square, as described by "The Tablet" reporter, in what she calls "an impassioned plea for an end to "immense humanitarian tragedies." He wanted to urge:

"'Christians to remember that they must resist worldly pressures to make personal gain their first priority and "succeed at any cost." He said that "The world proposes that we put ourselves forward at all costs, that we compete, that we prevail... But ... CHRISTIANS ARE THE SEEDS OF ANOTHER HUMANITY IN WHICH WE SEEK TO LIVE IN SERVICE TO ONE ANOTHER... This is not weakness, but true strength. We ask today for the grace not to succumb to the pride which fuels violence and war, but to have the humble virtues of pardon and peace."[28]

He called for an end to violent attacks on Christians and expressed his solidarity with the families of the students massacred in Holy Week by Islamic terrorists at Garissa University in Kenya. He denounced the absurd bloodshed and barbarous acts of violence by groups such as Islamic State:

"We ask Jesus, the victor over death, to lighten the sufferings of our many brothers and sisters who are persecuted for his name, and of all those who suffer an injustice as a result of ongoing conflicts and violence, There are so many of them."[29]

28. From *The Tablet*.
29. Ibid.

He also made an impassioned appeal for peace in the Middle East, and other war-torn regions. He asked that peace be restored in the Holy Land and that in Syria and Iraq "the roar of arms may cease and that peaceful relations may be restored among the various groups which make up those beloved countries." He called on the international community to "not stand by before the immense humanitarian tragedy unfolding in these countries and the drama of the numerous refugees."

The 78 year old Pope looked visibly wearied by the weight of his serious message to mankind. He "implored" peace for Libya, Yemen, Nigeria, South Sudan and the Democratic Republic of Congo, as well as for the Ukraine. He was very pleased, however to give news of the nuclear deal signed by Iran, with the US, France, Russia, China and Germany during Easter Week, to treat Iran fairly, but to inhibit any extension of abilities to make a nuclear bomb. As it happens, Iran has since then, played an important part in preventing the extension of the "Islamic State" throughout Syria and Iraq.

On Maundy Thursday of this same week, Francis washed and kissed the feet of 12 prisoners at Rome's Rebibbia prison, plus those of a toddler living in the prison with his incarcerated mother. In his short and off-the-cuff homily he described the shock and incomprehension of the Apostles at the Last Supper, when, instead having a slave to wash their feet, Jesus performed the rite Himself. Then he said that "Jesus gave his life in order to give life to us . . . for you, for you, for me, for them", he said, pointing to the men and women inmates gathered in the chapel. To give meaning from the ceremony, Francis said "have the certainty . . . that when the Lord washes our foot, He washes away everything, He purifies us. He makes us feel His love once more."[30]

All of this reveals the emotional sincerity with which Francis explained the troubles of the World which he was facing, together with his great faith and hope in that love of Christ which can conquer everything. Again we see in his love for people and his wish to put things right for them, the need he has for the support of all people of good will behind him, both from the Church itself and the secular world which he strives to serve.

Perhaps the most important evidence of his strength, however, is an incident revealed by Austen Ivereigh in his biography of Francis, entitled "The Great Reformer."[31] The then Cardinal Jorge Bergoglio, Archbishop of

---

30. Ibid.
31. Ivereigh, *The Great Reformer*, 307–9.

Buenos Aires, was engaged in protecting the vulnerable people of the slums against the drug dealers. One of his young priests, Padre Pepe, was doing great work in his parish, in bringing his flock into a new and constructive way of life, when he came to see his Archbishop in some distress: "Look Boss, they've (drug dealers) threatened to kill me, and I think it could be serious": "The Cardinal fell silent for a time. "First of all, we have to be calm, because we are acting in accordance to the Gospel", he said, before adding: "If someone has to die. It should be me. I will ask God to take me, and not you." The Cardinal knew that these gangsters had already killed the saintly Archbishop Oscar Romero for his work against their atrocious and inhuman behaviour.

He decided to make the matter public. The following day, as it happened, he was in a huge gathering of people, with the public media in attendance and in his homily, he suddenly said:

"The priests in Villa21, ... recently opened three homes to help young addicts. The drug dealers did not like this. Some have got nervous and threatened to kill a priest ... We don't know how this will end."[32]

The next day, he went to Villa 21 to spend hours walking the streets with Padre Pepe and greeting people as they went round. The message was clear: "The shepherds were one with their flock and ready to die for them. There was huge publicity about it. The next day there were thousands of people gathered to support their pastors in their work. The story was picked up across the world. The threats which had been continuous now stopped completely.

He then immediately created a vicariate for slum priests and named Padre Pepe to lead it. This vicariate negotiated with public authorities to achieve improvements in the condition of the slums. The publicity had exposed how little the State had done before and they were now shamed into taking action to help them.

Another and immediately up-to-date example of his extraordinary courage and qualities of leadership has been his decision to visit a war-ridden part of Africa at the end of November, 2015. He became the first Pope in History to visit the war zone and troubled area of the Central African Republic (CAR). This was just a few days after the terrorist attacks on Paris and CAR was a former French colony. France said that it could not guarantee the Pope's safety, but it was enough for Francis to know that the leaders there wanted him to come to meet their people. He travelled throughout

32. Ibid.

Kenya and Uganda in an open Pope-mobile to bring peace and reconciliation between conflicting sects and between Muslim rebels and Christians. He refused to wear a bullet-proof vest. He sent a message to the Country, in advance of his trip:

"Your dear Country has far too long been affected by a violent situation and by insecurity of which many of you have been innocent victims. The goal of my visit is, above all, to bring to you, in the name of Christ, the comfort of consolation and hope."[33]

He wanted to show that the internal conflicts between Muslims and Christians were harmful and unnecessary; and could only be stopped by a rational acceptance of the need to pursue a policy of mercy, fraternity and reconciliation, by which they could live in peace to achieve the common good of all. In a message to Kenya and Uganda, he said:

"We are living at a time when religious believers... are called to foster mutual understanding and respect, and to support each other as members of our one human family. For all of us are God's children."[34]

Francis met the Interim President and administered the Sacrament of Reconciliation to young people during a prayer vigil in from of the Cathedral at Bangui, the CAR capital. He visited the Kangemi slum in the Kenyan Capital, Nairobi, which was the home of 100,000 of the Country's poorest people.

He met leading Muslim leaders at the central Koudoukou mosque and invited one of them to ride with him in the Pope mobile. In Uganda he took the opportunity to visit the shrines of 23 Anglican and 22 Catholic martyrs, which he turned into a significant ecumenical event.

This visit to central India contained many signs of Francis's character, mission, and outlook as Pope. He had chosen to come to a dangerous and very needy area, suffering from sectarian conflicts, particularly between Christians and the Islam rebels in the very the heart of India, to meet the people in his usual "heart to heart" manner, as a "pilgrim of peace" and "apostle of hope."

On his way from the airport, in his open Pope-mobile, he noticed among the crowds, a young man in a wheel chair, holding a flag to greet him. Francis stopped the procession to bless and greet him. He turned out to be Stanislaus Redepouzou, who had lost a leg in an attack by Muslim rebels killed his mother and father. He said afterwards that he was prepared

33. Cited in *The Tablet*.
34. Ibid.

to forgive those who were responsible. This typified what Francis wanted to do in Africa- to separate true religion from the idea of violence and oppression by warring sectarian parties. There had to be a form of forgiveness and mercy and dialogue, to achieve reconciliation between different faiths. Francis was repeating the action of St. Francis of Assisi who, in the medieval period, had risked his life by similarly walked into "enemy" lines during the Fifth Crusade to plead for peace between Muslim and Christian protagonists. Francis is renowned for preaching best by his symbolic actions, in addition to his inspiring words. In this instance, to quote the leading Catholic International Journal ("The Tablet") it was his symbolic action "to boldly go where no pope has gone." It also showed his determination to follow in the footsteps of the man whose special form of spirituality he had chosen to adopt.

He visited three "refugee camps" where people could find some safety against the conflicts. After visiting one of them, he went on to visit the Koudougou Mosque in central Bangui where Muslims had suffered from the conflicts and asked to pray with the imam; and after that he asked the imam to join him in the pope-mobile. He stressed that extremism was a disease that could affect all religions and could only be overcome by dialogue which centred on the goodness of the One God that they all worshipped.

It was on this visit to a marginalised country in one of the poorest parts of the World, that Francis chose to warn the world that it would be a great mistake if the 200 or so leaders of all the world's countries who were meeting in Paris at this time, failed to deal effectively with the problem of climate change. This warning was issued at the United Nations' Office in Nairobi, stressing the need to defend the poorest people in the world from the results of failure in respect; for poverty and frustration were among the major causes of world unrest and terrorism itself.

Finally Francis chose, unofficially, to open his "Jubilee Year of Mercy" in the World, by "opening the door to human Mercy" at the Cathedral in Bangui, an area of so much suffering, instead of the Vatican, to demonstrate the need for mercy and reconciliation among mankind in general. Afterwards, he repeated the message of forgiveness to one's enemies and starting anew, to the great gathering of young people on the steps of the Cathedral. They were thrilled that Francis had chosen them to be the centre of this great occasion.

Peace on Earth

On the plane, coming back from Africa, one observer stated that Francis had truly "given voice to the voiceless"; and that he seemed to be the only world leader who "is really trying to deal with people's problems at a global level." This, he said, is why Francis's visit had been so successful, meeting with cheering crowds and traditional African dancing and singing. It was because the Pope had chosen himself to come to see and encourage them, that it would be "unforgettable."

This says much, I believe, about the holiness, courage, wisdom, and determination of the man who had elected, unexpectedly, as leader of the Universal Church across the World in 2013. I hope that we have shown that he has also become the type of spiritual leader whom Toynbee predicted would be needed to play an important part in the revival and development of the West; but now we should speak of the World in general, as this is now seen as a "global village" in the new Millennium.

As I end this Essay, there are reports coming in of the extraordinary welcome being given to Pope Francis by many thousands of people wherever he goes, during his visit to his own Continent of South America. He went to Paraguay, Ecuador and Bolivia, all of which had never experienced such a wonderful occasion. As usual he chose to meet the poor and marginalised first always asked for him. He listened carefully to all who spoke to him and showed his sincere empathy, while responding with simple but wise words of sympathy and help. One of his keynote addresses was on the "tyranny of Mammon (Money)"; another was on the "grave sins that committed against the native peoples of." He spoke, too, of democracy, human rights, fellowship, faith and on "Mother Earth";

Perhaps the best report was from the English lady, Margaret Hebblethwaite, from Paraguay, the poorest of the poor

"The overwhelming sensation . . . is one of huge excited crowds, chants and shouting, climbing up to get a better view, and the waving of flags and balloons . . . also stretching out to touch the man whose goodness and compassion is so much greater than their own, in the hope that something will rub off. I will never read the gospels in the same way again . . . Pope Francis warm embracing of young people . . . they felt confident in going right up to him and putting their arms around him. It was the same with children . . . he embraced and blessed as many as he could all together . . . Actions speak louder than words."[35]

---

35. Ibid.

Pope Francis, "The Great Reformer"

He spoke too of the "corruption of politicians which is the gangrene of the people" and the people knew exactly whose side he was on.

Mrs. Hebblethwaite closed her report with: "Paraguay has indeed been showered with blessings in this visit, and Francis showed himself to be truly what the posters claimed –a "Messenger of Joy and Peace."

IX

Epilogue

In case any of our readers feel the need to "come down earth" on the subject we are dealing with, we might just end with reminding ourselves of the thoughts of some of the thoughts presented by some of our very "down to earth" scientists and one economist of distinction, in support of our thesis.

One of the great, if subconscious obstacles to World peace has been the idea that warfare is an unavoidable, if ugly, part of the human condition, because it has always been part of human history. It is part of a fatalist acceptance, disguised as "realism." It was a clear message of Pope John XXIII in his "Peace on Earth" encyclical, that War should no longer be part of the human agenda. This was a great break-through in human attitudes and thinking while we are all on the verge of the Third Millennium. It was supported in practice by the founders of the European Union, who showed what could happen, if there was a real attempt to put it into practice. It would necessarily entail a new cultural attitude towards the question; or a new phase in the "growing-up" of humanity.

This new cultural attitude was taken up by other very responsible people. It was the considered view of the scientists gathered together under the auspices of the United Nation Educational, Scientific and Cultural Organisation in 1986 that:

"We are not condemned to war and violence by our biology. Instead it is possible for us to end war and the suffering it causes."

And in 1996, Professor Rotblat, Nobel Prize Winner, repeated the challenge put forward in "Pacem in Terris":

Epilogue

"War must cease to be an admissible social institution. The abolition of war must be our ultimate goal."

Then there was a wonderful intervention by the distinguished economist, Barbara Jackson, Baroness Ward, who answered the sceptics, sometimes called "realists", by stating that there is no reason why people should not be able to extend their normal practice for establishing peace and unity in their own community or nation, to wider political and economic units, up to the scope of a global world, which, after all is now only a global "village" in terms of the ever increasing achievements of modern technology of instant communication throughout the world. One of the most important advantages achieved by this technology, when properly used, is to reduce the difficulties that used to be associated this kind of communication.

It is simply a challenge to the human will and intelligence to grow and adapt to this different perspective about the global world as just as much a manageable area as, say, any particular state would have been a hundred or more years ago. It is essentially a "growing" up process in human development, though it needs a special kind of creative, intelligent and spiritual leadership, to teach and spread the initial strides forward needed in this new development. Baroness Ward writes that:

"If freedom for us is no more than the right to pursue our own self-interest, personal or national, then we have no claim to the greatest vision of our society... There has to be a new start, new policies, a new approach. Otherwise we prepare for our own defeat, simply by default."[1]

She argues, too, that we are now in a period when scientists, having discovered the essential inter-dependence and delicate balance of the natural systems, are learning a greater humility and sensitivity handling their discoveries. Their work is inextricably linked with the great natural laws which govern the created world, just as human beings are also guided by the great moral laws which govern human relationships within the created human family.

The underlying unity of scientific law was known to the Greeks and the medieval humanistic scholars. The underlying laws of human brotherhood was proclaimed by the Hebrew Prophets, taught in a developed manner by Jesus Christ and expressed strongly by Christian humanists. This is proclaimed in the Catholic (Universal) Church's teaching on "solidarity" which means the simple but dynamic truth that we are all created to be responsible for one another in the human family. powerful and dynamic

---

1. Ward, *The Rich Nations and the Poor Nations*.

forces which have already energised peace and union in Europe; and which could go on to do the same throughout the world, if properly led by the same principles of Christian humanism.

Baroness Ward concluded in 1976, looking forward to the problems and opportunities for human development in the third Millennium, in which the technology exists to service and achieve our aims, and human beings have the intelligence to achieve them, by insisting that all will depend still on the free will of humans to choose the way forward which can accomplish the task. Technology in itself is a neutral instrument in the hands of human beings who can use it or abuse it. The fundamental laws which govern the brotherhood of man in the natural world, created for him

"Today they come together in a new fusion of vision and energy to remind us of our inescapable unity even as we stand on the very edge of annihilation. The scientist, the sage, the man of learning and the poet, the mathematician and the saint, repeats the same warning: "We must love each other, or we must die.""[2]

---

2. See Ward, *The Rich Nations and the Poor Nations*. And Ward, *The Home of Man*.

Appendix 1

Britain and Europe

"England once lay in the mainstream of European development and after the sixteenth century it became an eccentric tributary"

(V. BOGNADOR)

"It is in its Christian nature that the success of medieval society in shaping the future must lie."

(J. ROBERTS, "THE TRIUMPH OF THE WEST")

"The answers to modern man's problems lie in the medieval period"

(C.G. JUNG)

IT WAS A CONTINENTAL supra-national thinker and statesman who spent four years living in Britain during the Second World War and became a devoted admirer of its people and countryside, who wrote an extraordinary letter to an English Member of Parliament for the attention of the English Foreign Office in 1941. Paul Henri-Spaak was the Prime Minister of Belgium, and was later to become Secretary General of NATO and President of the first General Assembly of the United Nations in 1946. He

Appendix 1

had fled to England as a refugee from Hitler's invading army in 1941, and remained there until the War ended in 1945.

The letter is remarkable for two reasons. Firstly it was written at a very low point in Britain's seemingly lone stand against the might of Nazi Fascism. The USA had not yet come into the War to make its contribution and did not do so until the surprise Japanese attack on Pearl Harbour. Secondly, it contains some remarkably prophetic statements about later events in European history, particularly with regard to Britain and Germany.

Spaak speaks feelingly and very earnestly about the nature of English society and the character of the English people as he found them at one of the lowest points of the War in 1941:

"From the day I set foot on English soil I never doubted final victory. I knew I would see my country again, free and independent. I knew that life as it should be lived would begin again. I knew we would escape the Nazi horror and shame"

He describes later in his memoirs the great admiration he felt for the character of the English people, their courage, tenacity and firmness of character; and admired Winston Churchill as the supreme representative of these qualities. He also mentions, however, that he had found the English people to be "slow, hesitant, and unwilling to make the most of their opportunities."

He went on, in this letter of 1941, to say:

"The result of the last twenty months in Europe has shown me that its countries must unite. They have been shown to be dependent on each other for their security. After the War Europe will be glad to unite behind Britain's victorious leadership, providing that (1) Britain remains strong (2) Britain concerns herself with Europe. It will not be sufficient for Britain to establish and try to maintain a balance of power to offset a hegemony in Europe. She must herself assume the responsibility of her supremacy.

If Britain fails to recognize her duty to Europe, if she does not pursue a continental policy which makes her a strong leader of Europe, she must expect to be rapidly deprived of the fruits of her present efforts. Europe will organize itself against her, and I dare say that Germany, despite its defeat, will be the leader. The ideal solution would, of course, be a world organization, or failing this, an organization embracing all Europe.

The countries of Western Europe share political, legal and moral standards. They possess all that is necessary for close cooperation. A united or federal Europe must be the nucleus of post-war policy and reconstruction, and it is on this that Britain must lean."

Later in his Memoirs, his thinking becomes more specific. He makes a very important and insightful observation which is extremely relevant to the present problem facing the European Union, 62 years later. He refers to the League of Nations, established after the First World War to put an end to internecine warfare; but this proved to be a failure and was finally dissolved in 1946. By then Spaak, who was now holding important posts both in NATO and the UN, remarks:

> "Its (League of Nations) deference to national sovereignty was one of the prime reasons for its failure . . . the body must be superior to its individual members. No system is without its disadvantages. Order always involves some restriction on liberty."

As citizens of Britain we ought to attend to this question of Britain's avoidance of any really participative role in the movement for European Peace and Unity, in our interests as well as that of Europe and the wider world. Britain has much to gain and to offer as being an influential part of the "fraternity" of nations involved. It has great experience gained from its own work in the Empire and Commonwealth and wider world. Its people have shown great qualities of courage, creativity and determination when they are convinced of the purpose and meaning of what they have taken in hand, as shown in their willingness to face up to the evils of Hitler and the Nazi Party, even when they were doing it on their own.

I do not believe that the British, as a Nation, have had the chance to know what the European Movement for Peace and Unity is all about. It is a movement which has brought 500 million people unity and peace to live and work together as a Continental family of equal and inter-dependent human beings. This is its most important achievement and a great example for the rest of the World. Arnold Toynbee has identified "mimesis" (or imitation) as one of the best strategies in developing World development. It is fully in line with the new and exciting form of human development which we have in mind for the new world of the third Millennium.

Britain should be aware of the fact that we cannot deal with the major problems of the new Millennium without coming together as a United Body. Such problems as Climate Change; the gross and increasing inequality of the way the World's resources are divided between the very rich and very poor, even starving, when there is enough food for everyone to have a decent standard of life; the fear of return of warfare, but this time more terrible than ever before; together with the major developments in scientific and technological means of communication which really have made the World a much smaller place which we now call "the global village"; all point clearly to the need to establish a new way of looking outside ourselves from a "whole world" viewpoint. The world of "warring nationalisms" has gone hopefully, and our only chance of making the world a better place for all its people is to understand this and prepare for it. We just need to educate ourselves in what kind of preparations have to be made. It is exactly a "challenge and response" situation and humanity has the free will to decide which way it is going to go.

Britain has lost an Empire and failed to find a proper role in this new world, because it is not up-to-date with this new outlook and new needs. The European Union could well be regarded as providing a template for building the first new steps towards the full development of World Peace and Unity, by actually achieving this in one Continent of the World. Of course it is the beginning of a new phase of World history. Those leading it are in the vanguard of the future; that is if we have the courage and intelligence to respond to the challenge. If we decide not to accept the challenge, then it seems clear that we can be falling down a slippery slope which we have good reason to fear.

A great problem for Britain is that it has lost an Empire and failed to find a new vision for the future. So, apart from materialistic considerations, it is living in a vacuum as far as our human spirit and human values are concerned. The even greater problem is that Britain has been given a deep and enduring misunderstanding of its history. This is because in the sixteenth century, there took place a great revolution in which the first great nation state in Europe was established in England. England had been an important part of Christian Europe from the coming of Christianity, shortly after the start of the Roman period until 1530. Indeed it was a Devonshire monk and missionary, St. Boniface, who was largely responsible for the conversion of the Germanic lands to Christianity in the Anglo-Saxon period and their assimilation into European culture. This continued until the "Reformation" of the 1530's. It was only in its last 400 years that England had become separated from Europe and its culture, in the hands of the creators of the "Great Myth."

The "Reformation" initiated by Henry VIII, was to divide England from Europe and establish it as the first Nation State in which the ruler was in absolute control of all aspects of English life, material and spiritual. It was accomplished by the machinery, later to be used on other nation states, of State controlled propaganda, supported by drastic fear imposed by the death penalty for those who resisted. It was highly successful so that within a century the people had come to take it for granted that England had never been part of Europe, but a kingdom in its own right controlled by a King (indeed "Emperor"-according to the new statutes) who had a divine right to control everything. Henry VIII and Thomas Cromwell, his first minister until Henry decided to execute him, created the myth that England had been "stolen" by the Universal Church during the medieval period. Then, too, was imposed the idea of the "divine right of kings" which turned them into the representatives of God, fitted to rule absolutely over everybody and everything.

In this way England (and soon British) people were taught a false memory of the past for over four centuries. This was the source of "the Great Myth," identifying them as different, independent, and superior to others (See E. Jones, "The English Nation: the Great Myth," 3 editions, from 1998-2003). It was in fact the first and one of the most successful examples of a Government changing and shaping the memory of its people.

In spite of the gradual acceptance of the falsity of this myth by academic research in the second half of the twentieth century, it has still held its power, consciously or subconsciously in the minds of most British people who are outside the range of the academic world. It explains why they cannot accept that they have been identified as Europeans, as well as British, for much the greatest part of their history which they have forgotten all about. They have lost their true identity and destiny in the World. The recovery of this identity has become more important in the second part of the twentieth century when they have lost their Empire and have no positive or noble "vision" to follow, except to make as much money as they can. This is not the kind of "vision" without which people need and helped to create the, after virtue, culture in Britain.

It explains why Britain has forsaken many chances of taking a leading place in the European Movement for Peace and Unity from the start. It sought and still seeks continually to remain outside the Movement's main aims and to remain in it, only to gain their own narrow, British interests. It is not aware for the most part, of the humanistic and noble purpose for which that Movement has existed from the start.

These important reasons for the Movement's existence should play a crucially important part in the coming referendum on whether Britain should remain in or out of the Union. So far it has hardly been spoken of, because everyone now takes it for granted that Britain is only in it for its own purposes and advantages. As a Briton I am not happy to be thought of in this way; and I do not believe that most Britons would be either. The days of the old nationalisms are over. We are now having to face the dumb facts of reality that we are all together in a new World which is international in character and is also a "global village" Britain has lost many chances in the past to become a leading part of a new Movement which is intent on achieving a much more noble aim for the making of a better world for us all. This is why the Union's leaders want Britain to join them and play a very important part in it. I think that the best chance of us succeeding in this enterprise is contained in the philosophy of Christian Humanism as it has been outlaid in this essay. That is why I have written it.

There is still a chance for the British people to at last throw off the false notion of the "Great Myth" and attach itself to what can still be a leading role in the movement intent on leading us to "Peace on Earth" through the culture of Christian Humanism. This could redeem and restore our own culture to what it is capable of being. I think it could also bring out the best qualities in the British and in humanity as a whole. We should not be frightened of the new World, but see that it provides a wonderful opportunity to advance and develop humanity, by acquiring again, and this time following through, that "great vision" of Christian Humanism which our early ancestors and heritage thought to be essential "lest the people perish." We would have an important part to play in this mission and it would bring out the best in our own people and its culture. We should decide in the referendum to play a central and leading part with Germany, by proclaiming that we wanted to adopt a central and leading role with Germany, asking not what they can do for us, but what we can do for all of us Europeans and citizens of the world.

Appendix 2

The Encyclical Laudato si' (Praise be to You)

IT IS GOOD EVIDENCE of the part taken by Pope Francis as a world leader that on Saturday, 13th June, 2015 the following feature appeared in "The Guardian":

"Pope Francis's Edict on climate change will anger deniers and US Churches: Pontiff hopes to inspire action at UN meeting in Paris in December after his visits to Philippines and New York. Pope Francis was a key player in thawing relations between the US and Cuba.

He has been called the "superman pope" and it would be hard to deny that Pope Francis has had a good December. Cited by President Barrack Obama as key player in the thawing relations between the US and Cuba, the Argentine Pontiff followed that by lecturing the cardinals on the need to clean up Vatican politics. But can Francis achieve a feat that has so far eluded secular powers and inspire decisive action on climate change.

It looks as of if he will give it a go. In 2015, the pope will issue a length message on the subject to the world's 1.2 billion Catholics, give an address to the UN General Assembly and call a summit of the world's main religions.

The reason for such frenetic activity . . . is the pope's wish to directly influence . . .(the) crucial UN meeting in Paris, when countries will try to conclude 20 years of fraught negotiations with a universal commitment to reduce emissions:

"Our academics supported the pope's initiative to influence next year's crucial decisions, says Bishop Marcelo Sorondo, chancellor of the Vatican's

Appendix 2

Pontifical Academy of Sciences, as he told Cafod, the Catholic development agency, at a meeting in London:

"The idea is to convene a meeting with leaders of the main religions to make all people aware of the state of our climate and the tragedy of social exclusion"

Following a visit to Tacloban, the Philippine city devastated in 2012 by typhoon Haiyan, the pope will publish a rare encyclical on climate change and human ecology. Urging all Catholics to take action on moral and scientific grounds, the document will be sent to the world's 5,000 Catholic bishops and 400,000 priests, who will distribute it to parishioners.

In recent months, the pope has argued for a radical new financial and economic system to avoid human inequality and ecological devastation. In October he told a meeting of Latin American and Asian landless peasants and other social movements:

"An economic system centred on the god of money needs to plunder nature to sustain the frenetic rhythm of consumption that is inherent in it . . . The system continues unchanged, since what dominates are the dynamics of an economy and a finance that are lacking in ethics. It is no longer man who commands money. Cash commands . . . The monopolising of lands, deforestation, the appropriation of water, inadequate agro-toxics are some of the evils that tear man from the land of his birth. Climate change, the loss of biodiversity and deforestation are already showing their devastating effects in the great cataclysms we witness'

In Lima last month, bishops from every continent expressed their frustrations with the stalled climate talks and, for the first time, urged rich countries to act.

Sorondo, a fellow Argentinian who is known to be close to Pope Francis, said:

"Just as humanity confronted revolutionary change in the 19th century at the time of industrialisation, today we have changed the natural environment so much. If current trends continue, the century will witness unprecedented climate change and destruction with the ecosystem with tragic consequences"

According to Neil Thorns, head of advocacy at Cafod, said:

"The anticipation around Pope Francis's forthcoming encyclical is unprecedented. We have seen thousands of our supporters commit to making sure their MPs know climate change is affecting the poorest communities . . . A papal encyclical is rare. It is among the highest levels of a pope's authority. It will be 50-60 pages long."

Bibliography

Arnold-Baker, Charles. *Companion to British History*. Edited by Gardiner & Wenborn. New York: Routledge, 2015.

Betjeman, John. "Christmas." In *Great Christmas Compendium*. http://www.christmastime.com/cp-christ.html.

Botton, Alain de. *Religion for Atheists: A Non-believer's Guide to the Uses of Religion*. New York: Vintage, 2012.

Bognador, Vernon. *Twentieth Century British History*. Oxford: Oxford University Press, 1996.

Browing, Robert. *Men and Women*. Hamburg, Germany: Tredition GMBH, 1855.

Butterfield, Sir Hubert. *Man on His Past*. Cambridge: Cambridge University Press, 1955.

Clarke, Kenneth. *Civilisation*. London: BBC Books & John Murray, 1999.

Dawson, Christopher. *Understanding Europe*. London: Sheed and Ward, 1952.

Dessain, Charles Stephen. *The Mind of Cardinal Newman*. London: Catholic Truth Society, 1974.

Drabble, Margaret, ed. *The Oxford Companion to English Literature (1985)*. New York: Oxford University Press, 1985.

Draper, Robert. "Will the Pope Change the Vatican? Or will the Vatican change the Pope?" *National Geographic* (August 2015).

Duffy, Eamon. *Saints, Sacrilege and Sedition: Religion and Conflict in the Tudor Reformations*. London: Bloomsbury, 2012.

Eliot, T.S. *Notes Towards the Definition of Culture*. Cambridge: Cambridge University Press, 1948.

Fesquet, Henri. *Wit and Wisdom of Good Pope John*. London: Harvell, 1964.

Greengrass, Mark. *Christendom Destroyed: Europe 1517–1648*. New York: Penguin, 2014.

Hawkins, Joyce M., ed. *The Oxford Reference Dictionary*. New York: Oxford University Press, 1986.

Hobsbawm, Eric. *Fractured Times: Culture and Society in the Twentieth Century*. London: Little Brown, 2013.

Hutchinson. "Hutchinson Encyclopedia." Abingdon: Helicon, 1990.

Ivereigh, Austen. *The Great Reformer: Francis and the Making of a Radical Pope*. New York: Henry Holt, 2014.

Jones, Alexander, ed. *Jerusalem Bible*. London: Darton, Longman and Todd, 1968.

John XXIII, Pope. *Encyclical: Pacem in Terris*. London: Catholic Truth Society, 1963.

John XXIII, Pope. *Vatican 11 1963–65*. London: Fowler Wright, 1965.

Bibliography

Jones, Edwin. *The English Nation: the Great Myth*. London: Sutton, 2003.
Julian of Norwich. *Revelations of Divine Love*. Mineola, NY: Dover, 2006.
Jung, C. G. *The Essential Jung*. Edited by Anthony Storr. Princeton, NJ: Princeton University Press, 1983.
Jung, Carl Gustav. *Man and His Symbols*. New York: Doubleday, 1964.
Kershaw, Ian. *The End: The Defiance and Destruction of Hitler's Germany, 1944–1945*. New York: Penguin, 2011.
Llewelyn, Robert, ed. *Enfolded in Love: Daily Readings with Julian Norwich*. London: Seabury, 1980.
MacDougall, Hugh A. *The Acton-Newman Relations: The Dilemma of Christian Liberalism*, New York: Fordham University Press, 1962.
Mapp, Alf J. Jr. *Thomas Jefferson: Passionate Pilgrim: The Presidency, the Founding of the University, and the Private Battle*. Lanham, MD: Rowman and Littlefield, 2009.
McGilchrist, Iain. *The Master and His Emissary: The Divided Brain and the Making of the Western Word*. New Haven, CT: Yale University Press, 2009.
Maritain, Jacques. *Education at the Cross Roads*. New Haven, CT: Yale University Press, 1960.
New Scientist,'Images of the Mind' (London, October, 2013)
New Scientist, Article by Neuro-Surgeon, J.Duty on discoveries of Neuro-Science, October, 2013)
"Outlines of The Sixteen Documents of Vatican II." Prepared by Virginia Heffernan of the Long Island Catholic Rockville Centre, New York. London: Fowler Wright, 1965.
Pepinster, Catherine, ed. *The Tablet: The International Catholic Weekly*. London: Invicta.
Roberts, J. M. *The Triumph of the West: The Origin, Rise, and Legacy of Western Civilization*. London: BBC, 1995.
Southern, Sir R. W. *Scholastic Humanism and the Unification of Europe Foundations*. Malden, MA: Wiley-Blackwell, 1995.
Sertillanges, A. D. *The Thoughts of Leonardo da Vinci*. Temecula, CA: Le Clos-Luce, 2010.
Spaak, Paul-Henri. *The Continuing Battle: Memoirs of a European 1936–1966*. New York: Little Brown, 1971.
Schuman, Robert. *Pour l'Europe: Ecrits Politiques*. Paris: Editions Nagel Briquet, 2005.
Tillich, Paul. *The Theology of Culture*. Edited by Robert C. Kimball. New York: Oxford University Press, 1959.
Toynbee, Arnold J. *A Study of History*. Edited by D.C. Somervell. New York: Oxford University Press, 1957.
Vallely, Paul. *Pope Francis: Untying the Knots*. London: Bloomsbury, 2013.
Vernon, Mark. *The Big Questions: God*. London: Quercus, 2012.
Ward, Barbara. *The Rich Nations and the Poor Nations*. New York: W.W. Norton & Company, 1962.
———. *The Home of Man*. London: International Institute for Environment and Development, 1976.
Woodford, Linda. Sociology of Religion British Academy Lecture. "Sociology of Religion," London: 2015.
Zaehner, R.C. 'The Religious Instinct', The New Outline of Modern Knowledge. London: Victor Gollancz, 1931.

www.ingramcontent.com/pod-product-compliance
Lightning Source LLC
Chambersburg PA
CBHW071444150426
43191CB00008B/1234